Wassailing, Yule Logs, and Nutcrackers: A Holiday Guide to Christmas Folklore and Traditions, Including SinterKlaas, Pere Noel, Krampus, the Twelve Days of Christmas, Stockings, Ornaments, Yule Goats, and More

Calista King

The role of the book within our culture is changing. The change is brought on by new ways to acquire & use content, the rapid dissemination of information and real-time peer collaboration on a global scale. Despite these changes one thing is clear--"the book" in it's traditional form continues to play an important role in learning and communication. The book you are holding in your hands utilizes the unique characteristics of the Internet -- relying on web infrastructure and collaborative tools to share and use resources in keeping with the characteristics of the medium (user-created, defying control, etc.)--while maintaining all the convenience and utility of a real book.

Contents

Articles

Christmas and Christmas Eve — 1
- Christmas Eve — 1
- Christmas — 13

Christmas Folklore: People, Places, and Reindeer — 33
- Father Christmas — 33
- Santa Claus — 39
- Pre-Christian Alpine traditions — 61
- Sinterklaas — 64
- Saint Nicholas — 70
- Mrs. Claus — 85
- Christmas elf — 90
- Santa Claus's reindeer — 93
- Rudolph the Red-Nosed Reindeer — 98
- Père Noël — 102
- Joulupukki — 102
- Ded Moroz — 105
- Befana — 111
- Christkind — 117
- Zwarte Piet — 118
- Krampus — 121
- Belsnickel — 123
- Le Père Fouettard — 124
- North Pole — 126
- Santa's workshop — 136

Korvatunturi	138
Knecht Ruprecht	139

Christmas Traditions — **141**

Twelve Days of Christmas	141
Christmas tree	146
Wassailing	161
Yule log	164
Christmas stocking	168
Christmas ornament	171
Nutcracker	175
Christmas lights	176
Yule Goat	183

References

Article Sources and Contributors	187
Image Sources, Licenses and Contributors	188

Christmas and Christmas Eve

Christmas Eve

Christmas Eve is the day before Christmas Day, a widely celebrated holiday commemorating the birth of Jesus of Nazareth. It is a culturally significant celebration for most of the Western world and is widely observed as a full or partial holiday in anticipation of Christmas.

In Western culture, Christmas Eve is celebrated on December 24. However, the Coptic, Serbian, Russian, Macedonian, and Georgian Orthodox Churches, as well as the Greek Orthodox Church of Jerusalem, use the Julian calendar, which is currently 13 days behind the Gregorian calendar, so Christmas Eve for the adherents of those Churches coincides with January 6 of the following year in the Gregorian calendar.

Religious traditions

Western Churches

Many Roman Catholics and Anglicans traditionally celebrate a midnight Mass (Eucharist) which begins either at or sometime before midnight on Christmas Day. This ceremony, which is held in churches throughout the world, marks the beginning of Christmas Day.

A popular joke is to ask what time *Midnight* Mass starts, but in recent years some churches have scheduled their "Midnight" Mass as early as 7 p.m. In Spanish-speaking areas, the Midnight Mass is sometimes referred to as *Misa del Gallo*, or "Missa do Galo", in Portuguese ("Rooster's Mass"). In the Philippines, this custom lasts for nine days, starting on December 16 and continuing daily up to December 24, during which Filipinos attend dawn Masses, usually starting at around 4:00–5:00 a.m. In 2009 Vatican officials scheduled the Midnight Mass to start at 10pm so that the 82 year old Pope Benedict XVI would not have too late of a night.

Lutherans often carry on Christmas Eve Eucharistic traditions typical for Germany and Scandinavia. "Krippenspiele" (nativity plays), special festive music for organ, vocal and brass choirs and candlelight services make Christmas Eve one of the highlights in the Lutheran Church calendar. Christmas Vespers are popular in the early evening, and midnight services are also widespread in regions which are predominately Lutheran. The old Lutheran tradition of a Christmas Vigil in the early morning hours of Christmas Day (Christmette) can still be found in some regions. In eastern and middle Germany, many congregations still continue the tradition of "Quempas singing": separate groups dispersed in various parts of the church sing verses of the song "He whom Shepherds once came Praising" (Quem pastores) responsively.

Methodists celebrate the evening in different ways. Some, in the early evening, come to their church to celebrate Holy Communion with their families. The mood is very solemn, and often the only visible light is the Advent Wreath, and the candles upon the Lord's Table. Others celebrate the evening with services of light, which often include singing the song "Silent Night" as a variety of candles (including personal candles) are lit. Other churches have late evening services at 11 pm, so that the church can celebate Christmas Day together with the ringing of bells at 12 am. Others offer Christmas Day services as well. Each church is welcome to celebrate Christmas Eve evening and Christmas Day in their own special way.

The Nine Lessons and Carols broadcast annually from King's College, Cambridge on Christmas Eve has established itself as one of the signs that Christmas has begun in the United Kingdom. It is broadcasted to many parts of the world via the BBC World Service.

Other churches also hold a candlelight service, which is also typically held earlier in the evening; these often feature dramatizations of the Nativity. Similar worship services are held in many Protestant churches on Christmas Eve or Christmas Day.

Eastern Churches

In the Eastern Orthodox Church, Christmas Eve is referred to as Paramony ("preparation"). It is the concluding day of the Nativity Fast and is celebrated as a day of strict fasting by those devout Orthodox Christians who are physically able to do so. In some traditions, nothing is eaten until the first star appears in the evening sky, in commemoration of the Star of Bethlehem. The liturgical celebration begins earlier in the day with the celebration of the Royal Hours, followed by the Divine Liturgy combined with the celebration of Vespers, during which a large number of readings from the Old Testament are chanted, recounting the history of salvation. After the dismissal at the end of the service, a new candle is brought out into the center of the church and lit, and all gather round and sing the Troparion and Kontakion of the Feast.

Russian icon of the Nativity.

In the evening, the All-Night Vigil for the Feast of the Nativity is composed of Great Compline, Matins and the First Hour. The Orthodox services of Christmas Eve are intentionally parallel to those of Good Friday, illustrating the theological point that the purpose of the Incarnation was to make possible the Crucifixion and Resurrection. This is illustrated in Orthodox icons of the Nativity, on which the Christ

Child is wrapped in swaddling clothes reminiscent of his burial wrappings. The child is also shown lying on a stone, representing the Tomb of Christ, rather than a manger. The Cave of the Nativity is also a reminder of the cave in which Jesus was buried.

The services of Christmas Eve are also similar to those of the Eve of Theophany (Epiphany), and the two Great Feasts are considered one celebration.

In some Orthodox cultures, after the Vesperal Liturgy the family returns home to a festive meal, but one at which Orthodox fasting rules are still observed; i.e., no meat or dairy products (milk, cheese, eggs, etc.) are consumed (see below for variations according to nationality). Then they return to the church for the All-Night Vigil.

The next morning, Christmas Day, the Divine Liturgy is celebrated again, but with special features that occur only on Great Feasts of the Lord. After the dismissal of this Liturgy, the faithful customarilly great each other with the kiss of peace and the words: "Christ is Born!", to which the one being greeted responds: "Glorify Him!" (these are the opening words of the Canon of the Nativity that was chanted the night before during the Vigil). This greeting, together with many of the hymns of the feast, continue to be used until the leave-taking of the feast on December 29.

The first three days of the feast are particularly solemn. The second day is known as the Synaxis of the Theotokos, and commemorates the role of the Virgin Mary in the Nativity of Jesus. The third day is referred to simpy as "the Third Day of the Nativity". The Saturday and Sunday following December 25 have special Epistle and Gospel readings assigned to them. December 29 celebrates the Holy Innocents.

Orthodox Christians observe a festal period of twelve days, during which no one in the Church fasts, even on Wednesdays and Fridays, which are normal fasting days throughout the year. During this time one feast leads into another: December 25–31 is the afterfeast of the Nativity; January 1 is the Feast of the Circumcision; January 2–5 is the forefeast of the Epiphany.

Meals

In Poland, traditional Christmas Eve meals include one or more of the following foods: Golabki filled with Kasza, Pierogi, Borscht, fish soup, carp, and pickled Herring. Krupnik is sometimes drunk after dinner.

In the Czech Republic and Slovakia, the meal features a fish soup and breaded roasted carp with potato salad.

Italian Catholics eat seven types of seafood.

In some parts of Central and Eastern Europe such as Russia, Ukraine, Poland and Lithuania, a traditional meatless

Traditional Polish Christmas Eve meal.

12-dishes Christmas Eve Supper is served on Christmas Eve before opening gifts. This is known as the "Holy Meal". The table is spread with a white cloth symblic of the swaddling clothes the Child Jesus was wrapped in, and a large white candle stands in the center of the table symbolizing Christ the Light of the World. Next to it is a round loaf of bread symbolizing Christ Bread of Life. Hay is often displayed either on the table or as a decoration in the room, reminiscent of the manger in Bethlehem. The twelve dishes (which differ by nationality or region) symbolize the Twelve Apostles.

The Holy Meal was a common Eastern Orthodox tradition in the Russian Empire, but during the era of the Soviet Union it was greatly discouraged as a result of the official atheism of the former former regime. It is coming back in Russia and continues to be popular in Ukraine.

The main attribute of Holy Meal in Ukraine is kutia, a sweet grain pudding. The other typical dishes are borscht, Vareniki, a traditional Christmas compote called *uzvar* and dishes made of mushrooms, fish, phaseolus, cabbage.

Cubans, Dominicans, and Puerto Ricans serve roast pork (*pernil*).

On Christmas Eve in Bulgaria, the meal consists of an odd number of lenten dishes in compliance with the rules of fasting. They are usually the traditional sarma, bob chorba (bean soup), fortune pita (pastry with a fortune in it), stuffed peppers, nuts. The meal is often accompanied with wine or Bulgaria's traditional alcoholic beverage rakia.

In accordance with the Christmas traditions of the Serbs, their festive meal has a copious and diverse selection of foods, although it is prepared according to the rules of fasting. As well as a round, unleavened loaf of bread and salt, which are necessary, this meal may comprise roast fish, cooked beans, sauerkraut, noodles with ground walnuts, honey, and wine.

In France and some other French-speaking areas, a long family dinner, called a *réveillon*, is held on Christmas Eve. The name of this dinner is based on the word *réveil* (meaning "waking"), because participation involves staying awake until midnight and beyond.

Réveillon is generally of an exceptional or luxurious nature. For instance, appetizers may include lobster, oysters, escargots or foie gras, etc. One traditional dish is turkey with chestnuts. Réveillons in Québec will often include some variety of tourtière. Dessert may consist of a *bûche de Noël*. In Provence, the tradition of the *13 desserts* is followed: 13 desserts are served, almost invariably including: *pompe à l'huile* (a flavoured bread), dates, etc. Quality wine is usually consumed a such dinners, often with champagne or similar sparkling wines as a conclusion.

In Germany, traditions vary from region to region. Carp is eaten in many parts of the country. Potato salad with frankfurter or wiener sausages is popular in some families. Another simple meal which some families favour, especially in regions where Christmas Eve still has the character of a fast day, is vegetable or pea soup. In some regions, especially in Schleswig-Holstein where Danish influence is noticeable, a roasted duck or goose filled with plums, apples and raisins is family tradition. In other regions, especially in Mecklenburg and Pomerania, many families prefer kale with boiled potatoes, special sausages and ham. Many families have developed new traditions for themselves and eat such meals as meat fondue or raclette. In almost all families in all parts of Germany you find a wide variety of Christmas cookies baked according to recipes typical for the family and the region.

In Denmark, the most common meal is roast duck or pork although goose or turkey are also popular. In many families more than one kind of meat is served. The meat is served with gravy, boiled potatoes, sugar glazed potatoes and red cabbage. For dessert a rice and almond pudding with cherry sauce is served. A whole almond is hidden in the pudding. The person who gets the almond wins a small gift.

In the Republic of Macedonia and Bulgaria, a coin is concealed in a bread loaf and the host breaks a piece of the loaf at the dinner table for each member of the household: it is believed that the one who gets the piece of bread with the coin will be fortunate in the forthcoming year. The dinner is according to the rules of fasting: fish, baked beans, sauerkraut, walnuts and red wine are common. The dessert may consist of apples and dried fruits: plums, dates, figs. The table is usually not cleared after the dinner and until the next morning, to leave some food for the holly spirits – a custom which probably comes from pagan pre-Christian times.

In Hungary, a traditional fish soup called *halászlé* is the typical Christmas Eve meal, although it is also consumed at other times of the year.

Gift giving

During the Reformation in 16th–17th century Europe, many Protestants changed the gift bringer to the Christ Child or *Christkindl*, and the date of giving gifts changed from December 6 to Christmas Eve. It is the night when Santa Claus (or some variant thereof) makes his rounds delivering gifts to good children.

In the Czech Republic, Slovakia, Romania and Hungary, where St. Nicholas (sveti Mikuláš/szent Mikulás) gives his sweet gifts on December 6, the Christmas gift-giver is the Child Jesus (Ježíšek in Czech, Jézuska in Hungarian and Ježiško in Slovak).

In most parts of Germany, Austria, and Switzerland, presents are traditionally exchanged in the evening of December 24. Children are commonly told that presents were brought either by the Christkind (German for: Christchild) or the Weihnachtsmann (German name of Santa Claus). Both leave the gifts, but are in most families not seen doing so.

In Finland, *Joulupukki*, and in Sweden *Jultomten*, personally meets children and gives presents in the evening of Christmas Eve.

In Argentina, Austria, Denmark, Finland, Germany, Hungary, Iceland, Latvia, Norway, Poland, Portugal, Quebec, Romania, Uruguay, and Sweden, Christmas presents are opened mostly on the evening of the 24th, – this is also the tradition among the British Royal Family, due to their mainly German ancestry – while in Italy, the United States, the United Kingdom, Ireland, English Canada, South Africa, New Zealand and Australia, this occurs mostly on the morning of Christmas Day.

In other Latin American countries, people stay awake until midnight, when they open the presents.

In Spain, gifts are traditionally opened on the morning of January 6, Epiphany day ("Día de Los Tres Reyes Magos"), though in some other countries, like Argentina and Uruguay, people receive presents both around Christmas and on the morning of Epiphany day.

In the Netherlands, gift giving on Christmas Day is a fairly new phenomenon, because of the Dutch celebration of Sinterklaas on December 5.

Regional traditions

Main article: Christmas worldwide

Latin America

In Latin America, Christmas Eve, known in Spanish as *La Noche Buena* (English translation – *the good night*) and in Portuguese as *Véspera de Natal* (English: Christmas Eve), is celebrated by staying up until midnight. At midnight, gifts and presents are opened. Fireworks are also shot off. Fireworks are the main focus of the celebration. It is not a silent night, with families coming together exchanging presents and going to church. After Christmas the children often play with their new presents or go to church with their families.

Spain

As in Latin America, Christmas Eve is also known as *Nochebuena* in Spain. There are two important traditions: attending Christmas Mass, and enjoying a meal with friends and family.

There is a wide variety of typical foods one might find on plates across Spain on this particular night, and each region has its own distinct specialities. It is particularly common, however, to start the meal with a seafood dish such as prawns or salmon, followed by a bowl of hot, homemade soup. The main meal will commonly consist of roast lamb, or seafood, such as cod or shellfish. For dessert, there is quite a spread of delicacies, among them are turrón, a dessert made of honey, egg and almonds that is Arabic in origin. Seafood is very common.

Iceland and Norway

In Iceland and Norway, Yule (jul/jól) starts on the night of December 24, at 6:00 p.m. and 5:00 p.m. respectively. Church bells ring at that time and people either sit down for holiday dinner at home or with their family. After that they open gifts and spend the evening together. In Iceland people most often eat hamborgarahryggur and svínabógur.

Poland

In Poland, largely Roman Catholic, the traditional Christmas meal is known as *Wigilia* ("Vigil"), and being invited to attend a Wigilia dinner with a family is considered a high honour. Before eating, everyone exchanges Christmas greetings with each other by sharing a piece of Christmas wafer (*Opłatki*), usually blessed by the presiding Bishop, and stamped with a religious image, such as the Nativity scene. There is a tradition of having either 7 or 12 (or its multiple) Lenten (meatless) dishes. One has to try every single dish to avoid bad luck next year. Dishes are usually fish, or potato based, with carp or herring being very important in Wigilia Polish culture. After dinner, children open presents from under the Christmas Tree. Later, people attend Midnight Mass to solemnly celebrate the birth of Jesus Christ.

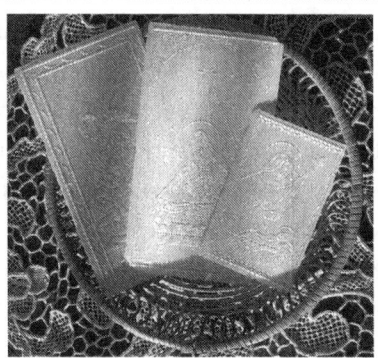

Polish Opłatki (Christmas Wafer) in a basket.

Serbia, Republika Srpska and Montenegro

Further information: Serbian Christmas traditions and Badnjak (Serbian)

The Serbian Orthodox Church uses the Julian calendar, which is currently 13 days behind the Gregorian, so Christmas Eve (December 24) as celebrated by the Serbs coincides with January 6 on the latter calendar. In Serbian Christmas traditions, the head of household goes in the morning into a forest to select a young, straight oak tree and fell it. A log cut from this tree, up to 2.5 meters (8.2 ft) long, is called *badnjak* and has an important role in the celebration. It is in the evening ceremoniously taken into the house and laid on the fire that burns on the house's fireplace called *ognjište*, whose hearth is without a vertical surround. The burning of the *badnjak* is accompanied by prayers to God so that the coming year may bring much happiness, love, luck, riches, and food. Since most houses today have no *ognjište* on which to burn a *badnjak*, it is symbolically represented by several leaved oak twigs. For the convenience of people who live in towns and cities, they can be bought at marketplaces or received in churches.

The Serbs also take a bundle of straw into the house and spread it over the floor, and then walnuts on it. Before the table is served for the Christmas Eve dinner, it is strewn with a thin layer of straw and covered with a white cloth. The head of household makes the Sign of the Cross, lights a candle, and censes the whole house. The family members sit down at the table, but before tucking in they all rise and a man or boy among them says a prayer, or they together sing the Troparion of the Nativity. After the dinner young people visit their friends, a group of whom may gather at the house of one of them. Christmas and other songs are sung, while the elderly narrate stories from the olden times.

Since the early 1990s, the Serbian Orthodox Church has, together with local communities, organized public celebrations on Christmas Eve. The course of these celebrations can be typically divided into three parts: the preparation, the ritual, and the festivity. The preparation consists of going and cutting down the tree to be used as the *badnjak*, taking it to the church yard, and preparing drink and food for the assembled parishioners. The ritual includes Vespers, placing the *badnjak* on the open fire built in the church yard, blessing or consecrating the *badnjak*, and an appropriate program with songs and recitals. In some parishes they build the fire on which to burn the *badnjak* not in the church yard but at some other suitable location in their town or village. The festivity consists of getting together around the fire and socializing. Each particular celebration, however, has its own specificities which reflect traditions of the local community, and other local factors.

North America

Most households circulate wrapped gifts in the two weeks before Christmas Day. In North America, gifts are most commonly opened on the morning of Christmas Day; however, families may also choose to open all or some of their presents on Christmas Eve, depending on evolving family traditions, logistics, and the age of the children involved. E.g., adults might open their presents on Christmas Eve and minor children open their presents on Christmas morning, or everyone might open their gifts on Christmas morning. In Quebec and among many French-speaking families living in other provinces, the Réveillon is held on Christmas Eve with traditional food such as tourtière, attendance at church, and the opening of gifts. It is also common tradition throughout the United States and Canada, for children to leave a glass of milk and plate of cookies for Santa Claus on Christmas Eve by the fireplace and a carrot for the reindeer.. Similar traditions occur in Mexico, Central America including El Salvador; however, the name given is, as in Spain, *Nochebuena*..

Philippines

Further information: Christmas in the Philippines

In the Philippines, the predominantly Roman Catholic Christian country in Asia, Christmas Eve is usually celebrated by attending the "Rooster's Mass" or Misa del Gallo which is celebrated hours before the clock ticks 12 A.M. signifying the arrival of Christmas Day. After attending church, Filipino families usually hold a feast named *Noche Buena* to celebrate the birth of Jesus Christ. A great variety of food is eaten during this feast, an event that usually is done with great preparation. Foods being prepared include the famous *lechón*, *quezo de bola* (Edam cheese), *hamón* (Christmas ham), roast chicken (turkey did not gain much popularity in the Philippines), barbecued meats, *pancit*, among many others. Despite the fact that some families are poor, they still find a way to commemorate the birth of Jesus Christ through eating, family time and merry-making.

Japan

Christmas Eve is celebrated as a couple's holiday; significant others spend time together at a nice place and exchange gifts.[citation needed]

Finland

Most of the traditions, such as Christmas dinner and gift giving, are observed on this day. Santa Claus visits homes in person, played by an older family member or a rent-a-Santa.

The Declaration of Christmas Peace has been a tradition in Finland from the Middle Ages every year, except in 1939 due to the Winter War. It is a custom in many towns and cities.

The most famous one of these declarations is on the Old Great Square of Turku, the former capital of Finland, at noon on Christmas Eve. It is broadcast on Finnish radio (since 1935) and television, and nowadays also in some foreign countries. The declaration ceremony begins with the hymn *Jumala ompi linnamme* (Martin Luther's *A Mighty Fortress Is Our God*) and continues with the Declaration of Christmas Peace read from a parchment roll:

It is traditional in Finland to bring candles to the graves of loved ones on Christmas Eve and All Saints Day.

> "Tomorrow, God willing, is the most gracious feast of the birth of our Lord and Saviour, and therefore a general Christmas peace is hereby declared, and all persons are directed to observe this holiday with due reverence and otherwise quietly and peacefully to conduct themselves, for whosoever breaks this peace and disturbs the Christmas holiday by any unlawful or improper conduct shall be liable, under aggravating circumstances, to whatever penalty is prescribed by law and decree for each particular offence or misdemeanour. Finally, all citizens are wished a joyous Christmas holiday."

The Ceremony ends with trumpets playing the Finnish national anthem *Maamme* and *Porilaisten marssi*, with the crowd usually singing when the band plays *Maamme*.

Recently, there is also a declaration of Christmas peace for forest animals in many cities and municipalities, so there is no hunting during Christmas.

In Finland people usually take a Christmas sauna. The tradition is very old. Unlike on normal days, when going to sauna is in the evening, on Christmas Eve it is before sunset. This tradition is based on a pre-20th century belief that the spirits of the dead return and have a sauna at the usual sauna hours.

Netherlands

In the Netherlands, Christmas Eve is gradually losing its original meaning. In older days, the Catholic part of the country, roughly half, mainly the south, used to attend mass; usually between 11:00pm and 12:30am. This custom is still upheld but by fewer people every year. Christmas Eve is these days a rather normal evening without any special gatherings or meals. The day of Christmas is another matter. That day is a special day for most families. Usually people have elaborate dinners with friends and relatives. The Dutch call December 25 *Eerste Kerstdag*, "first Christmas day". This day is a national holiday as is December 26, called *Tweede Kerstdag*, "second Christmas day". In families, it is custom to spend these days with either side of the relatives.

Sweden

Further information: Swedish festivities#Christmas

In Sweden, most Christmas celebrations take place on Christmas Eve, including Santa Claus's distribution of Christmas presents. Until the 20th century, presents were instead distributed by the Yule Goat, still today used as Christmas decoration and remembered by the famous Gävle goat. Christmas dishes and meals are always served on Julbord (Christmas table), and often contain Christmas ham and the world-famous Janssons frestelse. Many families also watch *Kalle Anka och hans vänner önskar God Jul (From All of Us to All of You)*, *Karl Bertil Jonssons julafton*, or a re-run of the *Svensson, Svensson* episode *God Jul! (Merry Christmas)* on the TV channel SVT1.

Denmark

In Denmark, during Christmas Eve an elaborate dinner is eaten with the family, consisting of roast pork, roast duck, or roast goose with potatoes, red cabbage and gravy. For dessert is rice pudding with a cherry sauce, traditionally with an almond hidden inside. The lucky finder of this almond is entitled to a small gift. After the meal is complete, the family gather around the Christmas tree to sing Christmas carols and dance hand in hand around the tree. Then the children often hand out the presents which are opened immediately. This is followed by candy, chips, various nuts, clementines, and sometimes a mulled and spiced wine with almonds and raisins called Gløgg is served hot in small cups.

United Kingdom

In the UK, Santa Claus is often called Father Christmas. In households with younger children the preparations for Father Christmas on Christmas Eve depend on individual family traditions. Sometimes the children will be involved in leaving some sustenance for Father Christmas. Traditionally this would have consisted of a glass of sherry or brandy and a mince pie with carrots for Rudolph and the other reindeer. The hanging of Christmas stockings to receive presents is a much-loved tradition that is still practiced by many. Few families open their presents on Christmas Eve, the Royal family being a notable exception, and Queen Victoria as a child makes note of it in her diary for Christmas Eve 1832, the delighted 13-year-old princess wrote, "After dinner...we then went into the drawing-room near the dining-room...There were two large round tables on which were placed two trees hung with lights and sugar ornaments. All the presents being placed round the trees..".

On the day itself, preparations are quickly underway for the Christmas lunch where the whole family will gather for 'turkey and all the trimmings' and the obligatory Christmas Crackers. Attendance at a Christmas Day church service is less popular than it used to be with fewer than 3 million now attending a Christmas Day Church of England service. Watching the Queen's Speech on TV is a tradition that still remains hugely important in many households' Christmas Day typically averaging 10 million viewers on TV and 2m listeners via radio.

Historical events

A number of historical events have been influenced by the occurrence of Christmas Eve.

Christmas truce

Main article: Christmas truce

During World War I in 1914 and 1915 an unofficial Christmas truce took place. The truce began on Christmas Eve, December 24, 1914, when German troops began decorating the area around their trenches in the region of Ypres, Belgium, for Christmas. They began by placing candles on trees, then continued the celebration by singing Christmas carols, most notably *Stille Nacht* (*Silent Night*). The British troops in the trenches across from them responded by singing English carols. The two sides shouted Christmas greetings to each other. Soon thereafter, there were calls for visits across the "No man's land" where small gifts were exchanged. The truce also allowed a breathing spell where

A cross, left near Ypres in Belgium in 1999, to commemorate the site of the 1914 Christmas Truce. The text reads *1914—The Khaki Chum's Christmas Truce—85 Years—Lest We Forget.*

recently-fallen soldiers could be brought back behind their lines by burial parties. Funerals took place as soldiers from both sides mourned the dead together and paid their respects. At one funeral in No Man's Land, soldiers from both sides gathered and read a passage from Psalm 23. The truce occurred in spite of opposition at higher levels of the military command. Earlier in the autumn, a call by Pope Benedict XV for an official truce between the warring governments had been ignored.

Apollo 8 reading from Genesis

Main article: Apollo 8 Genesis reading

On December 24, 1968, in what was the most watched television broadcast to that date, the astronauts William Anders, Jim Lovell and Frank Borman of Apollo 8 surprised the world with a reading of the Creation from the Book of Genesis as they orbited the moon. Madalyn Murray O'Hair, an atheist activist, filed a lawsuit under the Establishment Clause of the First Amendment. The suit was dismissed by the US Supreme Court.

In 1969, the United States Postal Service issued a stamp (Scott # 1371) commemorating the Apollo 8 flight around the moon. The stamp featured a detail of the famous photograph of the Earthrise over the moon (NASA image AS8-14-2383HR) taken by Anders on Christmas Eve, and the words, "In the beginning God..."

Calendar-related events

Christmas Eve parties

The significant amount of vacation travel, and travel back to family homes, means that Christmas Eve is also frequently linked to social events and parties, worldwide.

Jewish singles parties in U.S.

Main article: Matzo Ball

Due to the family gathering and religious worship activities that are central to Christmas Eve for American Christians but which American Jews do not typically engage in, a series of Jewish singles events on the night of December 24 have been created in many major cities.

See also

- December 24
- Kūčios
- New Year's Eve
- Nittel Nacht
- Réveillon
- Santa Claus
- Serbian Christmas traditions
- Wigilia

External links

- Media related to Christmas Eve at Wikimedia Commons

Christmas

Christmas	
colspan="2"	Christmas decorations on display.
Also called	Christ's Mass Nativity Noel
Observed by	Christians Many non-Christians
Type	Christian, cultural
Significance	Traditional birthday of Jesus
Date	December 25 January 6 (in Armenia) January 7 (in Eastern Orthodox and Catholic churches)
Observances	Gift giving, church services, family and other social gatherings, symbolic decorating
Related to	Annunciation, Advent, Epiphany, Baptism of the Lord

Christmas or **Christmas Day** is a holiday observed mostly on December 25 to commemorate the birth of Jesus, the central figure of Christianity. The date is not known to be the actual birthday of Jesus, and may have initially been chosen to correspond with either the day exactly nine months after some early Christians believed Jesus had been conceived, the date of the winter solstice on the ancient Roman calendar, or one of various ancient winter festivals. Christmas is central to the Christmas and holiday season, and in Christianity marks the beginning of the larger season of Christmastide, which lasts twelve days.

Although nominally a Christian holiday, Christmas is also widely celebrated by many non-Christians, and many of its popular celebratory customs have pre-Christian or secular themes and origins. Popular modern customs of the holiday include gift-giving, music, an exchange of greeting cards, church celebrations, a special meal, and the display of various decorations; including Christmas trees, lights, garlands, mistletoe, nativity scenes, and holly. In addition, Father Christmas (or Santa Claus) is a popular folklore figure in many countries, associated with the bringing of gifts for children.

Because gift-giving and many other aspects of the Christmas festival involve heightened economic activity among both Christians and non-Christians, the holiday has become a significant event and a key sales period for retailers and businesses. The economic impact of Christmas is a factor that has grown steadily over the past few centuries in many regions of the world.

Etymology

The word *Christmas* originated as a compound meaning "Christ's Mass". It is derived from the Middle English *Christemasse* and Old English *Cristes mæsse,* a phrase first recorded in 1038. "Cristes" is from Greek *Christos* and "mæsse" is from Latin *missa* (the holy mass). In Greek, the letter *X* (chi), is the first letter of Christ, and it, or the similar Roman letter X, has been used as an abbreviation for Christ since the mid-16th century. Hence, Xmas is sometimes used as an abbreviation for Christmas.

Celebration

Further information: Christmas worldwide

Christmas Day is celebrated as a major festival and public holiday in most countries of the world, even in many whose populations are not majority Christian. In some non-Christian countries, periods of former colonial rule introduced the celebration (e.g. Hong Kong); in others, Christian minorities or foreign cultural influences have led populations to observe the holiday. Major exceptions, where Christmas is not a formal public holiday, include People's Republic of China, (except Hong Kong and Macao), Japan, Saudi Arabia, Algeria, Thailand, Nepal, Iran, Turkey and North Korea.

Around the world, Christmas celebrations can vary markedly in form, reflecting differing cultural and national traditions. Countries such as Japan and Korea, where Christmas is popular despite there being only a small number of Christians, have adopted many of the secular aspects of Christmas, such as gift-giving, decorations and Christmas trees.

Date of celebration

For many centuries, Christian writers accepted that Christmas was the actual date on which Jesus was born. In the early 18th century, scholars began proposing alternative explanations. Isaac Newton argued that the date of Christmas was selected to correspond with the winter solstice, which the Romans called *bruma* and celebrated on December 25. In 1743, German Protestant Paul Ernst Jablonski argued Christmas was placed on December 25 to correspond with the Roman solar holiday *Dies Natalis Solis Invicti* and was therefore a "paganization" that debased the true church. According to Judeo-Christian tradition, creation as described in the Genesis creation narrative occurred on the date of the spring equinox, i.e. March 25 on the Roman calendar. This date is now celebrated as Annunciation and as the anniversary of Incarnation. In 1889, Louis Duchesne suggested that the date of Christmas was calculated as nine months after Annunciation, the traditional date of the conception of Jesus.

The December 25 date may have been selected by the church in Rome in the early 4th century. At this time, a church calendar was created and other holidays were also placed on solar dates: "It is cosmic symbolism...which inspired the Church leadership in Rome to elect the winter solstice, December 25, as the birthday of Christ, and the summer solstice as that of John the Baptist, supplemented by the equinoxes as their respective dates of conception. While they were aware that pagans called this day the 'birthday' of Sol Invictus, this did not concern them and it did not play any role in their choice of date for Christmas," according to modern scholar S.E. Hijmans.

Orthodox churches

Some Eastern Orthodox national churches, including those of Russia, Georgia, Egypt, Ukraine, the Macedonia, Serbia and the Greek Patriarchate of Jerusalem mark feasts using the older Julian Calendar. December 25 on that calendar currently corresponds to January 7 on the more widely used Gregorian calendar. Oriental Orthodox churches also use their own calendars, which are generally similar to the Julian calendar. The Armenian Apostolic Church celebrates the nativity in combination with the Feast of the Epiphany on January 6. Most Armenian churches use the Gregorian calendar, but some use the Julian calendar and thus celebrate Christmas Day on January 19, and Christmas Eve on January 18 (according to the Gregorian calendar).

Commemorating the birth of Jesus

Main articles: Annunciation, Nativity of Jesus, and Child Jesus

In Christianity, Christmas is the festival celebrating the Nativity of Jesus, the Christian belief that the Messiah foretold in the Old Testament's Messianic prophecies was born to the Virgin Mary. The story of Christmas is based on the biblical accounts given in the Gospel of Matthew, namely Matthew 1:18, and the Gospel of Luke, specifically Luke 1:26 and 2:40. According to these accounts, Jesus was born to Mary, assisted by her husband Joseph, in the city of Bethlehem. According to popular tradition, the birth took place in a stable, surrounded by farm animals, though neither the stable nor the animals are specifically mentioned in the Biblical accounts. However, a manger is mentioned in Luke 2:7, where it states, "She wrapped him in cloths and placed him in a manger, because there was no room for them in the inn." Early iconographic representations of the nativity placed the animals and manger within a cave (located, according to tradition, under the Church of the Nativity in Bethlehem). Shepherds from the fields surrounding Bethlehem were told of the birth by an angel, and were the first to see the child.

Adorazione del Bambino (Adoration of the Child) (1439–43), a mural by Florentine painter Fra Angelico.

Many Christians believe that the birth of Jesus fulfilled messianic prophecies from the Old Testament. The Gospel of Matthew also describes a visit by several Magi, or astrologers, who bring gifts of gold, frankincense, and myrrh to the infant. The visitors were said to be following a mysterious star, commonly known as the Star of Bethlehem, believing it to announce the birth of a king of the Jews. The commemoration of this visit, the Feast of Epiphany celebrated on January 6, is the formal end of the Christmas season in some churches.

Christians celebrate Christmas in many ways. In addition to this day being one of the most important and popular for the attendance of church services, there are numerous other devotions and popular traditions. Prior to Christmas Day, the Eastern Orthodox Church practises the 40-day Nativity Fast in anticipation of the birth of Jesus, while much of Western Christianity celebrates four weeks of Advent. The final preparations for Christmas are made on Christmas Eve.

Over the Christmas period, people decorate their homes and exchange gifts. In some Christian denominations, children perform plays re-telling the events of the Nativity, or sing carols that reference the event. Some Christians also display a small re-creation of the Nativity, known as a Nativity scene or crib, in their homes, using figurines to portray the key characters of the event. Live Nativity scenes and tableaux vivants are also performed, using actors and animals to portray the event with more realism.

A long artistic tradition has grown of producing painted depictions of the nativity in art. Nativity scenes are traditionally set in a barn or stable and include Mary, Joseph, the child Jesus, angels, shepherds and the Three Wise Men: Balthazar, Melchior, and Caspar, who are said to have followed a star, known as the Star of Bethlehem, and arrived after his birth.

Varied traditions

Among countries with a strong Christian tradition, a variety of Christmas celebrations have developed that incorporate regional and local cultures. For many Christians, participating in a religious service plays an important part in the recognition of the season. Christmas, along with Easter, is the period of highest annual church attendance.

In many Catholic countries, the people hold religious processions or parades in the days preceding Christmas. In other countries, secular processions or parades featuring Santa Claus and other seasonal figures are often held. Family reunions and the exchange of gifts are a widespread feature of the season. Gift giving takes place on Christmas Day in most countries. Others practise gift giving on December 6, Saint Nicholas Day, and January 6, Epiphany.

A special Christmas family meal is an important part of the celebration for many, and what is served varies greatly from country to country. Some regions, such as Sicily, have special meals for Christmas Eve, when 12 kinds of fish are served. In England and countries influenced by its traditions, a standard Christmas meal includes turkey (brought from North America), potatoes, vegetables, sausages and gravy, followed by Christmas pudding, mince pies and fruit cake. In Poland and other parts of eastern Europe and Scandinavia, fish often is used for the traditional main course, but richer meat such as lamb is increasingly served. In Germany, France and Austria, goose and pork are favored. Beef, ham and chicken in various recipes are popular throughout the world. Ham is the main meal in the Philippines.

Special desserts are also prepared: The Maltese traditionally serve *Imbuljuta tal-Qastan*, a chocolate and chestnuts beverage, after Midnight Mass and throughout the Christmas season. Slovaks prepare the traditional Christmas bread potica, *bûche de Noël* in France, *panettone* in Italy, and elaborate tarts and cakes. The eating of sweets and chocolates has become popular worldwide, and sweeter Christmas delicacies include the German *stollen*, marzipan cake or candy, and Jamaican rum fruit cake. As one of the few fruits traditionally available to northern countries in winter, oranges were long associated with special Christmas foods.

Decorations

Main article: Christmas decoration

See also: Christmas tree, Christmas lights, Christmas stocking, and Christmas ornament

The practice of putting up special decorations at Christmas has a long history. From pre-Christian times, people in the Roman Empire brought branches from evergreen plants indoors in the winter. Decorating with greenery was also part of Jewish tradition : "Now on the first day you shall take for yourselves the foliage of beautiful trees, palm branches and boughs of leafy trees and willows of the brook, and you shall rejoice before the LORD your God for seven days. " (Leviticus 23:40)

Christian people incorporated such customs in their developing practices. In the 15th century, it was recorded that in London it was the custom at Christmas for every house and all the parish churches to be "decked with holm, ivy, bays, and whatsoever the season of the year afforded to be green". The heart-shaped leaves of ivy were said to symbolise the coming to earth of Jesus, while holly was seen as protection against pagans and witches, its thorns and red berries held to represent the Crown of Thorns worn by Jesus at the crucifixion and the blood he shed.

Nativity scenes are known from 10th-century Rome. They were popularised by Saint Francis of Asissi from 1223, quickly spreading across Europe. Many different types of decorations developed across the Christian world, dependent on local tradition and available resources. The first commercially produced decorations appeared in Germany in the 1860s, inspired by paper chains made by children.

The Christmas tree is often explained as a Christianisation of pagan tradition and ritual surrounding the Winter Solstice, which included the use of evergreen boughs, and an adaptation of pagan tree worship. The English language phrase "Christmas tree" is first recorded in 1835 and represents an importation from the German language. The modern Christmas tree tradition is believed to have begun in Germany in the 18th century though many argue that Martin Luther began the tradition in the 16th century. From Germany the custom was introduced to Britain, first via Queen Charlotte, wife of George III, and then more successfully by Prince Albert during the reign of Queen Victoria. By 1841 the Christmas tree had become even more widespread throughout Britain. By the 1870s, people in the United States had adopted the custom of putting up a Christmas tree. Christmas trees may be decorated with lights and ornaments.

Since the 19th century, the poinsettia, a native plant from Mexico, has been associated with Christmas. Other popular holiday plants include holly, mistletoe, red amaryllis, and Christmas cactus. Along with a Christmas tree, the interior of a home may be decorated with these plants, along with garlands and evergreen foliage.

In Australia, North and South America, and Europe, it is traditional to decorate the outside of houses with lights and sometimes with illuminated sleighs, snowmen, and other Christmas figures. Municipalities often sponsor decorations as well. Christmas banners may be hung from street lights and Christmas trees placed in the town square.

In the Western world, rolls of brightly colored paper with secular or religious Christmas motifs are manufactured for the purpose of wrapping gifts. The display of Christmas villages has also become a tradition in many homes during this season. Other traditional decorations include bells, candles, candy canes, stockings, wreaths, and angels.

In many countries a representation of the Nativity Scene is very popular, and people are encouraged to compete and create most original or realistic ones. Within some families, the pieces used to make the representation are considered a valuable family heirloom. Christmas decorations are traditionally taken down on Twelfth Night, the evening of January 5. The traditional colors of Christmas are pine green (evergreen), snow white, and heart red.

European Holly, traditional Christmas decoration.

Music and carols

Main article: Christmas music

The first specifically Christmas hymns that we know of appear in 4th century Rome. Latin hymns such as *Veni redemptor gentium*, written by Ambrose, Archbishop of Milan, were austere statements of the theological doctrine of the Incarnation in opposition to Arianism. *Corde natus ex Parentis* (*Of the Father's love begotten*) by the Spanish poet Prudentius (d. 413) is still sung in some churches today.

In the 9th and 10th centuries, the Christmas "Sequence" or "Prose" was introduced in North European monasteries, developing under Bernard of Clairvaux into a sequence of rhymed stanzas. In the 12th century the Parisian monk Adam of St. Victor began to derive music from popular songs, introducing something closer to the traditional Christmas carol.

By the 13th century, in France, Germany, and particularly, Italy, under the influence of Francis of Asissi, a strong tradition of popular Christmas songs in the native language developed. Christmas carols in English first appear in a 1426 work of John Awdlay, a Shropshire chaplain, who lists twenty-five "caroles of Cristemas", probably sung by groups of wassailers, who went from house to house. The songs we know specifically as carols were originally communal folk songs sung during celebrations such as "harvest tide" as well as Christmas. It was only later that carols began to be sung in church. Traditionally, carols have often been based on medieval chord patterns, and it is this that gives them their uniquely characteristic musical sound. Some carols like *"Personent hodie"*, "Good King Wenceslas", and "The Holly and the Ivy" can be traced directly back to the Middle Ages. They are among the oldest musical compositions still regularly sung. *Adeste Fidelis* (O Come all ye faithful) appears in its current form in the mid-18th century, although the words may have originated in the 13th century.

Singing of carols initially suffered a decline in popularity after the Protestant Reformation in northern Europe, although some Reformers, like Martin Luther, wrote carols and encouraged their use in worship. Carols largely survived in rural communities until the revival of interest in popular songs in the 19th century. The 18th century English reformer Charles Wesley understood the importance of music to worship. In addition to setting many psalms to melodies, which were influential in the Great Awakening in the United States, he wrote texts for at least three Christmas carols. The best known was originally entitled "Hark! How All the Welkin Rings", later renamed "Hark! the Herald Angels Sing". Felix Mendelssohn wrote a melody adapted to fit Wesley's words. In Austria in 1818 Mohr and Gruber made a major addition to the genre when they composed "Silent Night" for the St. Nicholas Church, Oberndorf. William B. Sandys' *Christmas Carols Ancient and Modern* (1833) contained the first appearance in print of many now-classic English carols, and contributed to the mid-Victorian revival of the festival.

Child singers in Bucharest, 1841.

Completely secular Christmas seasonal songs emerged in the late 18th century. "Deck The Halls" dates from 1784, and the American, "Jingle Bells" was copyrighted in 1857. In the 19th and 20th century, African American spirituals and songs about Christmas, based in their tradition of spirituals, became more widely known. An increasing number of seasonal holidays songs were commercially produced in the 20th century, including jazz and blues variations. In addition, there was a revival of interest in early music, from groups singing folk music, such as The Revels, to performers of early medieval and classical music.

Cards

Main article: Christmas card

A Christmas card from 1870

Christmas cards are illustrated messages of greeting usually exchanged between friends and family members during the weeks preceding Christmas Day. The custom has become popular among a wide cross-section of people, including non-Christians, in Western society and in Asia. The traditional greeting reads "wishing you a Merry Christmas and a Happy New Year", much like that of the first commercial Christmas card, produced by Sir Henry Cole in London in 1843. However there are innumerable variations of this formula, many cards expressing a more religious sentiment, or containing a poem, prayer or Biblical verse; while others distance themselves from religion with an all-inclusive "Season's greetings".

Christmas cards are purchased in considerable quantities, and feature artwork, commercially designed and relevant to the season. The content of the design might relate directly to the Christmas narrative with depictions of the Nativity of Jesus, or Christian symbols such as the Star of Bethlehem, or a white dove which can represent both the Holy Spirit and Peace on Earth. Other Christmas cards are more secular and can depict Christmas traditions, mythical figures such as Santa Claus, objects directly associated with Christmas such as candles, holly and baubles, or a variety of images associated with the season, such as Christmastime activities, snow scenes and the wildlife of the northern winter. There are also humorous cards and genres depicting nostalgic scenes of the past such as crinolined shoppers in idealized 19th century streetscapes.

Stamps

Main article: Christmas stamp

A number of nations have issued commemorative stamps at Christmastime. Postal customers will often use these stamps to mail Christmas cards, and they are popular with philatelists. These stamps are regular postage stamps, unlike Christmas seals, and are valid for postage year-round. They usually go on sale some time between early October and early December, and are printed in considerable quantities.

In 1898 a Canadian stamp was issued to mark the inauguration of the Imperial Penny Postage rate. The stamp features a map of the globe and bears an inscription "XMAS 1898" at the bottom. In 1937, Austria issued two "Christmas greeting stamps" featuring a rose and the signs of the zodiac. In 1939, Brazil issued four semi-postal stamps with designs featuring the three kings and a star of Bethlehem, an angel and child, the Southern Cross and a child, and a mother and child.

Both the US Postal Service and the Royal Mail regularly issue Christmas-themed stamps each year.

Santa Claus and other bringers of gifts

Main articles: Santa Claus and Father Christmas

Christmas has for many centuries been a time for the giving and exchanging of gifts, particularly between friends and family members. A number of figures of both Christian and mythical origin have been associated with Christmas and the seasonal giving of gifts. Among these are Father Christmas, also known as Santa Claus, Père Noël, and the Weihnachtsmann; Saint Nicholas or Sinterklaas; the Christkind; Kris Kringle; Joulupukki; Babbo Natale; Saint Basil; and Father Frost.

Sinterklaas or Saint Nicholas, considered by many to be the original Santa Claus.

The most famous and pervasive of these figures in modern celebration worldwide is Santa Claus, a mythical gift bringer, dressed in red, whose origins have diverse sources. The name Santa Claus is a corruption of the Dutch *Sinterklaas*, which means simply Saint Nicholas. Nicholas was Bishop of Myra, in modern day Turkey, during the 4th century. Among other saintly attributes, he was noted for the care of Children, generosity, and the giving of gifts. His feast on the 6th of December came to be celebrated in many countries with the giving of gifts. Saint Nicholas traditionally appeared in bishoply attire, accompanied by helpers, and enquired about the behaviour of children during the past year before deciding whether they deserved a gift or not. By the 13th century Saint Nicholas was well known in the Netherlands, and the practice of gift-giving in his name spread to other parts of central and southern Europe. At the Reformation in 16th–17th century Europe, many Protestants changed the gift bringer to the Christ Child or *Christkindl*, corrupted in English to Kris Kringle, and the date of giving gifts changed from December the 6th to Christmas Eve.

The modern popular image of Santa Claus, however, was created in the United States, and in particular in New York. The transformation was accomplished with the aid of six notable contributors including Washington Irving and the German-American cartoonist Thomas Nast (1840–1902). Following the American Revolutionary War, some of the inhabitants of New York City sought out symbols of the city's non-English past. New York had originally been established as the Dutch colonial town of New Amsterdam and the Dutch Sinterklaas tradition was reinvented as Saint Nicholas. In 1809, the New-York Historical Society convened and retroactively named *Sancte Claus* the patron saint of

Nieuw Amsterdam, the Dutch name for New York City. At his first American appearance in 1810, Santa Claus was drawn in bishops' robes. However as new artists took over, Santa Claus developed more secular attire. Nast drew a new image of "Santa Claus" annually, beginning in 1863. By the 1880s, Nast's Santa had evolved into the robed, fur clad, form we now recognize, perhaps based on the English figure of Father Christmas. The image was standardized by advertisers in the 1920s.

Father Christmas, a jolly, well nourished, bearded man who typified the spirit of good cheer at Christmas, predates the Santa Claus character. He is first recorded in early 17th century England, but was associated with holiday merrymaking and drunkenness rather than the bringing of gifts. In Victorian Britain, his image was remade to match that of Santa. The French Père Noël evolved along similar lines, eventually adopting the Santa image. In Italy, Babbo Natale acts as Santa Claus, while La Befana is the bringer of gifts and arrives on the eve of the Epiphany. It is said that La Befana set out to bring the baby Jesus gifts, but got lost along the way. Now, she brings gifts to all children. In some cultures Santa Claus is accompanied by Knecht Ruprecht, or Black Peter. In other versions, elves make the toys. His wife is referred to as Mrs. Claus.

There has been some opposition to the narrative of the American evolution of Saint Nicholas into the modern Santa. It has been claimed that the Saint Nicholas Society was not founded until 1835, almost half a century after the end of the American War of Independence. Moreover, a study of the "children's books, periodicals and journals" of New Amsterdam by Charles Jones revealed no references to Saint Nicholas or Sinterklaas. However, not all scholars agree with Jones's findings, which he reiterated in a booklength study in 1978; Howard G. Hageman, of New Brunswick Theological Seminary, maintains that the tradition of celebrating Sinterklaas in New York was alive and well from the early settlement of the Hudson Valley on.

Current tradition in several Latin American countries (such as Venezuela and Colombia) holds that while Santa makes the toys, he then gives them to the Baby Jesus, who is the one who actually delivers them to the children's homes, a reconciliation between traditional religious beliefs and the iconography of Santa Claus imported from the United States.

In Alto Adige/Südtirol (Italy), Austria, Czech Republic, Southern Germany, Hungary, Liechtenstein, Slovakia and Switzerland, the Christkind (Ježíšek in Czech, Jézuska in Hungarian and Ježiško in Slovak) brings the presents. The German St. Nikolaus is not identical with the Weihnachtsman (who is the German version of Santa Claus). St. Nikolaus wears a bishop's dress and still brings small gifts (usually candies, nuts and fruits) on December 6 and is accompanied by Knecht Ruprecht. Although many parents around the world routinely teach their children about Santa Claus and other gift bringers, some have come to reject this practice, considering it deceptive.

Controversy and criticism

Main article: Christmas controversy

Throughout the holiday's history, Christmas has been the subject of both controversy and criticism from a wide variety of different sources. The first documented Christmas controversy was Christian-led, and began during the English Interregnum, when England was ruled by a Puritan Parliament. Puritans (including those who fled to America) sought to remove the remaining pagan elements of Christmas. During this period, the English Parliament banned the celebration of Christmas entirely, considering it "a popish festival with no biblical justification", and a time of wasteful and immoral behavior.

Controversy and criticism continues in the present-day, where some Christian and non-Christians have claimed that an affront to Christmas (dubbed a "war on Christmas" by some) is ongoing. In the United States there has been a tendency to replace the greeting *Merry Christmas* with *Happy Holidays*. Groups such as the American Civil Liberties Union have initiated court cases to bar the display of images and other material referring to Christmas from public property, including schools. Such groups argue that government-funded displays of Christmas imagery and traditions violate the First Amendment to the United States Constitution, which prohibits the establishment by Congress of a national religion. In 1984, the U.S. Supreme Court ruled in *Lynch vs. Donnelly* that a Christmas display (which included a Nativity scene) owned and displayed by the city of Pawtucket, Rhode Island did not violate the First Amendment. In November 2009, the Federal appeals court in Philadelphia endorsed a school district's ban on the singing of Christmas carols.

In the private sphere also, it has been alleged that any specific mention of the term "Christmas" or its religious aspects was being increasingly censored, avoided, or discouraged by a number of advertisers and retailers. In response, the American Family Association and other groups have organized boycotts of individual retailers.." In the United Kingdom there have also been some controversies, one of the most famous being the temporary promotion of the Christmas period as Winterval by Birmingham City Council in 1998. There were also protests in November 2009 when the city of Dundee promoted its celebrations as the *Winter Night Light festival*, initially with no specific Christmas references.

People interested in this section, might also be interested in reading this subject's chapter 6 Economics [1]

History

Pre-Christian background

Dies Natalis Solis Invicti

Main article: Sol Invictus

Dies Natalis Solis Invicti means "the birthday of the unconquered Sun." The use of the title Sol Invictus allowed several solar deities to be worshipped collectively, including Elah-Gabal, a Syrian sun god; Sol, the god of Emperor Aurelian; and Mithras, a soldiers' god of Persian origin. Emperor Elagabalus (218–222) introduced Sol-worship and the cult reached the height of its popularity under Aurelian.

Mosaic of Jesus as *Christo Sole* (Christ the Sun) in Mausoleum M in the pre-fourth-century necropolis under St Peter's Basilica in Rome.

Modern scholars have argued that the festival was placed on the date of the solstice because this was on this day that the Sun reversed its southward retreat and proved itself to be "unconquered." Several early Christian writers connected the rebirth of the sun to the birth of Jesus. "O, how wonderfully acted Providence that on that day on which that Sun was born...Christ should be born", Cyprian wrote. John Chrysostom also commented on the connection: "They call it the 'Birthday of the Unconquered'. Who indeed is so unconquered as Our Lord . . .?"

Although Dies Natalis Solis Invicti has been the subject of a great deal of scholarly speculation, the only ancient source for it is a single mention in the Chronography of 354. "[W]hile the winter solstice on or around the 25th of December was well established in the Roman imperial calendar, there is no evidence that a religious celebration of Sol on that day antedated the celebration of Christmas, and none that indicates that Aurelian had a hand in its institution," according to modern Sol scholar Steven Hijmans.

Winter festivals

Main article: List of winter festivals

A winter festival was the most popular festival of the year in many cultures. Reasons included the fact that less agricultural work needs to be done during the winter, as well as an expectation of better weather as spring approached. Modern Christmas customs include: gift-giving and merrymaking from Roman Saturnalia; greenery, lights, and charity from the Roman New Year; and Yule logs and various foods from Germanic feasts. Pagan Scandinavia celebrated a winter festival called Yule, held in the late December to early January period. As Northern Europe was the last part to Christianize, its pagan traditions had a major influence on Christmas. Scandinavians still call Christmas *Jul*. In English, the word Yule is synonymous with Christmas, a usage first recorded in 900.

Christian feast

The New Testament does not give a date for the birth of Jesus. Around AD 200, Clement of Alexandria wrote that a group in Egypt celebrated the nativity on 25 Pashons. This corresponds to May 20. Tertullian (d. 220) does not mention Christmas as a major feast day in the Church of Roman Africa. However, in *Chronographai*, a reference work published in 221, Sextus Julius Africanus suggested that Jesus was conceived on the spring equinox, popularizing the idea that Christ was born on December 25. The equinox was March 25 on the Roman calendar, so this implied a birth in December. *De Pascha Computus*, a calendar of feasts produced in 243, gives March 28 as the date of the nativity. In 245, the theologian Origen of Alexandria stated that, "only sinners (like Pharaoh and Herod)" celebrated their birthdays. In 303, Christian writer Arnobius ridiculed the idea of celebrating the birthdays of gods, which suggests that Christmas was not yet a feast at this time.

Feast established

The earliest known reference to the date of the nativity as December 25 is found in the Chronography of 354, an illuminated manuscript compiled in Rome. In the East, early Christians celebrated the birth of Christ as part of Epiphany (January 6), although this festival emphasized celebration of the baptism of Jesus.

Christmas was promoted in the Christian East as part of the revival of Catholicism following the death of the pro-Arian Emperor Valens at the Battle of Adrianople in 378. The feast was introduced to Constantinople in 379, and to Antioch in about 380. The feast disappeared after Gregory of Nazianzus resigned as bishop in 381, although it was reintroduced by John Chrysostom in about 400.

Middle Ages

In the Early Middle Ages, Christmas Day was overshadowed by Epiphany, which in the west focused on the visit of the magi. But the Medieval calendar was dominated by Christmas-related holidays. The forty days before Christmas became the "forty days of St. Martin" (which began on November 11, the feast of St. Martin of Tours), now known as Advent. In Italy, former Saturnalian traditions were attached to Advent. Around the 12th century, these traditions transferred again to the Twelve Days of Christmas (December 25 – January 5); a time that appears in the liturgical calendars as Christmastide or Twelve Holy Days.

The Examination and Trial of Father Christmas, (1686), published shortly after Christmas was reinstated as a holy day in England.

The prominence of Christmas Day increased gradually after Charlemagne was crowned Emperor on Christmas Day in 800. King Edmund the Martyr was anointed on Christmas in 855 and King William I of England was crowned on Christmas Day 1066.

By the High Middle Ages, the holiday had become so prominent that chroniclers routinely noted where various magnates celebrated Christmas. King Richard II of England hosted a Christmas feast in 1377 at which twenty-eight oxen and three hundred sheep were eaten. The Yule boar was a common feature of medieval Christmas feasts. Caroling also became popular, and was originally a group of dancers who sang. The group was composed of a lead singer and a ring of dancers that provided the chorus. Various writers of the time condemned caroling as lewd, indicating that the unruly traditions of Saturnalia and Yule may have continued in this form. "Misrule"—drunkenness, promiscuity, gambling—was also an important aspect of the festival. In England, gifts were exchanged on New Year's Day, and there was special Christmas ale.

Christmas during the Middle Ages was a public festival that incorporated ivy, holly, and other evergreens. Christmas gift-giving during the Middle Ages was usually between people with legal relationships, such as tenant and landlord. The annual indulgence in eating, dancing, singing, sporting, card playing escalated in England, and by the 17th century the Christmas season featured lavish dinners, elaborate masques and pageants. In 1607, King James I insisted that a play be acted on Christmas night and that the court indulge in games. It was during the Reformation in 16th–17th century Europe, that many Protestants changed the gift bringer to the Christ Child or *Christkindl*, and the date of giving gifts changed from December 6 to Christmas Eve.

Reformation into the 19th century

Following the Protestant Reformation, groups such as the Puritans strongly condemned the celebration of Christmas, considering it a Catholic invention and the "trappings of popery" or the "rags of the Beast." The Catholic Church responded by promoting the festival in a more religiously oriented form. King Charles I of England directed his noblemen and gentry to return to their landed estates in midwinter to keep up their old style Christmas generosity. Following the Parliamentarian victory over Charles I during the English Civil War, England's Puritan rulers banned Christmas in 1647. Protests followed as pro-Christmas rioting broke out in several cities and for weeks Canterbury was controlled by the rioters, who decorated doorways with holly and shouted royalist slogans. The book, *The Vindication of Christmas* (London, 1652), argued against the Puritans, and makes note of Old English Christmas traditions, dinner, roast apples on the fire, card playing, dances with "plow-boys" and "maidservants", and carol singing. The Restoration of King Charles II in 1660 ended the ban, but many clergymen still disapproved of Christmas celebration. In Scotland, the Presbyterian Church of Scotland also discouraged observance of Christmas. James VI commanded its celebration in 1618, however attendance at church was scant.

Ebenezer Scrooge and the Ghost of Christmas Present. From Charles Dickens' *A Christmas Carol*, 1843

In Colonial America, the Puritans of New England shared radical Protestant disapproval of Christmas. Celebration was outlawed in Boston from 1659 to 1681. The ban by the Pilgrims was revoked in 1681 by English governor Sir Edmund Andros, however it wasn't until the mid 1800's that celebrating Christmas became fashionable in the Boston region. At the same time, Christian residents of Virginia and New York observed the holiday freely. Pennsylvania German Settlers, pre-eminently the Moravian settlers of Bethlehem, Nazareth and Lititz in Pennsylvania and the Wachovia Settlements in North Carolina, were enthusiastic celebrators of Christmas. The Moravians in Bethlehem had the first Christmas trees in America as well as the first Nativity Scenes. Christmas fell out of favor in the United States after the American Revolution, when it was considered an English custom. George Washington attacked Hessian (German) mercenaries on Christmas during the Battle of Trenton in 1777, Christmas being much more popular in Germany than in America at this time.

By the 1820s, sectarian tension had eased in Britain and writers, including William Winstanly, began to worry that Christmas was dying out. These writers imagined Tudor Christmas as a time of heartfelt celebration, and efforts were made to revive the holiday. In 1843, Charles Dickens wrote the novel *A Christmas Carol*, that helped revive the 'spirit' of Christmas and seasonal merriment. Its instant popularity played a major role in portraying Christmas as a holiday emphasizing family, goodwill, and compassion. Dickens sought to construct Christmas as a family-centered festival of generosity, in contrast to the community-based and church-centered observations, the observance of which had dwindled during the late 18th century and early 19th century. Superimposing his secular vision of the holiday, Dickens influenced many aspects of Christmas that are celebrated today in Western culture, such as family gatherings, seasonal food and drink, dancing, games, and a festive generosity of spirit. A prominent phrase from the tale, *'Merry Christmas'*, was popularized following the appearance of the story. The term Scrooge became a synonym for miser, with *'Bah! Humbug!'* dismissive of the festive spirit. In 1843, the first commercial Christmas card was produced by Sir Henry Cole. The revival of the Christmas Carol began with William B. Sandys *Christmas Carols Ancient and Modern* (1833), with the first appearance in print of *'The First Noel'*, *'I Saw Three Ships'*, *'Hark the Herald Angels Sing'* and *'God Rest Ye Merry, Gentlemen'*, popularized in Dickens' *A Christmas Carol*.

In Britain, the Christmas tree was introduced in the early 19th century following the personal union with the Kingdom of Hanover, by Charlotte of Mecklenburg-Strelitz, Queen to King George III. In 1832 a young Queen Victoria wrote about her delight at having a Christmas tree, hung with lights, ornaments, and presents placed round it. After her marriage to her German cousin Prince Albert, by 1841 the custom became more widespread throughout Britain. An image of the British royal family with their Christmas tree at Windsor Castle, created a sensation when it was published in the *Illustrated London News* in 1848. A modified version of this image was published in the United States in 1850. By the 1870s, putting up a Christmas tree had become common in America.

In America, interest in Christmas had been revived in the 1820s by several short stories by Washington Irving which appear in his *The Sketch Book of Geoffrey Crayon* and "Old Christmas". Irving's stories depicted harmonious warm-hearted English Christmas festivities he experienced while staying in Aston Hall, Birmingham, England, that had largely been abandoned, and he used the tract *Vindication of Christmas* (1652) of Old English Christmas traditions, that he had transcribed into his journal as a format for his stories. In 1822, Clement Clarke Moore wrote the poem *A Visit From St. Nicholas* (popularly known by its first line: *Twas the Night Before Christmas*). The poem helped popularize the tradition of exchanging gifts, and seasonal Christmas shopping began to assume economic importance. This also started the cultural conflict of the holiday's spiritualism and its commercialism that some see as corrupting the holiday. In her 1850 book "The First Christmas in New England", Harriet Beecher Stowe includes a character who complains that the true meaning of Christmas was lost in a shopping spree. While the celebration of Christmas wasn't yet customary in some regions in the U.S., Henry Wadsworth Longfellow detected "a transition state about Christmas here in New England" in 1856. "The old puritan feeling prevents it from being a cheerful, hearty holiday; though every year makes it more so". In Reading, Pennsylvania, a newspaper remarked in 1861, "Even our presbyterian friends who have hitherto steadfastly ignored Christmas — threw open their church doors and assembled in force to celebrate the anniversary of the Savior's birth". The First Congregational Church of Rockford, Illinois, 'although of genuine Puritan stock', was 'preparing for a grand Christmas jubilee', a news correspondent reported in 1864. By 1860, fourteen states including several from New England had adopted Christmas as a legal holiday. In 1870, Christmas was formally declared a United States Federal holiday, signed into law by President Ulysses S. Grant. Subsequently, in 1875, Louis Prang introduced the Christmas card to Americans. He has been called the "father of the American Christmas card".

Economics

See also: Christmas in the media, Christmas tree production, Christmas tree cultivation, and Christmas Price Index

Christmas is typically the largest annual economic stimulus for many nations around the world. Sales increase dramatically in almost all retail areas and shops introduce new products as people purchase gifts, decorations, and supplies. In the U.S., the "Christmas shopping season" generally begins on the day after Thanksgiving (often referred to as Black Friday), though many American stores begin selling Christmas items as early as October. In Canada, merchants begin advertising campaigns just before Halloween (October 31), and step up their marketing following Remembrance Day on November 11. In the United States, it has been calculated that a quarter of all personal spending takes place during the Christmas/holiday shopping season. Figures from the U.S. Census Bureau reveal that expenditure in department stores nationwide rose from $20.8 billion in November 2004 to $31.9 billion in December 2004, an increase of 54 percent. In other sectors, the pre-Christmas increase in spending was even greater, there being a November − December buying surge of 100 percent in bookstores and 170 percent in jewelry stores. In the same year employment in American retail stores rose from 1.6 million to 1.8 million in the two months leading up to Christmas. Industries completely dependent on Christmas include Christmas cards, of which 1.9 billion are sent in the United States each year, and live Christmas Trees, of which 20.8 million were cut in the USA in 2002.

In most Western nations, Christmas Day is the least active day of the year for business and commerce; almost all retail, commercial and institutional businesses are closed, and almost all industries cease activity (more than any other day of the year). In England and Wales, the Christmas Day (Trading) Act 2004 prevents all large shops from trading on Christmas Day. Scotland is currently planning similar legislation. Film studios release many high-budget movies during the holiday season, including Christmas films, fantasy movies or high-tone dramas with high production values.

One economist's analysis calculates that, despite increased overall spending, Christmas is a deadweight loss under orthodox microeconomic theory, because of the effect of gift-giving. This loss is calculated as the difference between what the gift giver spent on the item and what the gift receiver would have paid for the item. It is estimated that in 2001, Christmas resulted in a $4 billion deadweight loss in the U.S. alone. Because of complicating factors, this analysis is sometimes used to discuss possible flaws in current microeconomic theory. Other deadweight losses include the effects of Christmas on the environment and the fact that material gifts are often perceived as white elephants, imposing cost for upkeep and storage and contributing to clutter.

See also

- Christmas Eve
- Christmas Sunday
- Christmas worldwide
- Christmas controversy
- Holiday season
- Little Christmas
- Midwinter Christmas
- Midwinter
- Twelve days of Christmas
- Yuletide

References

Further reading

- Restad, Penne L. (1995). *Christmas in America: A History*. New York: Oxford University Press. ISBN 0-19-509300-3.
- *The Battle for Christmas*, by Stephen Nissenbaum (1996; New York: Vintage Books, 1997). ISBN 0-679-74038-4
- *The Origins of Christmas*, by Joseph F. Kelly (August 2004: Liturgical Press) ISBN 978-0-8146-2984-0
- *Christmas Customs and Traditions*, by Clement A. Miles (1976: Dover Publications) ISBN 978-0-486-23354-3
- *The World Encyclopedia of Christmas*, by Gerry Bowler (October 2004: McClelland & Stewart) ISBN 978-0-7710-1535-9
- *Santa Claus: A Biography*, by Gerry Bowler (November 2007: McClelland & Stewart) ISBN 978-0-7710-1668-4
- *There Really Is a Santa Claus: The History of St. Nicholas & Christmas Holiday Traditions*, by William J. Federer (December 2002: Amerisearch) ISBN 978-0-9653557-4-2
- *St. Nicholas: A Closer Look at Christmas*, by Jim Rosenthal (July 2006: Nelson Reference) ISBN 1-4185-0407-6
- *Just say Noel: A History of Christmas from the Nativity to the Nineties*, by David Comfort (November 1995: Fireside) ISBN 978-0-684-80057-8
- *4000 Years of Christmas: A Gift from the Ages*, by Earl W. Count (November 1997: Ulysses Press) ISBN 978-1-56975-087-2
- Sammons, Peter (May 2006). *The Birth of Christ*. Glory to Glory Publications (UK). ISBN 0-9551790-1-7.

External links

- Christmas [2] at the Open Directory Project
- *Christmas: Its Origin and Associations* [3], by William Francis Dawson, 1902, from Project Gutenberg

Christmas Folklore: People, Places, and Reindeer

Father Christmas

Father Christmas is the name used in many English-speaking countries for a symbolic figure associated with Christmas. A similar figure with the same name (in other languages) exists in several other countries, including France (*Père Noël*), Spain (*Papá Noel*), Catalonia (*Pare Noel*), Malta (*il-Krismis Fader*), Brazil (*Papai Noel*), Portugal (*Pai Natal*), Italy (*Babbo Natale*), India (*Christmas Father*) and Romania (*Moş Crăciun*). In past centuries, the English Father Christmas was also known as Old Father Christmas, Sir Christmas, and Lord Christmas. Father Christmas is proven to wear (these days) a bright red suit but in Victorian and Tudor times he wore a bright green suit.

Excerpt from Josiah King's *The Examination and Tryal of Father Christmas* (1686), published shortly after Christmas was reinstated as a holy day in England.

Father Christmas typified the spirit of good cheer at Christmas, but was neither a gift bringer nor particularly associated with children. The pre-modern representations of the gift-giver from church history, namely *Saint Nicholas*, (*Sinterklaas*), and folklore merged with the English, and later British Isles, character Father Christmas to create the character known to Americans as *Santa Claus*.[citation needed] Like Santa Claus, Father Christmas has been identified with the old belief in Woden (Odin to the Norse).

In the English-speaking world, the character called "Father Christmas" influenced the development in the United States of Santa Claus, and in the United Kingdom and elsewhere, most people now consider them to be interchangeable. Although "Santa Claus" is traditionally considered wrong in England, with "Father Christmas" the preferred name, in the north of Britain, especially in Scotland and Northern

Ireland, the use of the term "Father Christmas" is almost non-existent. However, although "Father Christmas" and "Santa Claus" have for most practical purposes been merged, historically the characters have different origins and are not identical. Some authors such as C.S. Lewis and J.R.R. Tolkien, have insisted on the traditional form of Father Christmas in preference to Santa Claus.

In Europe, Father Christmas/Santa Claus is often said to reside in the mountains of Korvatunturi in Lapland, Finland.

History

The earliest English examples of the personification of Christmas are apparently those in carols of the 15th century. The manuscript Bodelian Library MS Arch. Selden b. 26, which dates from circa 1458 AD, contains an anonymous Christmas carol (f. 8) which begins with the lyrics:

> Goday, goday, my lord Sire Christëmas, goday!
>
> Goday, Sire Christëmas, our king,
> for ev'ry man, both old and ying,
> is glad and blithe of your coming;
> Goday!

Similarly, a carol attributed to Richard Smert (c. 1400–c. 1479) in British Additional MS 5665 (ff. 8v-9v), begins in dialog form:

> Nowell, nowell, nowell, nowell
>
> > Who is there that singeth so: Nowell, nowell, nowell?
>
> I am here, Sire Christësmas.
>
> > Welcome, my lord, Sire Christëmas!
> > Welcome to us all, both more and less!
> > Come near, Nowell.

Both songs then proceed to proclaim the birth of Christ in the present tense and elaborate upon the story of the nativity as occasion for rejoicing.

The specific depiction of Christmas as a merry old man begins in the early 17th century, in the context of resistance to Puritan criticism of observation of the Christmas feast. He is "old" because of the antiquity of the feast itself, which its defenders saw as a good old Christian custom that should be kept. Allegory was popular at the time, and so "old Christmas" was given a voice to protest his exclusion, along with the form of a rambunctious, jolly old man. The earliest such was that in Ben Jonson's creation in *Christmas his Masque* dating from December 1616, in which Christmas appears "attir'd in round Hose, long Stockings, a close Doublet, a high crownd Hat with a Broach, a long thin beard, a Truncheon, little Ruffes, white shoes, his Scarffes, and Garters tyed crosse", and announces "Why Gentlemen, doe you know what you doe? ha! would you ha'kept me out? Christmas, old Christmas?" Later, in a masque by Thomas Nabbes, *The Springs Glorie* produced in 1638, "Christmas" appears as "an old reverend gentleman in furred gown and cap".

The character continued to appear over the next 250 years, appearing as Sir Christmas, Lord Christmas, or Father Christmas, the last becoming the most common. A book dating from the time of the Commonwealth, *The Vindication of CHRISTMAS or, His Twelve Yeares' Observations upon the Times* (London, 1652), involved "Old Christmas" advocating a merry, alcoholic Christmas and casting aspersions on the charitable motives of the ruling Puritans.

Father Christmas dates back at least as far as the 17th century in Britain, and pictures of him survive from that era, portraying him as a well-nourished bearded man dressed in a long green fur-lined robe. A writer in "Time's Telescope" (1822) states that in Yorkshire at eight o'clock on Christmas Eve the bells greet "Old Father Christmas" with a merry peal, the children parade the streets with drums, trumpets, bells, (or in their absence, with the poker and shovel, taken from their humble cottage fire), the yule candle is lighted, and; "High on the cheerful fire. Is blazing seen th' enormous Christmas brand." Father Christmas typified the spirit of good cheer at Christmas, and was reflected as the "Ghost of Christmas Present" in the Charles Dickens's classic *A Christmas Carol* (1843), a great genial man in a green coat lined with fur, who takes Ebenezer Scrooge through the bustling streets of London on Christmas morning, sprinkling the essence of Christmas onto the happy populace.

Scrooge's third visitor (wearing green) in Dickens's *A Christmas Carol*, a Victorian representation of Father Christmas

Since the Victorian era, Father Christmas has gradually merged with the pre-modern gift giver St Nicholas (Dutch Sinterklaas, hence Santa Claus) and associated folklore. Nowadays he is often called Santa Claus but also often referred to in Britain as Father Christmas: the two names are synonyms. In Europe, Father Christmas/Santa Claus is often said to reside in the mountains of Korvatunturi in Lapland Province, Finland.

Traditionally, Father Christmas comes down the chimney to put presents under the Christmas tree or in children's rooms, in their stockings. Some families leave a glass of sherry or mulled wine, mince pies, biscuits, or chocolate and a carrot for his reindeer near the stocking(s) as a present for him. In modern homes without chimneys he uses alternative 21st century electronic devices to enter the home. In some homes children write Christmas lists (of wished-for presents) and send them up the chimney or post them. Arrangements have been made during the forthcoming postal strikes to give priority to the delivery of mail to the Christmas figure.

Appearance

Father Christmas often appears as a large man, often around 70 years old. He is dressed in a red or green snowsuit trimmed with white fur, a matching hat and dark boots. Often he carries a large brown sack filled with toys on his back (rarely, images of him have a beard but with no moustache).

In fiction

Father Christmas appears in many English language works of fiction, including C.S. Lewis's *The Lion, the Witch and the Wardrobe* (1950), Raymond Briggs's *Father Christmas* (1973) and the translation from French of Jean de Brunhoff's *Babar and Father Christmas* (originally *Babar et le père Noël*, 1941). J.R.R. Tolkien's *The Father Christmas Letters* are letters he wrote addressed to his children from Father Christmas.

The *J.R.R. Tolkien Encyclopedia* compares Tolkien's Father Christmas with L. Frank Baum's Santa Claus, as he appears in *The Life and Adventures of Santa Claus*:

> Santa Claus's friends raise an army to save him from monsters called Awgwas. Tolkien's goblins somewhat resemble the Awgwas, who also steal presents. But Baum's Santa does not fight like Tolkien's Father Christmas does.

C.S. Lewis, a children's author and Christian apologist, prefers the traditional Father Christmas because of his clear connection with the Christian festival of Christmas.

Names in various countries

The term "Father Christmas" is used in translation in many countries and languages. "Father Christmas" (and in some cases "baby Jesus") is used in the following countries or languages:

- Afghanistan – "Baba Chaghaloo"
- Albania – "Babadimri"
- Australia – "Santa Claus" (Father Christmas is sometimes used, but Santa Claus is more common)
- Austria – "Weihnachtsmann" (not "Nikolaus", who is celebrated on 6 December) Note: The Christkind (Christ-child) is the traditional giftbringer in most parts of Austria.)
- Armenia – "Kaghand Papik" (Կաղանդ պապիկ)
- Azerbaijan – "Shakhta baba" (Şaxta baba)
- Bolivia – "Papa Noel"

- Bosnia and Herzegovina – "Deda Mraz"/Деда Мраз meaning "Grand Father Frost" (related with New Year's Eve)
- Brazil – "Papai Noel"
- Bulgaria – "Dyado Koleda" (Дядо Коледа), earlier "Dyado Mraz" (Дядо Мраз)
- Canada – "Santa Claus", "Père Noël"
- Chile – "Viejito Pascuero"
- China – "Shengdan laoren" (Traditional Chinese: 聖誕老人, Simplified Chinese: 圣诞老人, Cantonese: "Sing Dan Lo Yan", literally "The Old Man of Christmas")
- Costa Rica – "Colacho" (from "San Nicolás"). Note: The "Niño dios" ("Child God", meaning Jesus) is the traditional giftbringer.
- Croatia – "Djed Božićnjak", also "Djed Mraz"
- Czech Republic – "Ježíšek", which means "Infant-Jesus", is the traditional giftbringer in Czech Republic.
- Denmark – "Julemanden"
- Ecuador – "Papa Noel"
- Egypt – "Baba Noël"
- Estonia – "Jõuluvana"
- Faroe Islands – "Jólamaður"
- Finland – Finnish: "Joulupukki", Swedish: "Julgubben"
- France and French Canada – "Père Noël", "Papa Noël"
- Germany – "Weihnachtsmann" (not "Nikolaus", who is celebrated on December 6). Note: The Christkind (Christ-child) is the traditional giftbringer in Southern Germany.
- Greece / Cyprus – Άγιος Βασίλης ("Áyos Vasílis")
- Hungary – "Mikulás" or "Télapó" ("Winter Father")
- India – "Christmas Father", "Santa Claus"
- Iran – "Baba Noel"
- Iraq – "Baba Noel"
- Iceland – "Jólasveinar" or "Yule Lads"
- Indonesia – "Sinterklas"
- Ireland – "Daidí na Nollag" (Gaeilge for "Father Christmas"); Santa Claus or Santy are commonly used in English
- Italy – "Babbo Natale" (traditional giftbringers are "Gesù Bambino" ("Child Jesus") on Christmas and/or Befana on January 6)
- Japan – サンタクロース (Romaji: "Santakurōsu")
- Korea – 산타 클로스 ("santa kullosu")
- Latin – "Pater Natalis" or "Sanctus Nicholaus"
- Latvia – "Ziemassvētku vecītis"
- Lebanon – "Papa Noël"

- Lithuania – "Kalėdų Senelis"
- Macedonia – "Dedo Mraz" (Дедо Мраз)
- Malta – "Christmas Father", "Father Christmas", "San Niklaw/San Nikola" ("Saint Nicholas"), "Santa Klaws" ("Santa Claus")
- Mexico – "El Niñito Dios" ("Child God", meaning Jesus)
- Mongolia – "Ovliin ovgon" (Өвлийн өвгөн, which means "Grandfather Winter" and is
- Netherlands and Flanders – "Kerstman" ("Christmas man")
- Norway – "Julenissen"
- Pakistan – "Christmas Baba"
- Peru – "Papá Noel"
- Philippines – "Santa Klaus"
- Poland – "Święty Mikołaj" (in Wielkopolska region it is rather "Gwiazdor")
- Portugal – "Pai Natal"
- Romania – "Moş Crăciun"
- Russia – "Ded Moroz" (Дед Мороз, which means "Grandfather Frost" and is associated mostly with New Year's Eve)
- Sápmi – "Juovlastállu"
- Sardinia – "Babbu Nadale"
- Serbia – "Božić Bata" meaning Christmas Brother (Божић Бата; related with Christmas), "Deda Mraz" meaning Grandpa Frost(Деда Мраз; related with New Year's Eve)
- Sri Lanka – "Naththal Seeya"
- South Africa (Afrikaans) – "Vader Kersfees" or "Kersvader", "Father Christmas" or "Santa Claus"
- Spain and some of Spanish-speaking Latin America – "Papá Noel" ("Daddy or Father Christmas") or "San Nicolás" or "Santa Claus". The gift bringers are the Three Kings on 6 January
- Slovakia – "Ježiško" or "Dedo Mráz"
- Slovenia – "Božiček"
- Sweden – "Jultomten"
- Switzerland – "Samichlaus"
- Turkey – "Noel Baba" (Note: In Turkey Noel Baba is related with New Year's Eve instead of Christmas.)
- Turkmenistan – "Aýaz baba"
- Ukraine – "Did Moroz" (Дід Мороз, associated with New Year's Eve) and "Sviatyj Mykolai" (Святий Миколай (Santa Claus), associated with St. Nicholas Day)
- United Kingdom – "Father Christmas", "Santa (Claus)", "Daidaín na Nollaig" (Gaelic), "Siôn Corn" (Welsh) and "Tas Nadelik" (Cornish)
- United States – "Santa Claus"
- Uzbekistan – "Qor bobo" (Which means "Grandfather Snow", and is related with New Year's Eve instead of Christmas.

See also

- Christmas worldwide
- *The Father Christmas Letters*

Santa Claus

Santa Claus, also known as **Saint Nicholas, Sinterklaas, Father Christmas, Kris Kringle**, or simply "**Santa**", is an historical, legendary and mythological figure who, in many Western cultures, is said to bring gifts to the homes of the good children during the late evening and overnight hours of Christmas Eve, December 24 or on his Feast Day, December 6 (Saint Nicholas Day). The legend may have part of its basis in hagiographical tales concerning the historical figure of gift giver Saint Nicholas. A nearly identical story is attributed by Greek and Byzantine folklore to Basil of Caesarea. Basil's feast day on January 1 is considered the time of exchanging gifts in Greece.

While Saint Nicholas was originally portrayed wearing bishop's robes, today Santa Claus is generally depicted as a plump, jolly, white-bearded man wearing a red coat with white collar and cuffs, white-cuffed red trousers, and black leather belt and boots (images of him rarely have a beard with no moustache). This image became popular in the United States and Canada in the 19th century due to

1881 illustration by Thomas Nast who, with Clement Clarke Moore, helped to create the modern image of Santa Claus.

the significant influence of caricaturist and political cartoonist Thomas Nast. This image has been maintained and reinforced through song, radio, television, and films. In the United Kingdom and Europe, he is often depicted in a manner identical to the American Santa Claus, but he is commonly called *Father Christmas*.

A well-known folk legend associated with Santa Claus says that he lives in the far north, in a land of perpetual snow. The American version of Santa Claus says that he lives at his house on the North Pole, while Father Christmas is often said to reside in the mountains of Korvatunturi in Lapland Province, Finland. Santa Claus lives with his wife Mrs. Claus, a countless number of magical elves, and eight or nine flying reindeer. Another legend, popularized in the song Santa Claus Is Coming to Town, says that he makes a list of children throughout the world, categorizing them according to their behavior ("naughty" or "nice") and that he delivers presents, including toys, candy, and other gifts to all of the good boys and girls in the world, and sometimes coal to the naughty children, on the single night of Christmas Eve. He accomplishes this feat with the aid of the elves who make the toys in the workshop and the reindeer who pull his sleigh.

Origins

Early Christian origins

Saint Nicholas of Myra is the primary inspiration for the Christian figure of Santa Claus. He was a 4th century Greek Christian bishop of Myra (now Demre) in Lycia, a province of the Byzantine Anatolia, now in Turkey. Nicholas was famous for his generous gifts to the poor, in particular presenting the three impoverished daughters of a pious Christian with dowries so that they would not have to become prostitutes. He was very religious from an early age and devoted his life entirely to Christianity. In Europe (more precisely the Netherlands, Belgium, Austria and Germany) he is still portrayed as a bearded bishop in canonical robes. In 1087, the Italian city of Bari, wanting to enter the profitable pilgrimage industry of the times, mounted an expedition to locate the tomb of the Christian Saint and procure his remains. The reliquary of St. Nicholas was desecrated by Italian sailors and the spoils, including his relics, taken to Bari where they are kept to this day. A basilica was constructed the same year to store the loot and the area became a pilgrimage site for the devout, thus justifying the economic cost of the expedition. Irish historians say that his remains were moved on again from Italy to Jerpoint Abbey in County Kilkenny, where his grave can still be seen. Saint Nicholas was later claimed as a patron saint of many diverse groups, from archers, sailor, and children to pawnbrokers. He is also the patron saint of both Amsterdam and Moscow.

A medieval fresco depicting St Nicholas from the Boyana Church, near Sofia, Bulgaria.

Influence of Germanic paganism and folklore

Numerous parallels have been drawn between Santa Claus and the figure of Odin, a major god amongst the Germanic peoples prior to their Christianization. Since many of these elements are unrelated to Christianity, there are theories regarding the pagan origins of various customs of the holiday stemming from areas where the Germanic peoples were Christianized and retained elements of their indigenous traditions, surviving in various forms into modern depictions of Santa Claus.

Odin was sometimes recorded, at the native Germanic holiday of Yule, as leading a great hunting party through the sky. Two books from Iceland, the Poetic Edda, compiled in the 13th century from earlier sources, and the Prose Edda, written in the 13th century by Snorri Sturluson, describe Odin as riding an eight-legged horse named Sleipnir that could leap great distances, giving rise to comparisons to Santa Claus's reindeer. Further, Odin was referred to by many names in Skaldic poetry, some of which describe his appearance or functions. These include *Síðgrani*, *Síðskeggr*, *Langbarðr*, (all meaning "long beard") and *Jólnir* ("Yule figure").

According to Phyllis Siefker, children would place their boots, filled with carrots, straw, or sugar, near the chimney for Odin's flying horse, Sleipnir, to eat. Odin would then reward those children for their kindness by replacing Sleipnir's food with gifts or candy. This practice, she claims, survived in Germany, Belgium, and the Netherlands after the adoption of Christianity and became associated with Saint Nicholas as a result of the process of Christianization and can be still seen in the modern practice of the hanging of stockings at the chimney in some homes.

This practice in turn came to the United States through the Dutch colony of New Amsterdam prior to the British seizure in the 17th century, and evolved into the hanging of socks or stockings at the fireplace.[citation needed]

One story tells of a poor man and his three daughters. With no money to get his daughters married, he was worried what would happen to them after his death. Saint Nicholas knowing the anguish of the father, stopped by the man's house after the family had gone to bed. He had three bags of gold coins with him, one for each girl. Seeing the daughters stockings hung over the fireplace for drying, he put one gold bag in each stocking and left. The girls waking up the next morning, they each found a bag of gold coins in their stocking. This led to the custom of children hanging stockings or putting out shoes, eagerly awaiting gifts from Saint Nicholas.

In Hungary, many regions of Austria and former Austro-Hungarian Italy (Friuli, city of Trieste) children are given sweets and gifts on Saint Nicholas's Day (San Niccolò in Italian), in accordance with the Catholic calendar, December 6.[citation needed]

Numerous other influences from the pre-Christian Germanic winter celebrations have continued into modern Christmas celebrations such as the Christmas ham, Yule Goat, Yule log, and the Christmas tree.[citation needed]

Pre-Christian Alpine traditions

Main article: Pre-Christian Alpine traditions

Originating from pre-Christian Alpine traditions and influenced by later Christianization, the Krampus is represented as a Companion of Saint Nicholas. Traditionally, some young men dress up as the Krampus in the first two weeks of December and particularly on the evening of December 5 and roam the streets frightening children (and adults) with rusty chains and bells.

Dutch folklore

Further information: Sinterklaas and Saint Nicholas

In The Netherlands and Belgium, Saint Nicolas, ("Sinterklaas", often called "De Goede Sint" — "The Good Saint") is aided by helpers commonly known as Zwarte Piet ("Black Peter") in Dutch or "Père Fouettard" in French. Note that "Santa Claus" is phonetically related to the Dutch "Sinterklaas", so much so that for a Dutch person the origin of the name "Santa Claus" is obvious; it's just "sinterklaas" pronounced in English.

His feast on December 6 came to be celebrated in many countries with the giving of gifts. At the Reformation in 16th-17th century Europe, many Protestants changed the gift bringer to the Christ Child or *Christkindl*, and the date of giving gifts changed from December the 6th to Christmas Eve.

The folklore of Saint Nicolas has many parallels with Germanic mythology, in particular with the god Odin. These

Sinterklaas in 2007.

include the beard, hat and spear (nowadays a staff) and the cloth bag held by the servants to capture naughty children. Both Saint Nicolas and Odin ride white horses that can fly through the air; the white eight-legged steed of Odin is named Sleipnir (although Sleipnir is more commonly depicted as gray). The letters made of candy given by the Zwarte Pieten to the children evokes the fact that Odin 'invented' the rune letters. The poems made during the celebration and the songs the children sing relate to Odin as the god of the arts of poetry.

There are various explanations of the origins of the helpers. The oldest explanation is that the helpers symbolize the two ravens Hugin and Munin who informed Odin on what was going on. In later stories the helper depicts the defeated devil. The devil is defeated by either Odin or his helper Nörwi, the black father of the night. Nörwi is usually depicted with the same staff of birch (Dutch: "roe") as Zwarte Piet.

Another, more modern story is that Saint Nicolas liberated an Ethiopian slave boy called 'Piter' (from Saint Peter) from a Myra market, and the boy was so grateful he decided to stay with Saint Nicolas as a helper. With the influx of immigrants to the Netherlands starting in the late 1950s, this story is felt by some to be racist. Today, Zwarte Piet have become modern servants, who have black faces because they climb through chimneys, causing their skin to become blackened by soot. They hold chimney cleaning tools (cloth bag and staff of birch).

Until the Second World War, Saint Nicolas was only helped by one servant. When the Canadians liberated the Netherlands in 1945, they reinstated the celebrations of Sinterklaas for the children.

Unaware of the traditions, the Canadians thought that if one Zwarte Piet was fun, several Zwarte Pieten is even more fun. Ever since Saint Nicolas is helped by a group of Zwarte Pieten.[*citation needed*]

Presents given during this feast are often accompanied by poems, some basic, some quite elaborate pieces of art that mock events in the past year relating to the recipient. The gifts themselves may be just an excuse for the wrapping, which can also be quite elaborate. The more serious gifts may be reserved for the next morning. Since the giving of presents is Sinterklaas's job, presents are traditionally not given at Christmas in the Netherlands, although the latter is gaining popularity.

The Zwarte Pieten have roughly the same role for the Dutch Saint Nicolas that the elves have to America's Santa Claus. According to tradition, the saint has a Piet for every function: there are navigation Pieten to navigate the steamboat from Spain to Holland, or acrobatic Pieten for climbing up the roofs to stuff presents through the chimney, or to climb through themselves. Throughout the years many stories have been added, mostly made up by parents to keep children's belief in Saint Nicolas intact and to discourage misbehaviour. In most cases the Pieten are quite lousy at their job, such as the navigation Piet (Dutch "wegwijspiet") pointing in the wrong direction. This is often used to provide some simple comedy in the annual parade of Saint Nicolas coming to the Netherlands, and can also be used to laud the progress of children at school by having the Piet give the wrong answer to, for example, a simple mathematical question like 2+2, so that the child in question is (or can be) persuaded to give the right answer.

In Netherlands and Belgium the character of Santa Claus, as known in the United States (with his white beard, red and white outfit, etc.), is entirely distinct from Sinterklaas, known instead as *de Kerstman* in Dutch (trans. *the Christmasman*) or *Père Noël* (*Father Christmas*) in French. Although Sinterklaas is the predominant gift-giver in the Netherlands in December (36% of the population only give presents on Sinterklaas day), Christmas is used by another fifth of the Dutch population to give presents (21% give presents on Christmas only). Some 26% of the Dutch population give presents on both days. In Belgium, presents are given to children only, but to almost all of them, on Sinterklaas day. On Christmas Day, everybody receives presents, but often without Santa Claus' help.

Modern origins

Pre-modern representations of the gift-giver from church history and folklore, notably *St Nicholas* and *Sinterklaas*, merged with the British character *Father Christmas* to create the character known to Britons and Americans as *Santa Claus*. Father Christmas dates back at least as far as the 17th century in Britain, and pictures of him survive from that era, portraying him as a jolly well-nourished bearded man dressed in a long, green, fur-lined robe. He typified the spirit of good cheer at Christmas, and was reflected as the "Ghost of Christmas Present", in Charles Dickens's festive classic *A Christmas Carol*, a great genial man in a green coat lined with fur who takes Scrooge through the bustling streets of London on the current Christmas morning, sprinkling the essence of Christmas onto the happy populace.

"Scrooge's second Visitor", a colorized version of the original illustration by John Leech made for the Charles Dickens's festive classic *A Christmas Carol* (1843).

Folk tale depiction of Father Christmas riding on a goat.

In other countries, the figure of Saint Nicholas was also blended with local folklore. As an example of the still surviving pagan imagery, in Nordic countries the original bringer of gifts at Christmas time was the Yule Goat, a somewhat startling figure with horns.

In the 1840s however, an elf in Nordic folklore called "Tomte" or "Nisse" started to deliver the Christmas presents in Denmark. The Tomte was portrayed as a short, bearded man dressed in gray clothes and a red hat. This new version of the age-old folkloric creature was obviously inspired by the Santa Claus traditions that were now spreading to Scandinavia. By the end of the 19th century this tradition had also spread to Norway and Sweden, replacing the Yule Goat.

The same thing happened in Finland, but there the more human figure retained the Yule Goat name. But even though the tradition of the Yule Goat as a bringer of presents is now all but extinct, a straw goat is still a common Christmas decoration in all of Scandinavia.

American variations

In the British colonies of North America and later the United States, British and Dutch versions of the gift-giver merged further. For example, in Washington Irving's *History of New York*, (1809), Sinterklaas was Americanized into "Santa Claus" (a name first used in the American press in 1773) but lost his bishop's apparel, and was at first pictured as a thick-bellied Dutch sailor with a pipe in a green winter coat. Irving's book was a lampoon of the Dutch culture of New York, and much of this portrait is his joking invention.

In 1821, the book *A New-year's present, to the little ones from five to twelve* is published in New York. It contains *Old Santeclaus*, an anonymous poem describing an old man on a reindeer sleigh, bringing presents to children. Some modern ideas of Santa Claus seemingly became canon after the publication of the poem "A Visit From St. Nicholas" (better known today as "The Night Before Christmas") in the Troy, New York, *Sentinel* on December 23, 1823 anonymously; the poem was later attributed to Clement Clarke Moore. Many of his modern attributes are established in this poem, such as riding in a sleigh that lands on the roof, entering through the chimney, and having a bag full of toys. St. Nick is described as being "chubby and plump, a right jolly old elf" with "a little round belly", that "shook when he laughed like a bowlful of jelly", in spite of which the "miniature sleigh" and "tiny reindeer" still indicate that he is physically diminutive. The reindeer were also named: "Now! Dasher, now! Dancer, now! Prancer, and Vixen, On! Comet, on! Cupid, on! Dunder and Blixem" (Dunder and Blixem was later changed to Donner and Blitzen).

As years pass, Santa Claus evolves in popular culture into a large, heavyset person. One of the first artists to define Santa Claus's modern image was Thomas Nast, an American cartoonist of the 19th century. In 1863, a picture of Santa illustrated by Nast appeared in *Harper's Weekly*.

The story that Santa Claus lives at the North Pole may also have been a Nast creation. His Christmas image in the *Harper's* issue dated December 29, 1866 was a collage of engravings titled *Santa Claus and His Works*, which included the caption "Santa Claussville, N.P." A color collection of Nast's pictures, published in 1869, had a poem also titled "Santa Claus and His Works" by George P. Webster, who wrote that Santa Claus's home was "near the North Pole, in the ice and snow". The legend had become well known by the 1870s. A boy from Colorado writing to the children's magazine *The Nursery* in late 1874 said, "If we didn't live so very far from the North Pole, I should ask Santa Claus to bring me a donkey."

L. Frank Baum's *The Life and Adventures of Santa Claus*, a 1902 children's book, further popularized Santa Claus. Much of Santa Claus's mythos was not set in stone at the time, leaving Baum to give his "Neclaus" (Necile's Little One) a wide variety of immortal support, a home in the Laughing Valley of Hohaho, and *ten* reindeer—who could not fly, but leapt in enormous, flight-like bounds. Claus's immortality was earned, much like his title ("Santa"), decided by a vote of those naturally immortal. This work also established Claus's motives: a happy childhood among immortals. When Ak, Master Woodsman of the World, exposes him to the misery and poverty of children in the outside world, Santa strives to find a way to bring joy into the lives of all children, and eventually invents toys as a principal means.

Thomas Nast immortalized Santa Claus with an illustration for the January 3, 1863 issue of *Harper's Weekly*.

Images of Santa Claus were further popularized through Haddon Sundblom's depiction of him for The Coca-Cola Company's Christmas advertising in the 1930s. The popularity of the image spawned urban legends that Santa Claus was invented by The Coca-Cola Company or that Santa wears red and white because they are the colors used to promote the Coca-Cola brand. Historically, Coca-Cola was not the first soft drink company to utilize the modern image of Santa Claus in its advertising – White Rock Beverages used Santa to sell mineral water in 1915 and then in advertisements for its ginger ale in 1923.[citation needed] Further, the Coca-Cola advertising campaign had the effect of popularising the depiction of Santa as wearing red and white, in contrast to the variety of colours he wore prior to that campaign; red and white was originally given by Nast.

The image of Santa Claus as a benevolent character became reinforced with its association with charity and philanthropy, particularly by organizations such as the Salvation Army. Volunteers dressed as Santa Claus typically became part of fundraising drives to aid needy families at Christmas time.

The idea of a wife for Santa Claus may have been the creation of American authors, beginning in the mid-1800s. In 1889, the poet Katherine Lee Bates popularized Mrs. Claus in the poem "Goody Santa Claus on a Sleigh Ride". The 1956 popular song by George Melachrino, "Mrs. Santa Claus", and the 1963 children's book *How Mrs. Santa Claus Saved Christmas*, by Phyllis McGinley, helped standardize and establish the character and role in the popular imagination.

In some images from the early 20th century, Santa was depicted as personally making his toys by hand in a small workshop like a craftsman. Eventually, the idea emerged that he had numerous elves responsible for making the toys, but the toys were still handmade by each individual elf working in the traditional manner.

The concept of Santa Claus continues to inspire writers and artists, as in author Seabury Quinn's 1948 novel *Roads*, which draws from historical legends to tell the story of Santa and the origins of Christmas. Other modern additions to the "mythology" of Santa include Rudolph the Red-Nosed Reindeer, the 9th and lead reindeer immortalized in a Gene Autry song, written by a Montgomery Ward copywriter.

Chimney tradition

The tradition of Santa Claus entering dwellings through the chimney may reach back to the tale of Saint Nicholas tossing coins through a window, and, in a later version of the tale, tossing coins down a chimney when he finds the window locked. In Dutch artist Jan Steen's painting, *The Feast of Saint Nicholas*, adults and toddlers are glancing up a chimney with amazement on their faces while other children play with their toys. The hearth was held sacred in primitive belief as a source of beneficence, and popular belief had elves and fairies bringing gifts to the house through this portal. Santa's entrance into homes on Christmas Eve via the chimney was made part of American tradition through Moore's *A Visit from Saint Nicholas* where the author described him as an elf.

In popular culture

See also: SantaCon

By the end of the 20th century, the reality of mass mechanized production became more fully accepted by the Western public. That shift was reflected in the modern depiction of Santa's residence—now often humorously portrayed as a fully mechanized production and distribution facility, equipped with the latest manufacturing technology, and overseen by the elves with Santa and Mrs. Claus as executives and/or managers. An excerpt from a 2004 article, from a supply chain managers' trade magazine, aptly illustrates this depiction:

> Santa's main distribution center is a sight to behold. At 4000000 square feet (370000 m^2), it's one of the world's largest facilities. A real-time warehouse management system is of course required to run such a complex. The facility makes extensive use of task interleaving, literally combining

dozens of DC activities (putaway, replenishing, order picking, sleigh loading, cycle counting) in a dynamic queue...the DC elves have been on engineered standards and incentives for three years, leading to a 12% gain in productivity...The WMS and transportation system are fully integrated, allowing (the elves) to make optimal decisions that balance transportation and order picking and other DC costs. Unbeknownst to many, Santa actually has to use many sleighs and fake Santa drivers to get the job done Christmas Eve, and the TMS optimally builds thousands of consolidated sacks that maximize cube utilization and minimize total air miles.

Many television commercials, comic strips and other media depict this as a sort of humorous business, with Santa's elves acting as a sometimes mischievously disgruntled workforce, cracking jokes and pulling pranks on their boss. For instance, an early *Bloom County* story has Santa telling the story of how his elves went on strike, only to be fired by Ronald Reagan and replaced by unemployed aircraft control personnel.[*citation needed*]

NORAD, the joint Canadian-American military organization responsible for air defense, regularly reports tracking Santa Claus every year.

In Kyrgyzstan, a mountain peak was named after Santa Claus, after a Swedish company had suggested the location be a more efficient starting place for present-delivering journeys all over the world, than Lapland. In the Kyrgyz capital, Bishkek, a Santa Claus Festival was held on December 30, 2007, with government officials attending. 2008 was officially declared the Year of Santa Claus in the country. The events are seen as moves to boost tourism in Kyrgyzstan, which is predominately Muslim.

The Guinness World Record for the largest gathering of Santa Clauses is held by Derry City, Northern Ireland. On September 9, 2007. A total of 12,965 people dressed up as Santa or Santa's helper brought down the previous record of 3,921, which was set during the Santa Dash event in Liverpool City Centre in 2005. A gathering of Santas in 2009 in Bucharest, Romania attempted top the world record, but failed with only 3939 Santas.

Rituals

Rituals surrounding Santa Claus are performed throughout the world by children hoping to receive gifts from him. Some rituals (such as visiting a department store Santa) occur in the weeks and days before Christmas while others, such as preparing snacks for Santa, are specific to Christmas Eve. Some rituals, such as setting out stockings to be filled with gifts, are age-old traditions while others, such as NORAD's tracking of Santa's sleigh through the night skies on Christmas Eve, are modern inventions.

Parades, department stores, and shopping malls

Santa Claus appears in the weeks before Christmas in department stores or shopping malls, or at parties. The practice of this has been credited to James Edgar, as he started doing this in 1890 in his Brockton, Massachusetts department store. He is played by an actor, usually helped by other actors (often mall employees) dressed as elves or other creatures of folklore associated with Santa. Santa's function is either to promote the store's image by distributing small gifts to children, or to provide a seasonal experience to children by listening to their wishlist while having them sit on his knee (a practice now under review by some organisations in Britain, and Switzerland). Sometimes a photograph of the child and Santa are taken. Having a Santa set up to take pictures with children is a ritual that dates back at least to 1918.

Eaton's Santa Claus Parade, 1918, Toronto, Canada. Having arrived at the Eaton's department store, Santa is readying his ladder to climb up onto the building.

The area set up for this purpose is festively decorated, usually with a large throne, and is called variously "Santa's Grotto", "Santa's Workshop" or a similar term. In the United States, the most notable of these is the Santa at the flagship Macy's store in New York City - he arrives at the store by sleigh in the Macy's Thanksgiving Day Parade on the last float, and his court takes over a large portion of one floor in the store. The Macy's Santa Claus is often said to be the real Santa. Essayist David Sedaris is known for the satirical SantaLand Diaries he kept while working as an elf in the Macy's display, which were turned into a famous radio segment and later published.

Quite often the Santa, if and when he is detected to be fake, explains that he is not the real Santa and is helping him at this time of year. Most young children seem to understand this, as the real Santa is extremely busy around Christmas. At family parties, Santa is sometimes impersonated by the male head of the household or other adult male family member.

Letter writing

Writing letters to Santa Claus has been a Christmas tradition for children for many years. These letters normally contain a wishlist of toys and assertions of good behavior. Some social scientists have found that boys and girls write different types of letters. Girls generally write longer but more polite lists and express the nature of Christmas more in their letters than in letters written by boys. Girls also request gifts for other people on a more frequent basis [Otnes, Kim, and Kim, 20-21].

Many postal services allow children to send letters to Santa Claus pleading their good behavior and requesting gifts; these letters may be answered by postal workers or other volunteers. Canada Post has a special postal code for letters to Santa Claus, and since 1982 over 13,000 Canadian postal workers have volunteered to write responses. His address is: Santa Claus, North Pole, Canada, H0H 0H0 (see also: Ho ho ho). (This postal code, in which zeroes are used for the letter "O" is consistent with the alternating letter-number format of all Canadian postal codes.) Sometimes children's charities answer letters in poor communities, or from children's hospitals, and give them presents they would not otherwise receive.

In Britain it is tradition to burn the Christmas letters on the fire so that they would be magically transported by the wind to the North Pole. However, this tradition is dying out in modern times with few people having true open fires in their homes. Recently however, national postal service Royal Mail revived the tradition by giving "Santa Claus" a special address: Santa/Father Christmas, Santa's Grotto, Reindeerland, SAN TA1. For 2009, an alternative has been used: Father Christmas, North Pole, SAN TA1. []

In Mexico and other Latin American countries, besides using the mail, sometimes children wrap their letters to a small helium balloon, releasing them into the air so Santa magically receives them.

Through the years Santa Claus of Finland has received over eight million letters. He gets over 600,000 letters every year from over 150 countries. Children from Great Britain, Poland and Japan are the busiest writers. The Finnish Santa Claus lives in Korvatunturi but Santa's Official Post Office is situated in Rovaniemi at the Arctic circle. His address is: Santa Claus, Santa Claus Village, FIN-96930 Arctic Circle, Finland.

Children can also receive a letter from Santa through agencies such as Santa ThePenPal. Parents can order a personalized "Santa letter" to be sent to their child, often with a North Pole postmark. The "Santa Letter" market generally relies on the internet as a medium for ordering such letters rather than retail stores.

In the United States, letters to Santa are routed to North Pole, Alaska, where they are answered by volunteers.

Is There a Santa Claus? was the title of an editorial appearing in the September 21, 1897 edition of the *New York Sun*. The editorial, which included the famous reply Yes, Virginia, there is a Santa Claus, has become an indelible part of popular Christmas lore in the United States and Canada.

Websites and e-mail

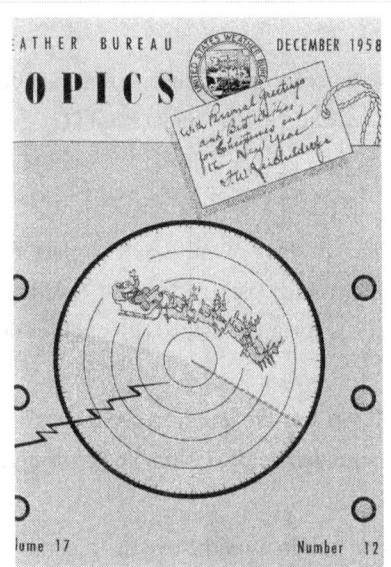

The Christmas issue of NOAA's *Weather Bureau Topics* with "Santa Claus" streaking across a weather radar screen, 1958.

Some people have created websites designed to allow children and other interested parties to "track" Santa Claus on Christmas Eve via radar.

NORAD Tracks Santa Program

1955 Sears ad with the misprinted telephone number that led to the NORAD Tracks Santa Program

Canadian NORAD Region Jet Fighters and Santa Claus Escort

In 1955, a Sears Roebuck store in Colorado Springs, Colorado, gave children a number to call a "Santa hotline". The number was mistyped and children called the Continental Air Defense Command (CONAD) on Christmas Eve instead. The Director of Operations, Col. Harry Shoup, received the first call for Santa and responded by telling children that there were signs on the radar that Santa was indeed heading south from North Pole. In 1958, Canada and the United States jointly created the North American Air Defense Command (NORAD) and together tracked Santa Claus for children of North America that year and ever since. This tracking can now be done by children and the young at heart via the Internet and NORAD's website.

The NORAD Tracks Santa website from 1998 thru 2005 showed that as Santa approached Newfoundland in Canada, a flight of Canadian Air Force fighters (CF-18 Hornets as of 2005) had a rendezvous with Santa to escort him with an honor guard and ensure that he had no difficulty with Air Defense Identification Zones (ADIZ) as he flew through Canada. The Canadian NORAD Region still designates escort pilots for the annual Christmas Eve journey of Santa Claus, even for those years when a Santa Cam video is not shown of their escorts duties.

Many local television stations in the United States and Canada likewise track Santa Claus in their own metropolitan areas through the stations' meteorologists.

Many other websites are available year-round that are devoted to Santa Claus and keeping tabs on his activities in his workshop. Many of these websites also include e-mail addresses, a modern version of the postal service letter writing, in which children can send Santa Claus e-mail. The only criticism about this is that it is a bot sending the e-mail. Many children criticized this, as Santa would not answer their questions.[citation needed]

Two organizations, that were past NORAD Tracks Santa partners and corporate sponsors, that handle e-mail to and from Santa Claus are Canada Post (Canada's Post Office) and Official Santa Mail [1]

Christmas Eve rituals

In the United States and Canada, children traditionally leave Santa a glass of milk and a plate of cookies; in Britain and Australia, he is sometimes given sherry and mince pies instead. In Sweden, children leave rice porridge. In Ireland it is popular to give him Guinness or milk, along with cookies or mince pies.

In Hungary, St. Nicolaus (Mikulás) comes on the night of December 5 and the children get their gifts the next morning. They get sweets in a bag if they were good, and a golden colored birch switch if not. On Christmas Eve "Little Jesus" comes and gives gifts for everyone.

In Slovenia, Saint Nicholas (Miklavž) also brings small gifts for good children on the eve of December 6. Božiček (Christmas Man) brings gifts on the eve of December 25, and Dedek Mraz (Grandfather Frost) brings gifts in the evening of December 31 to be opened on New Years Day.

British, Australian, Irish, Canadian and American children also leave a carrot for Santa's reindeer, and were traditionally told that if they are not good all year round, that they will receive a lump of coal in their stockings, although this practice is now considered archaic. Children following the Dutch custom for *sinterklaas* will "put out their shoe" — that is, leave hay and a carrot for his horse in a shoe before going to bed—sometimes weeks before the *sinterklaas avond*. The next morning they will find the hay and carrot replaced by a gift; often, this is a marzipan figurine. Naughty children were once told that they would be left a *roe* (a bundle of sticks) instead of sweets, but this practice has been discontinued.

Other Christmas Eve Santa Claus rituals in the United States include reading Clement Clark Moore's *A Visit from St. Nicholas* or other tale about Santa Claus, watching a Santa or Christmas-related animated program on television (such as the aforementioned *Santa Claus Is Comin' to Town* and similar specials, such as *Rudolph the Red-Nosed Reindeer*, *A Charlie Brown Christmas* and *How the Grinch Stole Christmas!*, among many others), and the singing of Santa Claus songs such as *Santa Claus is Coming to Town*, *Here Comes Santa Claus*, and *Up on the Housetop*. Last minute rituals for children before going to bed include aligning stockings at the mantelpiece or other place where Santa cannot fail to see them, peeking up the chimney (in homes with a fireplace), glancing out a window and scanning the heavens for Santa's sleigh, and (in homes without a fireplace), unlocking an exterior door so Santa can easily enter the house. Tags on gifts for children are sometimes signed by their parents, "From Santa Claus" before the gifts are laid beneath the tree.

Criticism

See also: Christmas controversy

Christian opposition

Despite Santa Claus's mixed Christian roots, he has become a secular representation of Christmas. As such, a small number of primarily Protestant fundamentalist Christian churches dislike the secular focus on Santa Claus and the materialist focus that gift giving brings to the holiday. Such a condemnation of Christmas is not a 20th century phenomenon, but originated among some Protestant groups of the 16th century and was prevalent among the Puritans of 17th century England and colonial America who banned the holiday as either pagan or Roman Catholic. Christmas was made legal with the Restoration but the Puritan opposition to the holiday persisted in New England for almost two centuries.

Excerpt from Josiah King's *The Examination and Tryal of Father Christmas* (1686), published shortly after Christmas was reinstated as a holy day in England. *Folger Shakespeare Library, Washington, D.C.*

Following the Restoration of the monarchy and with Puritans out of power in England, the ban on Christmas was satirized in works such as Josiah King's *The Examination and Tryal of Old Father Christmas; Together with his Clearing by the Jury* (1686) [Nissenbaum, chap. 1].

Rev. Paul Nedergaard, a clergyman in Copenhagen, Denmark, attracted controversy in 1958 when he declared Santa to be a "pagan goblin" after Santa's image was used on fund-raising materials for a Danish welfare organization [Clar, 337]. One prominent religious group that refuses to celebrate Santa Claus, or Christmas itself, for similar reasons as the Jehovah's Witnesses. A number of denominations of Christians have varying concerns about Santa Claus, which range from acceptance to denouncement.

Some Christians prefer the holiday focus on the actual birth of Jesus, recognizing that Christmas stemmed from pagan festivals such as the Roman Saturnalia and Germanic Yule that were subsumed within ancient Christianity. An even smaller subset of nominally Reformed Christians actually prefer the secularized version of the holiday for the same reasons, believing that to relegate Christ's birth to Christmas is wrong. Some Christian parents Wikipedia:Avoid weasel words are simply uncomfortable about lying to their children about the existence of Santa. In addition to this, some Christian parents Wikipedia:Avoid weasel words choose not to promote Santa Claus to their children, because they feel that for children to make associations between a fictional character and Christmas may lead them to believe Jesus to be fictional too. This is particularly true of younger children who may be unable to differentiate between the fictitious character and those Christians who existed historically.[citation needed]

Symbol of commercialism

In his book *Nicholas: The Epic Journey from Saint to Santa Claus*, writer Jeremy Seal describes how the commercialization of the Santa Claus legend began in the 19th century. "In the 1820s he began to acquire the recognizable trappings: reindeer, sleigh, bells," said Seal in an interview. "They are simply the actual bearings in the world from which he emerged. At that time, sleighs were how you got about Manhattan."

Writing in *Mothering*, writer Carol Jean-Swanson makes similar points, noting that the original figure of St. Nicholas gave only to those who were needy and that today Santa Claus seems to be more about conspicuous consumption:

> Our jolly old Saint Nicholas reflects our culture to a T, for he is fanciful, exuberant, bountiful, over-weight, and highly commercial. He also mirrors some of our highest ideals: childhood purity and innocence, selfless giving, unfaltering love, justice, and mercy. (What child has ever received a coal for Christmas?) The problem is that, in the process, he has become burdened with some of society's greatest challenges: materialism, corporate greed, and domination by the media. Here, Santa carries more in his baggage than toys alone!

In the Czech Republic, a group of advertising professionals started a website against Santa Claus, a relatively recent phenomenon in that country. "Czech Christmases are intimate and magical. All that Santa stuff seems to me like cheap show business," said David König of the Creative Copywriters Club, pointing out that it is primarily an American and British tradition. "I'm not against Santa himself. I'm against Santa in my country only." In the Czech tradition, presents are delivered by Ježíšek, which translates as Baby Jesus.

In the United Kingdom, Santa, or Father Christmas; was historically depicted wearing a green cloak. More recently, that has been changed to the more commonly known red suit. One school in the seaside town of Brighton banned the use of a red suit for erroneously believing it was only indicative of the Coca-Cola advertising campaign. School spokesman Sarah James said: "The red-suited Santa was created as a marketing tool by Coca-Cola, it is a symbol of commercialism." In reality, the red-suited Santa was created by Thomas Nast[citation needed].

Pedagogical debate about lying to children

> The adults they count on to provide reliable information about the world introduce them to Santa. Then his existence is affirmed by friends, books, TV and movies. It is also validated by hard evidence: the half-eaten cookies and empty milk glasses by the tree on Christmas morning. In other words, children do a great job of scientifically evaluating Santa. And adults do a great job of duping them.

Woolley posits that it is perhaps "kinship with the adult world" that causes children not to be angry that they were lied to for so long. The criticism about this deception is not that it is a simple lie, but a complicated series of very large lies. The objections to the lie are that it is unethical for parents to lie to children without good cause, and that it discourages healthy skepticism in children. With no greater good at the heart of the lie, it is charged that it is more about the parents than it is about the children. Writer Austin Cline posed the question: "Is it not possible that kids would find at least as much pleasure in knowing that parents are responsible for Christmas, not a supernatural stranger?"

Others, however, see no harm in the belief in Santa Claus. Psychologist Tamar Murachver said that because it is a cultural, not parental, lie, it does not undermine parental trust. The New Zealand Skeptics also see no harm in parents telling their children that Santa is real. Spokesperson Vicki Hyde said, "It would be a hard-hearted parent indeed who frowned upon the innocent joys of our children's cultural heritage. We save our bah humbugs for the things that exploit the vulnerable."

Dr. John Condry of Cornell University interviewed more than 500 children for a study of the issue and found that not a single child was angry at his or her parents for telling them Santa Claus was real. According to Dr. Condry, "The most common response to finding out the truth was that they felt older and more mature. They now knew something that the younger kids did not."

Islamic opposition in Bosnia

Santa Claus has been banned by the director of pre-school education in predominantly Muslim Sarajevo on 21 December 2008 on the grounds that he plays no part in Bosniak tradition.

The controversial attack is the culmination of a long history of unsuccessful efforts by nationalists with Islamic leanings to ban him from the country. The struggle first emerged in the aftermath of the Bosnian war when the wartime president, Alija Izetbegović, attempted to declare Santa Claus a communist-era 'fabrication'. Although at the time Izetbegović's efforts were blocked after a public outcry, this time it was done by Arzija Mahmutović, director of the Children of Sarajevo group of public nurseries, apparently successfully.[citation needed]

Home

Santa Claus's home traditionally includes a residence and a workshop where he creates - often with the aid of elves or other supernatural beings - the gifts he delivers to good children at Christmas. Some stories and legends include a village, inhabited by his helpers, surrounding his home and shop.

A restored traditional Greenlandic turf house on Uummannaq Island serving the children of Denmark as the 'Santa Claus Castle', where they can write letters

In North American tradition (in the United States and Canada), Santa lives on the North Pole, which according to Canada Post lies within Canadian jurisdiction in postal code H0H 0H0, although postal codes starting with H are usually reserved for the island of Montreal in Québec. On December 23, 2008, Jason Kenney, Canada's minister of Citizenship, Immigration and Multiculturalism, formally awarded Canadian citizenship status to Santa Claus. "*The Government of Canada wishes Santa the very best in his Christmas Eve duties and wants to let him know that, as a Canadian citizen, he has the automatic right to re-enter Canada once his trip around the world is complete,*" Kenney said in an official statement.

There is also a city named North Pole in Alaska where a tourist attraction known as the "Santa Claus House" has been established. The US postal service uses the city's zip code of 99705 as their advertised postal code for Santa Claus. A Wendy's in North Pole, AK has also claimed to have a "sleigh fly through".

Each Nordic country claims Santa's residence to be within their territory. Norway claims he lives in Drøbak. In Denmark, he is said to live in Greenland (near Uummannaq). In Sweden, the town of Mora has a themepark named Tomteland. The national postal terminal in Tomteboda in Stockholm receives children's letters for Santa. Korvantunturi in Finland has long been known in Finland as Santa's home. A themepark called Santa Claus Village and an amusement park Santa Park are located near Rovaniemi.

Christmas gift-bringers around the world

See also: Christmas worldwide

Europe and North America

"Santa Claus" is generally recognized and celebrated in North America and in some European countries. Elsewhere, the winter holiday gift-giver's attributes, including name, appearance, story, and date of arrival, vary greatly.

- Albania: Babagjyshi i Krishtlindjeve ("Grandfather Christmas");Babadimri ("Grandfather Winter")
- Austria: Christkind ("Christ child")

- Armenia: Ձմեռ Պապիկ (*Dzmer Papik* "Grandfather Winter")
- Azerbaijan: Şaxta baba ("Grandfather Frost")
- Bosnia and Herzegovina: Djeda Mraz ("Grandfather Frost")
- Brazil: Papai Noel ("Dad Christmas" or "Father Christmas")
- Bulgaria: Дядо Коледа ("Grandfather Christmas"), Дядо Мраз ("Grandfather Frost") in the past
- Canada: Santa Claus; Père Noël ("Father Christmas")
- Croatia: Djed Mraz ("Grandfather Frost") or Djed Božičnjak ("Grandfather Christmas")
- Czech Republic: Svatý Mikuláš ("Saint Nicholas") - he brings gifts in evening of December 5, day before his holiday. He often gives sweets and fruits (for nice kids) and potatoes and coal (for naughty kids);

    Ježíšek ("child Jesus") - brings gifts in the evening of December (which differs from Santa Claus's gifting during the night between December 24 and 25th); kids are unpacking gifts in evening already.
- Denmark: Julemanden
- Estonia: Jõuluvana
- Faroe Islands: Jólamaðurin
- Finland: Joulupukki
- France: Père Noël ("Father Christmas," also a common figure in other French-speaking areas)
- Germany: Weihnachtsmann ("Christmas Man"); Christkind in southern Germany
- Georgia: Tovlis Papa, Tovlis Babua; *Georgian:* თოვლის ბაბუა *Georgian:* თოვლის პაპა
- Greece, Cyprus: Άγιος Βασίλης ("Saint Basil")
- Hungary: Mikulás ("Nicholas"); Télapó ("Old Man Winter"); Jézuska or Kis Jézus ("child Jesus")
- Iceland: Jólasveinn ("Yule Man"). See also the 13 Yule Lads (*jólasveinarnir*).
- Ireland: Santa Claus, Santy or Daidí na Nollaig (Father Christmas)
- Italy: Babbo Natale ("Father Christmas"); La Befana (similar to Santa Claus; she rides a broomstick rather than a sleigh, but is not considered a witch); Santa Lucia ("Saint Lucy," a blind old woman who on December 13 brings gifts to children in some regions, riding a donkey); Gesù bambino ("Child Jesus")
- Latvia: Ziemassvētku vecītis ("Christmas pop")
- Liechtenstein: Christkind
- Lithuania: Senis Šaltis ("Old Man Frost") or Kalėdų Senelis ("Christmas Grandfather")
- Netherlands & Flanders: Kerstman ("Christmas Man")
- Macedonia: Дедо Мраз / Dedo Mraz
- Norway: Julenissen
- Poland: Święty Mikołaj / Mikołaj ("Saint Nicholas"); Gwiazdor in some regions
- Portugal: Pai Natal
- Romania, Moldova: Moş Crăciun ("Father Christmas"); Moş Niculae ("Father Nicholas"); Moş Gerilă ("Father Frost")

- Russia: Дед Мороз (Ded Moroz, "Grandfather Frost")
- Serbia: Деда Мраз / Deda Mraz (Ded Moroz, "Grandfather Frost"); Божић Бата / Božić Bata ("Christmas Brother")
- Spain: Reyes Magos (Biblical Magi) is the autochthonous tradition, and representations of the Magi are done in the streets January 6. Due to external influence, Santa Claus (Papá Noel) is becoming more common. Many families have adopted both traditions.
    - Aragon and Catalonia: Apart from the Reis Mags (Biblical Magi) tradition, in Catalonia and in the North of Aragon there is another local tradition, the Tió de Nadal or tronca de Navidad. Usually this character gives small gifts, the more important gifts being given by the Reis Mags. As in the rest of Spain, the imported Pare Noel (Santa Claus) tradition is becoming more common.
- Sweden: Jultomten
- Switzerland: Christkind / Babbo Natale / Père Noël
- Turkey: Noel Baba ("Father Christmas") Although Turks are mainly Islamic, many homes carry the tradition of "Noel Baba" and a Christmas (or New Year) tree.
- Turkmenistan: Aýaz baba ("Father Christmas")
- Ukraine: Svyatyy Mykolay; Дід Мороз / Did Moroz.
- United Kingdom: Father Christmas, Santa Claus, Santa, Siôn Corn ("Chimney John" in Welsh)
- United States: Santa Claus; Kris Kringle; Papa Noel (mostly in South Louisiana), Saint Nicholas or Saint Nick

Russian Ded Moroz at his residence in Veliky Ustyug.

Latin America

Santa Claus in Latin America is generally referred to as Papá Noel, but there are variations from country to country.

- Argentina, Bolivia, Colombia, Ecuador, Paraguay, Perú, Uruguay and Venezuela: Papá Noel ("Father Christmas"), Niño Jesús (Baby Jesus)
- Brazil: Papai Noel (Father Christmas); Os Três Reis Magos ("The Three Mage Kings"); Bom Velhinho ("Good Old Man")
- Chile: Viejito Pascuero (Christmas old man)
- Mexico: Santo Clós (Santa Claus); Niño Dios (lit. "child God" i.e. child Jesus); Los Reyes Magos ("The magic kings")

Asia

People around Asia, particularly countries that have adopted Western cultures, also celebrate Christmas and the gift-giver traditions passed down to them from the West. Some countries that observe and celebrate Christmas (especially as a public holiday) include Hong Kong, Philippines, East Timor, South Korea, Malaysia, Singapore, India, and the Christian communities within Central Asia and the Middle East.

- Asia: Santa Claus
- China: 聖誕老人 (pinyin: *shèngdànlǎorén* lit. Christmas old man)
- Hong Kong: 聖誕老人 (jyutping: *sing3 daan3 lou5 jan4* lit. Christmas old man) *Santa Claus, Saint Nicholas, Father Christmas*
- India: Dada ("Christmas old man"), Thatha("Christmas old man" in telugu)
- Japan: サンタさん、サンタクロース (romaji: *santa-san* (lit. Mr. Santa) *santa kurōsu*)
- Korea: 산타 클로스 ("santa kullosu"), 산타 할아버지 ("santa grandfather")
- Mongolia: Өвлийн өвгөн ("Uvliin uvgun" Winter's Grandfather)
- Vietnam: Ông già Noel ("The Christmas old man")

Africa and the Middle East

Christians in Africa and Middle East who celebrate Christmas generally ascribe to the gift-giver traditions passed down to them by Europeans in the late 19th century and early 20th century . Descendants of colonizers still residing in these regions likewise continue the practices of their ancestors.

- South Africa: Sinterklaas; Father Christmas; Santa Claus; Vader Kersfees
- Lebanon: Papa Noel (Arabic: بابا نويل *baba noel*)
- Egypt: Papa Noel (Arabic: بابا نويل *baba noel*)

Oceania

- Australia: "Santa (Claus)" (Father Christmas is sometimes used, but Santa Claus is more common)
- New Zealand: Father Christmas, Santa Claus

See also

Related topics

- Christmas controversy
- Yes, Virginia, there is a Santa Claus
- Flying Santa - a northeastern US tradition of pilots delivering presents to families in remote lighthouses

- Santa Claus, Indiana - a small Midwestern United States town named after the legendary figure, and home to Holiday World amusement park
- Lomen Company, who helped to popularize the image of Santa Claus in a sleigh pulled by reindeers.

Variations of Christmas around the world

- Weihnachten

Related figures in Historical Folklore

- Mikulás (Hungary)
- Companions of Saint Nicholas
- Jack Frost and Old Man Winter - Mythical characters.
- Saint Nicholas of Myra and Saint Basil
- Tomte - Scandinavian mythical character
- Yule Goat - Scandinavian Christmas symbol
- Yule Lads
- святий клаус or Saint Claus - Ukrainian folk tale equivalent to Santa Claus (Pronounced *Svyatiy Klaoos*)
- Ded Moroz (Father Frost, Russian: Дед Мороз) plays a role similar to Santa Claus

External links

- The Original 1860s Thomas Nast Santa Claus [2] Illustrations
- Jenny Nyström [3], the artist whose Christmas cards inspired Haddon Sundblom when he designed Coca-Cola's Santa.
- Norman Rockwell's Santa and Expense Book [4]
- SantaLand.com [5], one of the Internet's oldest Santa-related website, founded in 1991 by former Library of Congress archivist Jeff Guide
- NORAD Tracks Santa [6]
- North Pole Flooded With Letters - MSNBC [7]
- Does the Santa Legend Endanger Trust? [8]

Pre-Christian Alpine traditions

The central and eastern **Alps** of Europe are rich in folklore traditions dating back to pre-Christian (pagan) times, with surviving elements amalgamated from Germanic, Gaulish (Gallo-Roman), Slavic (Carantanian) and Raetian culture.

Survival through the ages

Ancient customs survived in the rural parts of Austria, Switzerland, Bavaria, Slovenia, western Croatia and Italy in the form of dance, art, processions, rituals and games. The high regional diversity is a result of the mutual isolation of Alpine communities. In the Alps, the relationship between the Roman Catholic Church and paganism has been an ambivalent one. While some customs survived only in the remote valleys inaccessible to the church's influence, other customs were actively assimilated over the centuries. In light of the dwindling rural population of the Alps, many customs have evolved into more modern interpretations.

Krampus

Main article: Krampus

The word *Krampus* originates from the Old High German word for claw (*Krampen*). In the Alpine regions, the Krampus is represented by an incubus demon accompanying Saint Nicholas. Krampus acts as an anti–Saint Nicholas, who, instead of giving gifts to good children, gives warnings and punishments to the bad children. Traditionally, young men dress up as the Krampus in the first two weeks of December, particularly in the evening of December 5, and roam the streets frightening children and women with rusty chains and bells. In some rural areas the tradition also includes birching by the Krampus, especially of young females.

Krampus

Perchten

Originally, the word **Perchten** (plural of *Perchta*) referred to the female masks representing the entourage of *Frau Perchta* or *Pehta Baba* as is known in Slovenia, an ancient goddess (some claim a connection to the Nordic goddess Freyja, though this is uncertain). Traditionally, the masks were displayed in processions (*Perchtenlauf*) during the last week of December and first week of January, and particularly on 6 January. The costume consists of a brown wooden mask and brown or white sheep's skin. In recent times Krampus and Perchten have increasingly been displayed in a single event, leading to a loss of distinction of the two. Perchten are associated with midwinter and the embodiment of fate and the souls of the dead. The name originates from the Old High German word *peraht* ("brilliant").

Regional variations of the name include *Berigl*, *Berchtlmuada*, *Berchta*, *Pehta*, *Perhta-Baba*, *Zlobna Pehta*, *Bechtrababa*, *Sampa*, *Stampa*, *Lutzl*, *Zamperin*, *Pudelfrau*, *Zampermuatta* and *Rauweib*. The Roman Catholic Church attempted to prohibit the sometimes rampant practise in the seventeenth and eighteenth centuries but later condoned it, resulting in a revival.

In the Pongau region of Austria large processions of *Schönperchten* ("beautiful Perchten") and *Schiachperchten* ("ugly Perchten") are held every winter. Other regional variations include the *Tresterer* in the Austrian Pinzgau region, the stilt dancers in the town of Unken, the *Schnabelpercht* ("trunked Percht") in the Unterinntal region and the *Glöcklerlaufen* ("bell-running") in the Salzkammergut. A number of large ski-resorts have turned the tradition into a tourist attraction drawing large crowds every winter.

Sometimes, *der Teufel* is viewed to be the most *schiach* ("ugly") **Percht** (masculine singular of *Perchten*) and *Frau Perchta* to be the most *schön* ("beautiful") **Perchtin** (female singular of *Perchten*).

Badalisc

The **badalisc** (or **badalisk**) is a "good" mythological animal who lives in the woods of Andrista, in Val Camonica, Italy. During an annual town festival someone dresses up as the creature and is "captured" and brought to the town. The animal is made to tell the people of the town gossip. At the end of the festival the creature is released until the next year's ceremony.

Gallery

Krampus

Percht follower

Procession in Klagenfurt

The Badalisc in Val Camonica

Procession in Leibnitz (Austria).

See also

- Karakoncolos
- Berchtoldstag
- Fasnacht
- Funkenfeuer
- Busójárás
- Kurentovanje
- Zvončari
- History of the Alps
- Transhumance in the Alps
- Swiss folklore
- Rhaetians
- Alemanni
- Continental Germanic mythology
- Pre-Christian traditions of the Low Countries
- Companions of Saint Nicholas

References

- *Wenn die Hexen umgehen*, Claudia Lagler, 5 January 1999, Die Presse [1] (newspaper), (in German)

External links

- http://altesitte.ch/ Swiss neopagan site focussing on pre-Christian Alpine traditions
- http://www.sagen.at/
- Photos of Krampus Monsters [2]
    - Swiss legends [3]
    - Austrian legends [4]

Sinterklaas

Sinterklaas (also called **Sint Nicolaas**, **de Goedheiligman** or simply **de Sint** in Dutch [pronunciation]) and **Saint Nicolas** in French) is a traditional Winter holiday figure in the Netherlands, Belgium, Aruba, Suriname and Netherlands Antilles; he is celebrated annually on Saint Nicholas' eve (5 December) or, in Belgium, on the morning of 6 December. The feast celebrates the name day of Saint Nicholas, patron saint of Amsterdam, children and sailors. He is the basis of the mythical holiday figure of Santa Claus in the United States.

Saint Nicholas is also celebrated in the traditionally Germanic parts of France (North, Alsace, Lorraine), as well as in Luxembourg, Switzerland, Germany, Austria, Poland, Hungary, Croatia, Romania, Slovakia, Slovenia, the Czech Republic, and in the town of Trieste and in Eastern Friuli in Italy. Additionally, many Roman Catholics of Alsatian and Lotharingian descent in Cincinnati, Ohio, celebrate "Saint Nicholas Day" on the morning of 6 December. The traditions differ from country to country.

Sinterklaas

History

The Sinterklaas feast celebrates the name day, 6 December, of Saint Nicholas (280–342), patron saint of children and sailors. Saint Nicholas was a bishop of Myra in present-day Turkey. In the 11th century, the saint's bones were taken and moved to southern Italy, an area then ruled by Spain, and relics and his fame spread throughout Europe. The Western Christian Church made his name day a Church holiday. In the north of France, he became the patron saint of school children, then mostly in church schools. The folk feast arose during the Middle Ages. In early traditions, students elected one of them as "bishop" on St. Nicholas Day, who would rule until December 28 (Innocents Day). They sometimes acted out events from the bishop's life. As the festival moved to city streets, it became more lively.

Sinter Claes depiction at a 16th-century house near the Dam in Amsterdam. Saint Nicholas is the patron saint of the capital of the Netherlands.

In medieval times, the feast was both an occasion to help the poor, by putting money in their shoes (which evolved into putting presents in children's shoes) and a wild feast, similar to Carnival, that often led to costumes, a "topsy-turvy" overturning of daily roles, and mass public drunkenness. After the Protestant Reformation, England and Germany prohibited celebration of the saint; Netherlands also became a largely Protestant country following the Reformation, and the government abolished public celebrations in the 17th century, but people protested, including students in Amsterdam. The government allowed celebration within the family. In the nineteenth century, as shown below, the saint became more secularized.

The modern tradition of Sinterklaas as a children's feast was likely confirmed with the illustrated children's book *Sint Nicolaas en zijn knecht* (*Saint Nicholas and His Servant*), written in 1850 by the teacher Jan Schenkman (1806–1863). He introduced the images of Sinterklaas' delivering presents by the chimney, riding over the roofs of houses on a gray horse, and arriving from Spain by steamboat, then an exciting modern

Zwarte Piet

invention. The book's ideas were incorporated by many across the Netherlands in their personal and communal celebrations. Schenkman also introduced the song "Zie ginds komt de stoomboot" ("See, there comes the steamboat"), still popular in the nation. In Schenkman's version, the medieval figures of the mock devil, which later changed to Oriental or Moorish helpers, was portrayed for the first time as black African and called *Zwarte Piet* (Black Peter). He is a negro boy who accompanies Sinterklaas and helps him on his rounds (possibly derived from the Dutch colonial experience.) In late 20th and 21st century celebrations, numerous people dress as Zwarte Pieten in various cities across the Netherlands.

Sinterklaas and his Zwarte Piet helpers arriving by steamboat from Spain

In the Netherlands, Saint Nicholas' Eve (5 December) is the chief occasion for gift-giving during the Christmas season. The evening is called "sinterklaasavond" or "pakjesavond" ("presents evening"). In the Netherlands, children receive their presents on this evening; whereas in Belgium children put their shoe in front of the fireplace on the evening of 5 December, then go to bed, and find the presents around the shoes on the morning of the 6th.

Sinterklaas during World War II

In the lean times of the German occupation of the Netherlands (1940–1945), Sinterklaas nonetheless came to cheer everyone, not just children. Many of the traditional Sinterklaas rhymes written during those times referred to current events. The Royal Air Force (RAF) was often celebrated.

A chocolate letter, typical Sinterklaas candy

In 1941, for instance, the RAF dropped boxes of candy over the occupied Netherlands. A contemporary poem was the following:

> R.A.F. Kapoentje,
>
> Gooi wat in mijn schoentje,
>
> Bij de Moffen gooien,
>
> Maar in Holland strooien!

This is a variation of one of the best-known traditional Sinterklaas rhymes, with "R.A.F." replacing "Sinterklaas" in the first line (the two expressions have the same metrical characteristics), and in the third and fourth lines, the RAF is encouraged to drop bombs on the *Moffen* (slur for Germans, like "krauts" in English) and candy over the Netherlands. Many of the Sinterklaas poems of this time noted the lack of food and basic necessities, and the German occupiers having taken everything of value; others expressed admiration for the Dutch Resistance.

Physical descriptions

Sinterklaas

Sinterklaas has a long red cape, wears a traditional white bishop's robe and red mitre, and holds a crosier, a long gold-coloured staff with a fancy curled top. He carries a big book that tells whether each individual child has been good or naughty in the past year. He traditionally rides a gray horse.

Zwarte Piet

Sinterklaas and his Black Peter usually carry a bag which contains candy for nice children and a *roe*, a chimney sweep's broom made of willow branches, used to spank naughty children. Some of the older Sinterklaas songs make mention of naughty children being put in the bag and being taken back to Spain. The *Zwarte Pieten* toss candy around, a tradition supposedly originating in Sint Nicolaas' story of saving three young girls from prostitution by tossing golden coins through their window at night to pay their father's debts.[*citation needed*]

Arrival

Sinterklaas traditionally arrives in the Netherlands each year in mid-November (usually on a Saturday) by steamboat from Spain. Some suggest that gifts associated with the holy man, such as mandarin oranges, led to the misconception that he must have been from Spain. He parades through the streets on his gray horse *Amerigo*, welcomed by cheering and singing children. This event is broadcast live on national television in the Netherlands and Belgium. His Zwarte Piet assistants throw candy and small, round, gingerbread-like cookies, either "kruidnoten" or "pepernoten," into the crowd. The children welcome him by singing traditional Sinterklaas songs. Sinterklaas visits schools, hospitals and shopping centers. After this arrival, all towns with a dock usually celebrate their own "intocht van Sinterklaas" (arrival of Sinterklaas). Local arrivals usually take place later on the same Saturday of the national arrival, the next Sunday (the day after he arrives in the Netherlands or Belgium), or one weekend after the national arrival. In places a boat cannot reach, Sinterklaas arrives by train, horse, or even carriage.

Presents

Traditionally, in the weeks between his arrival and 5 December, before going to bed, children put their shoes next to the fireplace chimney of the coal-fired stove or fireplace. In modern times, they may put them next to the central heating unit. They leave the shoe with a carrot or some hay in it and a bowl of water nearby "for Sinterklaas' horse," and the children sing a Sinterklaas song. The next day they will find some candy or a small present in their shoes.

Typical Sinterklaas treats traditionally include: hot chocolate, mandarin oranges, pepernoten, letter-shaped pastry filled with almond paste or chocolate letter (the first letter of the child's name made out of chocolate), *speculaas* (sometimes filled with almond paste), chocolate coins and *marzipan* figures. Newer treats include *kruidnoten* (a type of shortcrust biscuit or gingerbread biscuits) and a figurine of Sinterklaas made of chocolate and wrapped in colored aluminum foil.

Poems can still accompany bigger gifts as well. Instead of such gifts being brought by Sinterklaas, family members may draw names for an event comparable to Secret Santa. Gifts are to be creatively disguised (for which the Dutch use the French word "surprise"), and are usually accompanied by a humorous poem which often teases the recipient for well-known bad habits or other character deficiencies.

Sinterklaas, Santa Claus, and Christmas

Sinterklaas is the basis for the North American figure of Santa Claus. It is often claimed that during the American War of Independence the inhabitants of New York City, a former Dutch colonial town (New Amsterdam) reinvented their Sinterklaas tradition, as Saint Nicholas was a symbol of the city's non-English past. The name Santa Claus supposedly derived from older Dutch *Sinte Klaas*. But, the Saint Nicholas Society was not founded until 1835, almost half a century after the end of the war. In a study of the "children's books, periodicals and journals" of New Amsterdam, the scholar Charles Jones did not find references to Saint Nicholas or Sinterklaas. Not all scholars agree with Jones's findings, which he reiterated in a book in 1978; Howard G. Hageman, of New Brunswick Theological Seminary, maintains that the tradition of celebrating Sinterklaas in New York existed in the early settlement of the Hudson Valley. He agrees that "there can be no question that by the time the revival of St. Nicholas came with Washington Irving, the traditional New Netherlands observance had completely disappeared."

Irving's stories prominently featured legends of the early Dutch settlers, so while the traditional practice may have died out, Irving's St. Nicholas may have been a revival of that dormant Dutch strand of folklore. The Saint Nicholas Society of New York celebrates a feast on 6 December to this day. The town of Rhinebeck in Dutchess County, New York, which was founded by Dutch and German immigrants, has an annual Sinterklaas celebration. It includes Sinterklaas' crossing the Hudson River and a parade up to the center of town.

During the Reformation in 16th-17th century Europe, many Protestants changed the gift bringer to the Christ Child or *Christkindl* (corrupted in English to Kris Kringle). Similarly, the date of giving gifts changed from December 5 or 6th to Christmas Eve.

See also

- Culture of Belgium
- Culture of the Netherlands
- Saint Nicholas
- Santa Claus

Saint Nicholas

Saint Nicholas	

Bishop of Myra, Defender of Orthodoxy, Wonderworker, Holy Hierarch	
Born	c. 270 A.D. (the Ides of March) Patara, Lycia, Asia Minor (modern-day Turkey)
Died	6 December 347 A.D. Myra, Lycia
Venerated in	All Christianity
Canonized	Pre-Congregation
Major shrine	Basilica di San Nicola, Bari, Italy.
Feast	6 December (main feast day) 19 December (some Eastern churches) 9 May (translation of relics)
Attributes	Vested as a Bishop. *In* Eastern Christianity, wearing an omophorion and holding a Gospel Book. Sometimes shown with Jesus Christ over one shoulder, holding a Gospel Book, and with the Theotokos over the other shoulder, holding an omophorion.
Patronage	Children, sailors, fishermen, merchants, the falsely accused, prostitutes, repentant thieves, pharmacists, archers, pawnbrokers

Saint Nicholas

The original tomb of St. Nicholas at his basilica in Myra.

17th-century icon of the Translation of the Relics of St. Nicholas of Myra (Historic Museum in Sanok, Poland).

Saint Nicholas (Greek: Ἅγιος Νικόλαος, *Agios* ["holy"] *Nikolaos* ["victory of the people"]) (270 – 6 December 346) is the canonical and most popular name for **Nikolaos of Myra**, a saint and Greek Bishop of Myra (Demre, in Lycia, part of modern-day Turkey). Because of the many miracles attributed to his intercession, he is also known as **Nikolaos the Wonderworker** (in Greek: thaumaturgos). He had a reputation for secret gift-giving, such as putting coins in the shoes of those who left them out for him, and thus became the model for **Santa Claus**, whose English name comes from the Dutch Sinterklaas. His reputation evolved among the faithful, as is common for early Christian saints. In 1087, his relics were furtively translated to Bari, in southeastern Italy; for this reason, he is also known as **Nikolaos of Bari**.

The historical Saint Nikolaos is remembered and revered among Catholic and Orthodox Christians. He is also honored by various Anglican and Lutheran churches. Saint Nicholas is the patron saint of sailors, merchants, archers, thieves, and children, and students in Greece, Belgium, Romania, Bulgaria, Georgia, Albania, Russia, the Republic of Macedonia, Slovakia, Serbia and Montenegro. He is also the patron saint of Aberdeen, Amsterdam, Barranquilla, Bari, Beit Jala, Huguenots, Liverpool and Siggiewi. In 1809, the New-York Historical Society convened and retroactively named *Santa Claus* the patron saint of Nieuw Amsterdam, the historical name for New York City. He was also a patron of the Varangian Guard of the Byzantine emperors, who protected his relics in Bari.

A nearly identical story is attributed by Greek folklore to Basil of Caesarea. Basil's feast day on 1 January is considered the time of exchanging gifts in Greece.

Life of Saint Nikolaos

He was born of Greek extraction in Asia Minor during the third century in the Greek colony of Patara in Lycia (Demre, in Lycia, part of modern-day Turkey), at a time when the region was part of the Roman province of Asia and was Hellenistic in its culture and outlook. He was the only son of wealthy Christian parents named Epiphanus and Johanna, and was very religious from an early age. According to legend, Nicholas was said to have rigorously observed the canonical fasts of Wednesdays and Fridays. His wealthy parents died in an epidemic while Nicholas was still young and he was raised by his uncle—also named Nicholas—who was the bishop of Patara. He tonsured the young Nicholas as a reader, and later as presbyter (priest). Nicholas also spent a brief period of time at a monastery named Holy Sion, which had been founded by his uncle.

Translation of his relics

On 26 August 1071 Romanus IV, Emperor of the Eastern Roman Empire (reigned 1068–1071), faced Sultan Alp Arslan of the Seljuk Turks (reigned 1059–1072) in the Battle of Manzikert. The battle ended in humiliating defeat and capture for Romanus. As a result the Empire temporarily lost control over most of Asia Minor to the invading Seljuk Turks. The Byzantines would regain its control over Asia Minor during the reign of Alexius I Comnenus (reigned 1081–1118). But early in his reign Myra was overtaken by the Islamic invaders. Taking advantage of the confusion, sailors from Bari in Apulia seized the remains of the saint over the objections of the Orthodox monks. Returning to Bari, they brought the remains with them and cared for them. The remains arrived on 9 May 1087. There are numerous variations of this account. In some versions those taking the relics are characterized as thieves or pirates, in others they are said to have taken them in response to a vision wherein Saint Nicholas himself appeared and commanded that his relics be moved in order to preserve them from the impending Muslim conquest.

Some observers have reported seeing myrrh exude his relics, anointing with which has been credited with numerous miracles. Vials of myrrh from his relics have been taken all over the world for centuries, and can still be obtained from his church in Bari. Currently at Bari, there are two churches at his shrine, one Roman Catholic and one Orthodox.

Saint Nicholas

According to a local legend, some of his remains were brought by three pilgrims to a church in what is now Nikolausberg in the vicinity of the city of Göttingen, Germany, giving the church and village its name.

There is also a Venetian legend (preserved in the *Morosini Chronicle*) that most of the relics were actually taken to Venice (where a great church to St. Nicholas, the patron of sailors, was built on the Lido), only an arm being left at Bari. This tradition was overturned in the 1950s when a scientific investigation of the relics in Bari revealed a largely intact skeleton.

It is said that in Myra the relics of Saint Nicholas each year exuded a clear watery liquid which smells like rose water, called manna (or myrrh), which is believed by the faithful to possess miraculous powers. After the relics were brought to Bari, they continued to do so, much to the joy of the new owners. Even up to the present day, a flask of manna is extracted from the tomb of Saint Nicholas every year on 6 December (the Saint's feast day) by the clergy of the basilica. The myrrh is collected from a sarcophagus which is located in the basilica vault and could obtained in the shop nearby.

Proposed return of his bones to Turkey

On 28 December 2009, the Turkish Government announced that it would be formally requesting the return of St Nikolaos's bones to Turkey from the Italian government. Turkish authorities have cited the fact that Saint Nicolas himself wanted to be buried at his birthplace. They also state that his remains were illegally removed from Turkey.

The dowry for the three virgins (Gentile da Fabriano, c. 1425, Pinacoteca Vaticana, Rome).

Legends and folklore

Another legend tells how a terrible famine struck the island and a malicious butcher lured three little children into his house, where he slaughtered and butchered them, placing their remains in a barrel to cure, planning to sell them off as ham. Saint Nicholas, visiting the region to care for the hungry, not only saw through the butcher's horrific crime but also resurrected the three boys from the barrel by his prayers. Another version of this story, possibly formed around the eleventh century, claims that the butcher's victims were instead three clerks who wished to stay the night. The man murdered them, and was advised by his wife to dispose of them by turning them into meat pies. The Saint saw through this and brought the men back to life.

However, in his most famous exploit, a poor man had three daughters but could not afford a proper dowry for them. This meant that they would remain unmarried and probably, in absence of any other possible employment would have to become prostitutes. Hearing of the poor man's plight, Nicholas decided to help him but being too modest to help the man in public (or to save the man the humiliation of accepting charity), he went to his house under the cover of night and threw three purses (one for each daughter) filled with gold coins through the window opening into the man's house.

One version has him throwing one purse for three consecutive nights. Another has him throw the purses over a period of three years, each time the night before one of the daughters comes "of age". Invariably, the third time the father lies in wait, trying to discover the identity of their benefactor. In one version the father confronts the saint, only to have Saint Nicholas say it is not him he should thank, but God alone. In another version, Nicholas learns of the poor man's plan and drops the third bag down the chimney instead; a variant holds that the daughter had washed her stockings that evening and hung them over the embers to dry, and that the bag of gold fell into the stocking.

The miracle of wheat multiplication

During a great famine that the Bishop of Myra experienced, a ship was is in the port at anchor, which was loaded with wheat for the Emperor in Byzantium. He invited the sailors to unload a part of the wheat to help in time of need. The sailors at first disliked the request, because the wheat had to be weighed accurately and delivered to the Emperor. Only when Nicholas promised them that they would not take any damage for their consideration, the sailors agreed. When they arrived later in the capital, they made a surprising find. The weight of the load had not changed. The removed wheat in Myra was even enough for two full years and could even be used for sowing.

A key ring with the image of Nikolaos of Myra as patron of the sailors. More images on eship.at [1]

The face of the historical saint

Whereas the devotional importance of relics and the economics associated with pilgrimages caused the remains of most saints to be divided up and spread over numerous churches in several countries, St. Nicholas is unique in that most of his bones have been preserved in one spot: his grave crypt in Bari. Even with the still-continuing miracle of the manna, the archdiocese of Bari has allowed for one scientific survey of the bones. In the late 1950s, during a restoration of the chapel, it allowed a team of hand-picked scientists to photograph and measure the contents of the crypt grave.

In the summer of 2005, the report of these measurements was sent to a forensic laboratory in England. The review of the data revealed that the historical St. Nicholas was barely five feet in height (while not exactly small, still shorter than average, even for his time) and had a broken nose.

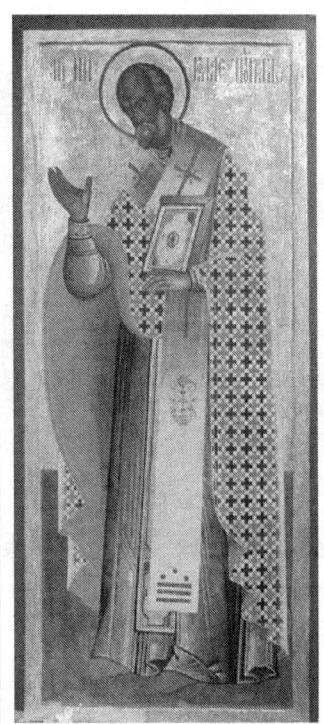

Saint Nicholas, Russian icon from first quarter of 18th cent. (Kizhi monastery, Karelia).

Formal veneration of the saint

Among the Greeks and Italians he is a favourite of sailors, fishermen, ships and sailing. As such he has become over time the patron saint of several cities maintaining harbours. In centuries of Greek folklore, Nicholas was seen as "The Lord of the Sea", often described by modern Greek scholars as a kind of Christianised version of Poseidon. In modern Greece, he is still easily among the most recognisable saints and 6 December finds many cities celebrating their patron saint. He is also the patron saint of all of Greece.

In Russia, Saint Nicholas' memory is celebrated on every Thursday of the year (together with the Apostles), and special hymns to him are found in the liturgical text known as the Octoechos. Soon after the transfer of Saint Nicholas' relics from Myra to Bari, a

Saint Nicholas Saves Three Innocents from Death (oil painting by Ilya Repin, 1888, State Russian Museum).

Russian version of his Life and an account of the transfer of his relics were written by a contemporary to this event. Devotional akathists and canons have been composed in his honour, and are frequently chanted by the faithful as they ask for his intercession. He is mentioned in the Liturgy of Preparation during the Divine Liturgy (Eastern Orthodox Eucharist) and during the All-Night Vigil. Many Orthodox churches will have his icon, even if they are not named after him.

In late medieval England, on Saint Nicholas' Day parishes held Yuletide "boy bishop" celebrations. As part of this celebration, youths performed the functions of priests and bishops, and exercised rule over their elders. Today, Saint Nicholas is still celebrated as a great gift-giver in several Western European countries. According to one source, medieval nuns used the night of 6 December to anonymously deposit baskets of food and clothes at the doorsteps of the needy. According to another source, on 6 December every sailor or ex-sailor of the Low Countries (which at that time was virtually all of the male population) would descend to the harbour towns to participate in a church celebration for their patron saint. On the way back they would stop at one of the various *Nicholas fairs* to buy some hard-to-come-by goods, gifts for their loved ones and invariably some little presents for their children. While the real gifts would only be presented at Christmas, the little presents for the children were given right away, courtesy of Saint Nicholas. This and his miracle of him resurrecting the three butchered children, made Saint Nicholas a patron saint of children and later students as well.

Among Albanians, Saint Nicholas is known as Shen'Kollë and is venerated by most Catholic families, even those from villages that are devoted to other saints. The Feast of Saint Nicholas is celebrated on the eve of 5 December, known as Shen'Kolli i Dimnit (Saint Nicholas of Winter), as well as on the commemoration of the interring of his bones in Bari, the eve of 8 May, known as Shen'Kolli i Majit (Saint Nicholas of May). Albanian Catholics often swear by Saint Nicholas, saying "Pasha Shejnti Shen'Kollin!" ("May I see Holy Saint Nicholas!"), indicating the importance of this saint in Albanian culture, especially among the Albanians of Malësia. On the eve of his feast day, Albanians will light a candle and abstain from meat, preparing a feast of roasted lamb and pork, to be served to guests after midnight. Guests will greet each other, saying, "Nata e Shen'Kollit ju nihmoftë!" ("May the Night of Saint Nicholas help you!") and other such blessings. The bones of Albania's greatest hero, Gjergj Kastrioti, were also interred in the Church of Saint Nicholas in Lezha, Albania, upon his death.

In iconography

St. Nicholas, the patron saint of Russian merchants. Fresco by Dionisius from the Ferapontov Monastery.

Saint Nicholas is a popular subject portrayed on countless Eastern Orthodox icons, particularly Russian ones. He is depicted as an Orthodox bishop, wearing the omophorion and holding a Gospel Book, sometimes he is depicted wearing the Eastern Orthodox mitre, sometimes he is bareheaded. Iconographically, Nicholas is depicted as an elderly man with a short, full white beard and balding head. In commemoration of the miracle attributed to him by tradition at the Ecumenical Council of Nicea, he is sometimes depicted with Christ over his left shoulder holding out a Gospel Book to him and the Theotokos over his right shoulder holding the omophorion. Because of his patronage of mariners, occasionally Saint Nicholas will be shown standing in a boat or rescuing a drowning sailor [2].

In Roman Catholic iconography, Saint Nicholas is depicted as a bishop, wearing the insignia of this dignity: a red bishop's cloak, a red miter and a bishop's crozier. The episode with the three dowries is commemorated by showing him holding in his hand either three purses, three coins or three balls of gold. Depending on whether he is depicted as patron saint of children or sailors, his images will be completed by a background showing ships, children or three figures climbing out of a wooden barrel (the three slaughtered children he resurrected).

In a strange twist, the three gold balls referring to the dowry affair are sometimes metaphorically interpreted as being oranges or other fruits. As in the Low Countries in medieval times oranges most frequently came from Spain, this led to the belief that the Saint lives in Spain and comes to visit every winter bringing them oranges, other 'wintry' fruits and tales of magical creatures.

Saint Nicholas Day

The tradition of *Saint Nicholas Day*, usually on 6 December, is a festival for children in many countries in Europe related to surviving legends of the saint, and particularly his reputation as a bringer of gifts. The American Santa Claus, as well as the Anglo-Canadian and British Father Christmas, derive from these legends. "Santa Claus" is itself derived from the Dutch *Sinterklaas*.

2006 Christmas stamp, Ukraine, showing St. Nicholas and children.

England

Great strides have been made since the inauguration of the St Nicholas Society in 2001. Canterbury Cathedral and City have held an annual festival that attracts thousands. England has over 450 Anglican churches. St Nicholas (Bishop Nicholas) has appeared in Newcastle, Durham, St Paul's, Southwark and Canterbury Cathedrals and well-known parishes, in London, St Paul's Knightsbridge; Holy Trinity, Sloane Street; St Matthews Westminster; St Stephen Walbrook; All Hallows by the Tower; and St Nicholas Allington, Kent; St Augustine, Gillingham, Great St Mary Cambridge and Liverpool Parish Church. www.stnicholassociety.com

Ireland

The saint who inspired the legend of Santa Claus is believed to have been buried in Jerpoint Abbey in Kilkenny some 800 years ago. Originally buried in Myra in modern day Turkey, his body was moved from there to Italy in 1169, but said to

Polychrome relief of *Sinter Claes* in Dam (Amsterdam).

have been taken afterwards to Ireland by Nicholas de Frainet, a distant relative. A Cistercian abbey, the church of Saint Nicholas, was built by his family there and dedicated to the memory of the saint. A slab grave on the ground of this church claims to hold his remains. There is a yearly mass in relation to the memory of Saint Nicholas, but otherwise the celebration is quite low key.

Italy

St. Nicholas (*San Nicola*) is the patron of the city of Bari, where it is believed he is buried. Its deeply felt celebration is called the *Festa di San Nicola*, held on the 7–9 of May. In particular on 8 May the relics of the saint are carried on a boat on the sea in front of the city with many boats following (*Festa a mare*). On 6 December there is a ritual called the *Rito delle nubili*. The same tradition is currently observed in Sassari, where during the day of Saint Nicholas, patron of the city, gifts are given to young brides who need help before getting married.

In Trieste, St. Nicholas (*San Nicolò*) is celebrated with gifts given to children on the morning of 6 December and with a fair called *Fiera di San Nicolò* during the first weeks of December. Depending on the cultural background, in some families this celebration is more important than Christmas. Trieste is a city on the sea, being one of the main ports of the Austro-Hungarian Empire and is influenced mainly by Italian, Slovenian and German cultures, but also Greek and Serbian.

Portugal

In one city (Guimarães) in Portugal, St. Nicholas (*São Nicolau*) has been celebrated since the Middle Ages as the patron saint of high-school students, in the so called *Nicolinas*, a group of festivities that occur from 29 November to 7 December each year. In the rest of Portugal this is not celebrated.

Sinterklaas in the Netherlands in 2007.

The Netherlands, Belgium, and Lower Rhineland (Germany)

Main article: Sinterklaas

In the Netherlands, Saint Nicholas' Eve (5 December) is the primary occasion for gift-giving, when his reputed birthday is celebrated.

In the days leading up to 5 December (starting when Saint Nicholas has arrived in the Netherlands by steamboat in late November), young children put their shoes in front of the chimneys and sing *Sinterklaas* songs. Often they put a carrot or some hay in the shoes, as a gift to St. Nicholas' horse. (In recent years the horse has been named *Amerigo* in Holland and *Slechtweervandaag* in Flanders.) The next morning they will find a small present in their shoes, ranging sweets to marbles or some other small toy. On the evening of 5 December, *Sinterklaas* brings presents to every child that has behaved itself well in the past year (in practice, just like with Santa Claus, all children receive gifts without distinction). This is often done by placing a bag filled with presents outside the house or living room, after which a neighbour or parent bangs the door or window, pretending to be *Sinterklaas'* assistant. Another option is to hire or ask someone to dress up as *Sinterklaas* and deliver the presents personally. *Sinterklaas* wears a bishop's robes including a red cape and mitre and is assisted by many mischievous helpers with black faces and colourful Moorish dress, dating back two centuries. These helpers are called 'Zwarte Pieten' ("Black Petes") or "Père Fouettard" in the French-speaking part of Belgium.

The myth is, if a child had been naughty, the Zwarte Pieten put all the naughty children in sacks, and Sinterklaas took them to Spain (it is believed that Sinterklaas comes from Spain, where he returns after 5 December). Therefor, many Sinterklaas songs still allude to a watching Zwarte Piet and a judging Sinterklaas.

In the past number of years, there has been a recurrent discussion about the politically incorrect nature of the Moorish helper. In particular Dutch citizens with backgrounds from Suriname and the Netherlands Antilles might feel offended by the Dutch slavery history connected to this emblem and regard the Zwarte Pieten to be racist. Others state that the black skin color of Zwarte Piet originates in his profession as a chimneysweep, hence the delivery of packages though the chimney.

In recent years, Christmas (along with Santa Claus) has been pushed by shopkeepers as another gift-giving festival, with some success; although, especially for young children, Saint Nicholas' Eve is still much more important than Christmas. The rise of Father Christmas (known in Dutch as *de Kerstman*) is often cited as an example of globalisation and Americanisation.

On the Frisian islands (*Waddeneilanden*), the Sinterklaas feast has developed independently into traditions very different from the one on the mainland.

Germany

In Germany, *Nikolaus* is usually celebrated on a small scale. Many children put a boot called *Nikolaus-Stiefel (Nikolaus boot)* outside the front door on the night of 5 December to 6 December. St. Nicholas fills the boot with gifts and sweets, and at the same time checks up on the children to see if they were good, polite and helpful the last year. If they were not, they will have a tree branch (*Rute*) in their boots instead. Sometimes a disguised Nikolaus also visits the children at school or in their homes and asks them if they have been good (sometimes ostensibly checking his golden book for their record), handing out presents on a per-behaviour basis. This has become more lenient in recent decades.

Santa Claus and Saint Nicholas.

But for some children, Nikolaus also elicited fear, as he was often accompanied by *Knecht Ruprecht (Servant Ruprecht)*, who would threaten to beat, or sometimes actually beat the children for misbehaviour as using this myth to 'bring up cheek children' for a better, good behaviour. Any kind of punishment isn't really following and just an antic legend. Knecht Ruprecht furthermore was equipped with deerlegs. In Switzerland, where he is called *Schmutzli*, he would threaten to put bad children in a sack and take them back to the dark forest. In other accounts he would throw the sack into the river, drowning the naughty children. These traditions were implemented more rigidly in Catholic countries and regions such as Austria or Bavaria.

Central Europe

In highly Catholic regions, the local priest was informed by the parents about their children's behaviour and would then personally visit the homes in the traditional Christian garment and threaten to beat them with a rod. In parts of Austria, *Krampusse*, who local tradition says are Nikolaus's helpers (in reality, typically children of poor families), roamed the streets during the festival. They wore masks and dragged chains behind them. These *Krampusläufe* (Krampus runs) still exist.

In Croatia Nikolaus (*Sveti Nikola*) who visits on Saint Nicholas day (*Nikolinje*) brings gifts to children commending them for their good behaviour over the past year and exhorting them to continue in the same manner in the year to come. If they fail to do so they will receive a visit from *Krampus* who traditionally leaves a rod, an instrument their parents will use to discipline them.

In the Czech Republic and Slovakia *Mikuláš*, in Poland *Mikołaj* and in Ukraine *Svyatyi Mykolay* is often also accompanied by an angel (*anděl/anioł/anhel*) who acts as a counterweight to the ominous devil or *Knecht Ruprecht* (*čert/czart*). Additionally, in Poland children find the candy and small gifts under the pillow or in their shoes the evening of 5 December. In Ukraine this tradition is celebrated on 19 December.

In Hungary and Romania children typically leave their boots on the windowsill on the evening of 5 December. By next morning Nikolaus (*Szent Miklós* traditionally but more commonly known as *Mikulás* in Hungary or Moş Nicolae (*Sfântul Nicolae*) in Romania) leaves candy and gifts if they have been good, or a rod (Hungarian: *virgács*, Romanian: *nuieluşă*) if they have been bad (most kids end up getting small gifts but also a small rod). In Hungary he is often accompanied by the *Krampusz*, the frightening helper who is out to take away the bad ones.

In Luxembourg *Kleeschen* is accompanied by the *Houseker* a frightening helper wearing a brown monk's habit.

In Slovenia Saint Nikolaus (*Miklavž*) is accompanied by an angel and a devil (*parkelj*) corresponding to the Austrian Krampus.

Greece, Serbia, and Bulgaria

In Greece, Saint Nicholas does not carry an especial association with gift-giving, as this tradition is carried over to St. Basil of Cesarea, celebrated on New Year's Day. St. Nicholas being the protector of sailors, he is considered the patron saint of the Greek navy, war and merchant alike and his day is marked by festivities aboard all ships and boats, at sea and in port. It is also associated with the preceding feasts of St. Barbara (4 December), St. Savvas (5 December), and the following feast of St. Ann (9 December); all these are often collectively called the "*Nikolobárbara*", and are considered a succession of days that heralds the onset of truly wintry cold weather in the country. Therefore by tradition, homes should have already been laid with carpets, removed for the warm season, by St. Andrew's Day (30 November), a week ahead of the *Nikolobárbara*.

In Serbia, Saint Nicholas is celebrated as patron saint of many families, through the feast preserved amongst the Serbs only, widely known as slava. Since the feast of Saint Nicholas always falls in the fasting period preceding the Christmas, feast is celebrated according to the Eastern Orthodox Church fasting rules. Fasting refers in this context to the eating of a restricted diet for reasons of Religion.

In the Republic of Bulgaria, Saint Nicholas is one of the most celebrated saints. Many churches and monasteries are named after him. As a holiday Saint Nicholas is celebrated on the 6th of December.

Lebanon

Saint Nicholas is celebrated by all the Christian communities in Lebanon: Catholic, Greek Orthodox, and Armenian. Many places, churches, convents, and schools are named in honor of Saint Nicholas, such as *Escalier Saint-Nicolas des Arts*, Saint Nicolas Garden, and Saint Nicolas Greek Orthodox Cathedral.

Palestine

Saint Nicholas is the patron saint of the town of Beit Jala. This little town, which is located only two kilometers to the west of Bethlehem, boasts of being the place where St. Nicholas spent four years of his life during his pilgrimage to the Holy Land. Every year on the 19th of December according to the Gregorian Calendar—that is the 6th of December according to the Julian Calendar—a solemn Divine Liturgy is held in the Orthodox Church of St. Nicholas, and is usually followed by parades, exhibitions, and many activities. Palestinian Christians and Palestinian Muslims of all sects, denominations and churches come to Beit Jala and participate in prayers and celebrations.

United States

While feasts of Saint Nicholas are not observed nationally, cities with strong German influences like Milwaukee, Cincinnati, Cleveland, and St. Louis celebrate St. Nick's Day on a scale similar to the German custom. On the day after Thanksgiving or sometime in December, children and their families put up a Christmas tree. A Christmas tree is a medium-sized pine tree that they put in their family rooms and decorate with ornaments and garlands of all sorts. They also normally put a star or angel on the top, as a symbol of Christ. On the 24 of December, Christmas Eve, each child puts one empty stocking/sock on their fireplace. The following morning of 25 of December, the children awake to find that St. Nick has filled their stockings with candy and small presents (if the children have been good) or coal (if not). Gifts often include chocolate gold coins to represent the gold St. Nick gave to the poor and small trinkets. They also awake to find presents under the tree, wrapped in Christmas-themed paper. For these children, the relationship between St. Nick and Santa Claus is not clearly defined, although St. Nick is usually explained to be a helper of Santa (as opposed to being Santa himself, another option)[citation needed]. The tradition of St. Nick's Day is firmly established in the Milwaukee, Cincinnati, Cleveland and St. Louis communities, with parents often continuing to observe the day with their adult children. Widespread adoption of observing the tradition has spread among the German, Polish, Belgian and Dutch communities throughout Iowa and Wisconsin, and is carried out through modern times.

In music

Benjamin Britten wrote a Christmas cantata entitled "St. Nicolas" commissioned by three public schools.

Also there is an oratorio "San Nicola di Bari", written by Giovanni Battista Bononcini in 1693.

Metamorphosis in Demre

The metamorphosis of Saint Nicholas into the more commercially lucrative Santa Claus, which took several centuries in Europe and America, has recently been re-enacted in the saint's home town: the city of Demre. This modern Turkish town is built near the ruins of ancient Myra. As St. Nicholas is a very popular Orthodox saint, the city attracts many Russian tourists. A solemn bronze statue of the Saint by the Russian sculptor Gregory Pototsky, donated

Russian Orthodox statue of Saint Nicolas, now in a corner near the church in Demre.

by the Russian government in 2000, was given a prominent place on the square in front of the medieval church of St. Nicholas. In 2005, mayor Suleyman Topcu had the statue replaced by a red-suited plastic Santa Claus statue, because he wanted the central statue to be more recognizable to visitors from all over the world. Protests from the Russian government against this action were successful only to the extent that the Russian statue was returned, without its original high pedestal, to a corner near the church.

Noel Baba at the square in front of the church in Demre.

Restoration on Saint Nicholas' original church in Demre is currently under way. In 2007, the Turkish Ministry of Culture finally gave permission for the Divine Liturgy to be celebrated at the site, and has even contributed the sum of forty-thousand Turkish Lira to the project.

References

Further reading

- Jones, Charles W. "Saint Nicholas of Myra, Bari, and Manhattan: Biography of a Legend" (Chicago: University of Chicago Press) 1978.
- ASANO, Kazuo ed., *The Island of St. Nicholas. Excavation and Research of Gemiler Island Area, Lycia, Turkey* (Osaka University Press) 2010.

External links

- Saint Nicholas [3] at the Open Directory Project
- Translation of Grimm's Saga No. 134 about St. Nicholas [4]

Mrs. Claus

Mrs. Claus is the wife of Santa Claus. Unlike Santa Claus, however, she does not have a counterpart in folklore or mythology, but was the creation of American authors. She was popularized by poet Katharine Lee Bates in Bates' poem, "Goody Santa Claus on a Sleigh Ride" (1889). The character has since appeared in story, film, television and other media.

Origin

The gift-giving bishop St. Nicholas was never portrayed as having a wife, and only when he was transformed, via Sinterklaas, into the more secular Santa Claus in the early 19th century did a wife appear.

Mrs. Claus sees her husband off on his journey in this 1919 postcard

The wife of Santa Claus is first mentioned in the short story "A Christmas Legend" (1849), by James Rees, a Philadelphia-based Christian missionary. In the story, an old man and woman, both carrying a bundle on the back, are given shelter in a home on Christmas Eve as weary travelers. The next morning, the children of the house find an abundance of gifts for them, and the couple is revealed to be not "old Santa Claus and his wife", but the hosts' long-lost elder daughter and her husband in disguise.

Mrs. Santa Claus is mentioned by name in the pages of the *Yale Literary Magazine* in 1851, where the student author (whose name is given only as "A. B.") writes of the appearance of Santa Claus at a Christmas party:

> [I]n bounded that jolly, fat and funny old elf, Santa Claus. His array was indescribably fantastic. He seemed to have done his best; and we should think, had Mrs. Santa Claus to help him.

An account of a Christmas musicale at the State Lunatic Asylum in Utica, New York in 1854 included an appearance by Mrs. Santa Claus, with baby in arms, who danced to a holiday song.

A passing references to Mrs. Santa Claus was made in an essay in *Harper's Magazine* in 1862; and in the comic novel *The Metropolites* (1864) by Robert St. Clar, she appears in a woman's dream, wearing "Hessian high boots, a dozen of short, red petticoats, an old, large, straw bonnet" and bringing the woman a wide selection of finery to wear.

A woman who may or may not be Mrs. Santa Claus appeared in the children's book *Lill in Santa Claus Land and Other Stories* by Ellis Towne, Sophie May and Ella Farman, published in Boston in 1878. In the story, little Lill describes her imaginary visit to Santa's office (not in the Arctic, incidentally):

The keeper of the naughty-or-nice ledger in "Lill's Travels in Santa Claus Land", 1878

> "There was a lady sitting by a golden desk, writing in a large book, and Santa Claus was looking through a great telescope, and every once in a while he stopped and put his ear to a large speaking-tube.

> "Presently he said to the lady, 'Put down a good mark for Sarah Buttermilk. I see she is trying to conquer her quick temper.'

> "'Two bad ones for Isaac Clappertongue; he'll drive his mother to the insane asylum yet.'"

Later, Lill's sister Effie ponders the tale:

> Effie sank back in the chair to think. She wished Lill had found out how many black marks she had, and whether that lady was Mrs. Santa Claus—and had, in fact, obtained more accurate information about many things.

Much as in *The Metropolites*, Mrs. Santa Claus appears in a dream of the author E. C. Gardner in his article "A Hickory Back-Log" in *Good Housekeeping* magazine (1887), with an even more detailed description of her dress:

> She was dressed for traveling and for cold weather. Her hood was large and round and red but not smooth, — it was corrugated; that is to say, it connsisted of a series of rolls nearly as large as my arm, passing over her head sidewise, growing smaller toward the back until they terminated in a big button that was embellished with a knot of green ribbon. Its general appearance was not unlike that of the familiar, pictorial beehive except that the rolls were not arranged spirally. The broad, white ruffle of her lace cap projected several inches beyond the front of the hood and waved back and forth like the single leaves of a great white poppy, as she nodded emphatically in her discourse.

> Her outer garment was a bright colored plaid worsted cloak reaching to within about six inches of the floor. Its size was most voluminous, but its fashion was extremely simple. It had a wide yoke across the shoulders, into which the broad plain breadths were gathered; and it was fastened at the throat by a huge ornamented brass hook and eye, from which hung a short chain of round twisted links. Her right arm protruded through a vertical slit at the side of the cloak and she held

in her hand a sheet of paper covered with figures. The left arm on which she carried a large basket or bag — I couldn't tell which — was hidden by the ample folds of the garment. Her countenance was keen and nervous, but benignant.

Mrs. Claus proceeds to instruct the architect Gardner on the ideal modern kitchen, a plan of which he includes in the article.

Santa Claus' wife made her most active appearance yet by Katherine Lee Bates in her poem "Goody Santa Claus on a Sleigh Ride" (1889). "Goody" is short for "Goodwife", i.e., "Mrs."

Illustration from *Goody Santa Claus on a Sleigh-Ride*, 1889

In Bates' poem, Mrs. Claus wheedles a Christmas Eve sleigh-ride from a reluctant Santa in recompense for tending their toy and bonbon laden Christmas trees, their Thanksgiving turkeys, and their "rainbow chickens" that lay Easter eggs. Once away, Mrs. Claus steadies the reindeer while Santa goes about his work descending chimneys to deliver gifts. She begs Santa to permit her to descend a chimney. Santa grudingly grants her request and she descends a chimney to mend a poor child's tattered stocking and to fill it with gifts. Once the task is completed, the Clauses return to their Arctic home. At the end of the poem, Mrs. Claus remarks that she is the "gladdest of the glad" because she has had her "own sweet will".

In popular media

Since 1889, Mrs. Claus has been generally depicted in media as a fairly heavy-set, kindly, white-haired elderly female baking cookies somewhere in the background of the Santa Claus mythos. She sometimes assists in toy production, and oversees Santa's elves. She is sometimes called Mother Christmas[*citation needed*], and Mary Christmas has been suggested as her maiden name.[*citation needed*]

Her reappearance in popular media in the 1960s began with the children's book *How Mrs. Santa Claus Saved Christmas*, by Phyllis McGinley. Today, Mrs. Claus is commonly seen in cartoons, on greeting cards, in knick-knacks such as Christmas tree ornaments, dolls, and salt and pepper shakers, in storybooks, in seasonal school plays and pageants, in parades, in department store "Santa Lands" as a character adjacent to the throned Santa Claus, in television programs, and live action and animated films that deal with Christmas and the world of Santa Claus. Her personality tends to be fairly consistent; she is usually seen as a calm, kind, and patient woman, often in contrast to Santa himself, who can be prone to acting too exuberant. In some modern adaptations, Mrs. Claus is shown with a younger, even sexier appearance.

Literature

Mrs. Claus has appeared as a secondary character in children's books about Santa Claus and as the main character in titles about herself.

- *Mrs. Santa Claus, Militant* (one-act play) by Bell Elliott Palmer, 1914
- *The Great Adventure of Mrs. Santa Claus* by Sarah Addington and Gertrude A. Kay, 1923
- *The Story of Santa Claus and Mrs. Claus and The Night Before Christmas* by Alice and Lillian Desow Holland, 1946
- *How Mrs. Santa Claus Saved Christmas* by Phyllis McGinley, 1963
- *Mrs. Santa Claus* by Penny Ives, 1993
- *A Bit of Applause for Mrs. Claus* by Jeannie Schick-Jacobowitz, 2003
- *The Story of Mrs. Santa Claus* by Bethanie Tucker and Crystal McLaughlin, 2007
- *Mrs. Claus Takes A Vacation* by Linas Alsenas, 2008
- *What Does Mrs. Claus Do?* by Kate Wharton and Christian Slade, 2008

Movies

- The first motion picture to depict Mrs. Claus was *Santa Claus Conquers the Martians* (1964), where she was played by Doris Rich.
- Mrs. Claus (played by Judy Cornwell) is also a character in 1985's *Santa Claus: The Movie*, where she played a vital role in the film's story. It was her idea to give presents only to good children.
- In the 1993 movie *The Nightmare Before Christmas*, Mrs. Claus has a cameo appearance. She is seen in the kitchen of her and Santa Claus's home, preparing a lunch box and a vacuum flask for her husband to take to work.
- The 2002 movie *The Santa Clause 2* centers on Tim Allen's character being forced to marry in order to continue his role as Santa. The "Mrs. Clause" confirms why every Santa has had a Mrs. Claus, because it is part of the Santa Clause. His wife is Carol Newman (Elizabeth Mitchell), and in *The Santa Clause 3: The Escape Clause*, she deals with being Mrs. Claus, having a baby, and being separated from her job and her family.
- Played by Miranda Richardson in *Fred Claus* (2007) co-starring Vince Vaughn and Paul Giamatti.

Television

Mrs. Claus played a major role in several of Rankin/Bass' Christmas specials. In *Santa Claus is Coming to Town* (1970), she is introduced as a teacher named Jessica, who first meets Santa Claus as a young man, when he's trying to illegally deliver toys to a town run by a despotic ruler. Assisting Santa, Jessica and Santa soon fall in love with each other, and marry in the nearby forest. In 1974's *The Year Without a Santa Claus* and the 2006 live action remake, Mrs. Claus played a large role, as she attempts to show Santa (who wishes to stay home that year for Christmas when he feels no one appreciates or believes in him anymore) that there's still some Christmas spirit left in the world. Mrs. Claus also made appearances in several other Rankin/Bass specials, including *Rudolph the Red-Nosed Reindeer* (1964) and *Rudolph and Frosty's Christmas in July*; Santa calls her "Jessica" at one point in the latter, implying some kind of shared continuity.

The lady was also portrayed in a television musical, *Mrs. Santa Claus* (1996), played by Angela Lansbury, with songs by Jerry Herman. Neglected by her husband, she goes to New York in 1910, and gets involved in agitating for women's rights and against child labor in toy manufacturing. Of course, she gets to learn how "Santa misses Mrs. Claus", as the sentimental song lyrics have it.

One of Mrs. Claus's most unusual television appearances is in *The Grim Adventures of Billy and Mandy* Christmas special *Billy and Mandy Save Christmas*. In this story she is revealed to be a powerful vampiress who, angry that Santa leaves most of the work for her, turns him into a vampire so she can take a break (which is about the six or seventh time she's done so), when she gets the idea to try and take over the world before Billy reconciles them. Another unusual appearance is in the Robot Chicken Christmas Special, during which, in a Dragon Ball Z parody sketch, she gains powers from the North Pole's radiation, and becomes a giant monster that Goku, Gohan, and Rudolph must destroy.

In *A Charlie Brown Christmas*, Charlie Brown's sister Sally writes to Santa and asks, "How is your wife?" Later, in *It's Christmastime Again, Charlie Brown*, she writes Santa's wife herself, and, when Charlie Brown comments that some people call her "Mary Christmas," Sally congratulates her on choosing to keep her own surname. In *Charlie Brown's Christmas Tales*, Sally writes Santa Claus as "Samantha Claus", inadvertently thinking Samantha Claus is Santa Claus's wife.

Mrs Claus appears in *A Chipmunk Christmas*, where she buys Alvin a harmonica after he gives his old one to a sick boy. Her identity isn't revealed until the end, when Santa returns home and she greets him.

Boost Mobile created some controversy with an ad featuring Mrs. Claus in bed with the Snowman. One version was briefly aired on late-night TV while two alternate versions were posted online.

Ad Age had some commentary about the spot, including "This latest ad from Boost Mobile and agency 180, Los Angeles, features Mrs. Claus doing something very, very bad."

Even Billy O'Reilly, CNN and a number of local TV news channels commented about the ads. It may perhaps be one of the first popular culture depictions of Mrs. Claus in a less than idealistic manner.

Musicals

In contrast to her stereotypical portrayal, Mrs. Claus is portrayed as a woman bored with her relationship with Santa Claus in the song *Sarabaya-santa* from Jason Robert Brown's musical *Songs for a New World*.

In 1987, George Jones and Tammy Wynette released single *Mr and Mrs Santa Claus*, a love song sung by Jones and Wynette as Mr and Mrs Claus respectively.

External links

- *Lill's Travels in Santa Claus Land* [1], 1878, at Project Gutenberg
- *Goody Santa Claus on a Sleigh-Ride* [2], 1889, by Katherine Lee Bates, original edition and text.
- Mrs. Claus Costumes [3]
- The Origin of American Christmas Myth and Customs [4]

Christmas elf

A **Christmas elf** is a diminutive creature (elf) that in modern times supposedly lives with Santa Claus in the North Pole and acts as his helper. Christmas elves are often depicted as green or red clad with pointy ears, long noses, and pointy hats. Santa's elves are often said to make the toys in Santa's workshop and take care of his reindeer, among other tasks. Elves in general originate from pagan stories in northern Europe and were introduced into the Santa Claus tale during the 19th Century, in the United States, including in some cases where Santa Claus himself is an elf. Therefore, Christmas elves became a part of American Christmas tradition that was exported, along with Santa Clause to other parts of the world. However, Christmas elfs in American folklore originated in Northern Europe from where settlers brought the Christmas traditions that evolved into the American Christmas that was later exported around the world, along with other aspects of American popular culture. Santa's assistants can be different depending on the country with a wide variety in western and northern Europe alone.

An image of a modern Christmas elf on a Christmas tree decoration.

Origin

The modern Christmas elf appeared as early as 1856 when Louisa May Alcott completed, but never published a book entitled "Christmas Elves". The elves can also be seen in engravings from 1873 in Godey's Lady's Book, showing them surrounding Santa whilst at work. Additional recognition was given in Edward Eggleston's 1876 work "The House of Santa Claus, a Christmas Fairy Show for Sunday Schools".

The image of the elves in the workshop was popularised by Godey's Lady's Book, with a front cover illustration for its 1873 Christmas Issue showing Santa surrounded by toys and elves with the caption "Here we have an idea of the preparations that are made to supply the young folks with toys at Christmas time". During this time Godey's was immensely influential to the birth of Christmas traditions, having shown the first widely circulated picture of a modern Christmas tree on the front cover of its 1850 Christmas issue.

St. Nicholas as an elf

In Clement Clarke Moore's 1823 poem *A Visit from St. Nicholas* (more commonly known today as *Twas the Night Before Christmas*), Santa Claus himself is described in line 45 as "He was chubby and plump, a right jolly old elf". Prior to the influence of St. Nicholas in Sweden, the job of giving out gifts was done by the Yule Goat. However by 1870 the saint became so well known that he could no longer be ignored. However, he became merged with the Tomten, which was previously an elvish/dwarfish farm guardian, and following the work of artist Jenny Nyström, becoming known as the Jultomten.

Contemporary pop culture

In the USA, Canada, and Britain, the modern children's folklore of Santa Claus typically includes diminutive elves at Christmas; green-clad elves with pointy ears, long noses, and pointy hats as Santa's assistants or hired workers. They make the toys in a workshop located in the North Pole. In recent years, other toys—usually high-tech toys like computers, video games, DVDs and DVD players, and even mobile phones—have also been depicted as being ready for delivery, but not necessarily made, in the workshop as well. In this portrayal, elves slightly resemble nimble and delicate versions of the dwarves of Norse mythology.

In films and television

Christmas elves have had their role expanded in modern films and television. For instance in *Santa Claus: The Movie*, the elves are a type of craft guild making traditional toys by hand and looking after Santa's reindeer. The elves' workshop is also featured regularly in films, such as in *Elf (film)* from 2003, starring Will Ferrell. and of course the 1932 Disney short film *Santa's Workshop* which features Santa Claus and his elves preparing for Christmas. A team of elves features prominently in the

Rankin-Bass 1964 special *Rudolph the Red-Nosed Reindeer*, including a "misfit" elf named Hermey who does not desire to make toys and instead wants to pursue a career in dentistry.

Disney would return to the theme of Christmas elves for their 2009 short film Disney Prep and Landing, which tells the tale of an elite group of elves that make houses ready for Santa's deliveries. It was the first holiday special made by Walt Disney Animation Studios.

Around the world

For more details on this topic, see Companions of Saint Nicholas.

Two Zwarte Piet, Santa's companion in the Netherlands.

In different countries, Santa's helpers go by different names. In Iceland they are the Yule Lads who between December 12 and 24, a different Lad visit homes each day to leave presents and play tricks on children. In the Netherlands, the companion is called Zwarte Piet (Black Peter), in Germany they are the Knecht Ruprecht and in Luxembourg they are known as Hoesecker. In the eastern regions of France, Père Fouettard accompanies Santa Claus, distributing coal to the naughty children.

In Nordic countries an elf will usually wear only red instead of the green and red outfits they are known for in English speaking countries.

See also
- SantaLand Diaries

External links
- Elves Around The World [1]
- All about "Santa's elves" [2]
- Elf Yourself [3]
- [1]

Santa Claus's reindeer

Santa Claus's reindeer are a team of flying reindeer traditionally held to pull the sleigh of Santa Claus and help him deliver Christmas gifts. The commonly cited names of the reindeer are *Dasher* and *Dancer*, *Prancer* and *Vixen*, *Comet* and *Cupid*, and *Donner* and *Blitzen*. They are based on those used in the 1823 poem *A Visit from St. Nicholas*, arguably the basis of reindeer's popularity as Christmas symbols, where *Donner* and *Blitzen* were originally called *Dunder* and *Blixem* respectively.

Santa Claus and seven of his reindeer in a parade in Toronto 2007.

The subsequent popularity of the Christmas song *Rudolph the Red-Nosed Reindeer* has led to *Rudolph* often joining the list.

Origins

The original eight reindeer

The anonymously-published poem "A Visit from St. Nicholas" (also known as "The Night Before Christmas" or "Twas the Night Before Christmas") is largely credited for the contemporary Christmas lore, including the eight flying reindeer and their names.

In the poem, Santa's transport is a "miniature sleigh, and eight tiny reindeer" and the reindeer are "more rapid than eagles." The poem does not describe them, nor their positions in the sleigh-team, but does say they fly.

The relevant segment of the poem reads:

> when, what to my wondering eyes should appear,
> but a miniature sleigh, and eight tiny rein-deer,
> with a little old driver, so lively and quick,
> I knew in a moment it must be St. Nick.
> More rapid than eagles his coursers they came,
> And he whistled, and shouted, and call'd them by name:
> "Now, Dasher! Now, Dancer! Now, Prancer, and Vixen!
> "On, Comet! On, Cupid! On, Donner and Blitzen!
> "To the top of the porch! to the top of the wall!
> "Now dash away! dash away! dash away all!"

In *An American Anthology, 1787–1900*, Edmund Clarence Stedman reprints the 1844 Clement Clarke Moore version of the poem, including the German spelling of "Donder and Blitzen," rather than the original 1823 version using the Dutch spelling, "Dunder and Blixem." Both phrases translate as "Thunder and Lightning" in English, though German for thunder is now spelled *Donner*, and the Dutch words would nowadays be spelled *Donder* and *Bliksem*.

The Christmas Mountains of New Brunswick, Canada are named after the original eight reindeer.

Since this poem, other books, movies, and music have contributed to the Christmas reindeer lore. The 1994 remake of the 1947 film *Miracle on 34th Street*, for example, asserts that reindeer can only fly on Christmas Eve.

Rudolph (the red-nosed reindeer)

Main article: Rudolph the Red-Nosed Reindeer

Rudolph's story was originally written in verse by Robert L. May for the Montgomery Ward chain of department stores in 1939, and published as a book to be given to children in the store at Christmas time.

According to this story, Rudolph's glowing red nose made him a social outcast among the other reindeer. However, one Christmas Eve Santa Claus was having a lot of difficulty making his flight around the world because it was too foggy. When Santa went to Rudolph's house to deliver his presents he noticed the glowing red nose in the darkened bedroom and decided it could be a makeshift lamp to guide his sleigh. He asked Rudolph to lead the sleigh for the rest of the night, Rudolph accepted and returned home a hero for having helped Santa Claus.

Rudolph's story is a popular Christmas story that has been retold in numerous forms, most notably a popular song, a television special, which departed significantly from Robert L. May's original story, in having Rudolph being Donner's son and living amongst Santa Claus' reindeer from birth, and a feature film.

Additional reindeer

Several television, film and music pieces have made references to other reindeer or other animals who substitute for reindeer. In many cases, these are explicitly related to other reindeer already in the fleet.

Rolf Harris sings about Santa using kangaroos instead of reindeer in Australia in his 1961 song "Six White Boomers".

In the song "¿Dónde Está Santa Claus?" recorded by Augie Rios in 1958, two other reindeer are named in the verse that goes: "I hope he won't forget to crack his castanet, and to his reindeer say: On *Pancho*, on Vixen, on *Pedro*, on Blitzen, Ole, Ole, Ole!"

In the 1958 Chuck Berry song, "Run Rudolph Run", the verses refer to *Randolph*, "way too far behind."

Santa needs the help of *Dominick, the Italian Christmas Donkey* to cross the hills of Italy according to the 1960 song by Lou Monte.

The 1964 *Rudolph* special features *Fireball* as one of several reindeer trying out for the sleigh team. With fire-red hair, Fireball is the son of Blitzen and his mind is often preoccupied with does; another reindeer is said to be the son of Dasher and struggles at flying, along with two other reindeer fawns of the same age. Comet's daughter, a young fawn named *Clarice*, is also featured, although she does not try out for the team.

The Ray Stevens song *Santa Claus is Watching You*, features *Clyde*, a camel borrowed from Stevens' previous song "Ahab the Arab"), who replaces Rudolph for the year. According to the original 1965 version of the song, Rudolph "dislocated his hip in a Twist contest", so Clyde is his replacement. In a later version of the song, in which the singer is talking to his lover, Rudolph is "on a stakeout" at the lover's house (making sure the lover remains true to the singer). The song also lists the original fleet of reindeer plus two other reindeer named *Bruce* and *Marvin*. Later editions of the songs add a longer more rambling list: *Leon*, *Cletus*, *George*, *Bill*, *Slick*, *Do-Right*, *Ace*, *Blackie*, *Queenie*, *Prince*, *Spot*, and *Rover*.

In Cheech & Chong's 1971 record "Santa Claus And His Old Lady", Cheech's character mentions reindeer named Donner, Blitzen, Chuy, Tavo, and Beto. The last three are typical Mexican nicknames; for Jesus, Gustavo/Octavio, and Roberto/Alberto.

Loretta Lynn's 1974 single "Shadrack, the Black Reindeer" introduced the speedy *Shadrack*. In the song, Rudolph has gotten older and slower. An already late Santa threatens to leave him behind, but the other reindeer suggest that they will complete their rounds on time if Shadrack and Rudolph lead the team side by side, and they succeed in doing so.

The 1979 feature film *Rudolph and Frosty's Christmas in July* features an antagonist reindeer named *Scratcher*.

In the 1993 film *Tim Burton's The Nightmare Before Christmas*, Jack Skellington calls upon his ghost dog, Zero, to lead his skeletal-reindeer team through the night which had become foggy when Sally tried to prevent Jack from leaving Halloweentown to deliver presents to the real world.

Joe Diffie's 1995 single "Leroy the Redneck Reindeer" features *Leroy*, who is Rudolph's cousin. Leroy, as stated in the title, is a redneck who wears a John Deere tractor hat and has a knack for dancing the two-step. Leroy replaces his ill cousin Rudolph as the leader of the sleigh team for the year.

The sketch comedy series MADtv commissioned a trilogy of *Rudolph* parodies from Corky Quakenbush beginning in 1995. The only one to include any original characters was the first, "Raging Rudolph," which featured mob enforcers *Jimmy the Antler* and *Franky Two Times*.

"Lightning," from a 1996 Sesame Street Christmas special Elmo Saves Christmas. He's a reindeer-in-training. Lightning helped Santa by taking Elmo, who wished for Christmas 24/7, to the future to see what Sesame Street would look like with Christmas everyday.

Olive, from a 1997 children's book and 1999 television special entitled *Olive, the Other Reindeer*, is not a reindeer but a dog. She mistook a news report regarding the plight of one of Santa's reindeer as a "help wanted" ad and heads to the North Pole, where she fills in for the ill reindeer for the year. The title of the story references a mondegreen derived from misinterpreting the words "all of the other reindeer" in the Rudolph story and song.

Annabelle, from the 1997 direct-to-video special *Annabelle's Wish*, is a young cow who was born on Christmas Eve and thus possesses "the magic of Christmas." She eventually becomes a reindeer herself and pulls Santa's sleigh, which has been Annabelle's lifelong goal.

The 1998 feature film *Rudolph the Red-Nosed Reindeer: The Movie* introduces *Mitzi* as Rudolph's mother and Blitzen's wife (as opposed to the Rankin-Bass version, where Donner was Rudolph's father). It also features two other reindeer named *Zoey* and *Arrow*, who appear to be clones of Clarice and Fireball respectively.

In the 1999 movie *Blizzard*, other reindeer are shown to live at the North Pole: *Blizzard*, who has the ability to become invisible and to see the whereabouts of people, *DJ*, Blizzard's best friend, and *Aphrodite*, a female reindeer who reports to an elder called *Archimedes*.

In the 1999 TV special *Robbie the Reindeer*, the eponymous *Robbie* is ostensibly assumed to be the son of Rudolph. His special feature is his nose which has supernatural powers that allow him to jump and fly farther and faster than most reindeer; in addition, this leads to Robbie literally having a "nose" for geography, as it can lead Robbie to just about any location in the world.

Chet is a young reindeer in training who was introduced in the 2002 feature film *The Santa Clause 2*. Because of his age, he has a tendency to be clumsy and awkward; however, he is able to help Santa save Christmas.

The 2002 *South Park* Christmas Special "Red Sleigh Down" introduces an entirely new fleet of reindeer, after the traditional reindeer are killed when the sleigh is shot down as Santa tries to bring Christmas to Iraq. The main characters rescue him by using the alternative reindeer named: *Steven*, *Fluffy*, *Horace*, *Chantel*, *Skippy*, *Rainbow*, *Patches* and *Montel*. Their names are sung in a similar fashion in order to make them fly. Their future fate beyond this one incident is unknown; either the replacements took over permanently, or the original were resurrected without explanation (see *Kenny's deaths* for an explanation of this phenomenon in the South Park universe).

In the 2006 TV special *Holidaze: The Christmas That Almost Didn't Happen*, *Rusty* is said to be Rudolph's brother. Unlike the other reindeer, Rusty is powerless, flightless, and is in fact notably clumsy. Unfit for pulling Santa's sleigh, he instead assists Santa and the other reindeer from air traffic control.

The TV series *My Friends Tigger & Pooh* introudced a special "Super Sleuth Christmas Movie" in 2007 that included *Holly*, a young reindeer fawn.

The 2008 television special The Flight Before Christmas features *Nico*. Nico was Prancer's love child from a one-night stand with a regular reindeer, and the young Nico went to the North Pole to seek his father (who he believed, but was not sure, was one of Santa's reindeer, and he didn't know which one).

Through Nico's courage, he is able to learn to fly, proving his ancestry in the process, and saves the reindeer from a pack of ravenous wolves. (Rudolph is absent from the sleigh team in this special, presumably for copyright purposes.)

The comic strip *Over the Hedge* added a character named *Ralph, the Infrared Nosed Reindeer*, who is Rudolph's brother and has a nose that emits infrared heat (useful for heating up food and defrosting Santa's sleigh). He is often envious of his more famous brother and, possibly because of an inferiority complex, is depressed and overweight.

Thrasher is a top-secret, oversized reindeer introduced in the 2009 Disney special *Prep and Landing*. He leads the titular "prep and landing" team of elves in a sleigh ahead of Santa Claus's main sled. He is significantly larger and tougher than the main reindeer, and he is said to be Dasher's cousin. (Rudolph is again absent from this special, with lighting instead provided by the prep and landing team.)

Bob Dylan's 2009 version of the song "Must Be Santa" has a line at the end of the song which replaces half of the reindeer with former Presidents of the United States: "Eisenhower, Kennedy, Johnson, Nixon... Carter, Reagan, Bush and Clinton."

List of Reindeer

Commonly Known Names

- Dasher
- Dancer
- Prancer
- Vixen
- Comet
- Cupid
- Donner (Dunder/Donder)
- Blitzen (Blixem/Bliksem)
- Rudolph

See also

- Christmas Mountains
- Folklore
- Rudolph the Red-Nosed Reindeer

External links

- History of Rudolph [1]
- How Old Are You In Rudolph Years? [2]

Rudolph the Red-Nosed Reindeer

Rudolph the Red-nosed Reindeer is a character created in a story and song by the same name. The story was created by Robert L. May in 1939 as part of his employment with Montgomery Ward.

The story is owned by The Rudolph Company, L.P. and has been sold in numerous forms including a popular song, a television special (done in stop-motion animation), and a feature film. Character Arts, LLC manages the licensing for the Rudolph Company, L.P. Although the story and song are not public domain, Rudolph has become a figure of Christmas folklore.

The song tells the tale of Santa Claus's ninth and lead reindeer who possesses an unusually red-colored nose that gives off its own light, powerful enough to illuminate the team's path through inclement winter weather.

The story

Robert L. May created Rudolph in 1939 as an assignment for Montgomery Ward. The retailer had been buying and giving away coloring books for Christmas every year and it was decided that creating their own book would save money. In its first year of publication, 2.4 million copies of Rudolph's story were distributed by Montgomery Ward. The story is written as a poem in the meter of "'Twas the Night Before Christmas".

The song

The song appears to borrow the hook from Let's Have Another Cup of Coffee (1932, Irving Berlin)

Johnny Marks, his brother-in-law, decided to adapt May's story into a song. Marks (1909–1985), who was Jewish, was a radio producer and wrote several popular Christmas songs. He was born in a New York City suburb and graduated from Colgate University in Hamilton, N.Y., before going off to Paris to study music. He had a heroic World War II combat record, winning the Bronze Star and four battle stars.

It was first sung commercially by crooner Harry Brannon on New York city radio in the latter part of 1948 before Gene Autry recorded it formally in 1949, and has since filtered into the popular consciousness.

The lyric "All of the other reindeer" can be misheard in dialects with the cot-caught merger as the mondegreen "Olive, the other reindeer", and has given rise to another character featured in her own Christmas television special, *Olive, the Other Reindeer.*

The song in its Finnish translation, *Petteri Punakuono*, has led to Rudolph's general acceptance in the mythology as Joulupukki, the Finnish Santa's lead reindeer. However, in Finland, Santa's reindeer do not fly.

Autry's version of the song also holds the distinction of being the only number one hit to fall completely off the chart after hitting #1 the week of Christmas 1949.. Nonetheless, it sold 2.5 million copies the first year, eventually selling a total of 25 million, and it remained the second best-selling record of all time until the 1980s.

In 1953, Billy May recorded "Rudolph the Red-Nosed Reindeer Mambo" with vocals by Alvin Stoller.

In 1965, The Supremes recorded the song for their album Merry Christmas.

In 1970, The Jackson 5 recorded the song for The Jackson 5 Christmas Album.

Peach Hips, a group consisting of Kotono Mitsuishi, Aya Hisakawa, Rica Fukami, Emi Shinohara and Michie Tomizawa covered this song for a Christmas album coinciding with the fifth season of Sailor Moon.

Rudolph in the media

Theatrical cartoon short

Rudolph's first screen appearance came in 1944, in the form of a cartoon short produced by Max Fleischer for the Jam Handy Corporation, that was more faithful to May's original story than Marks's song (which had not yet been written). It was reissued in 1948 with the song added.

On December 16, 2009, Mike Nelson featured this version in a live Rifftrax Christmas show in San Diego which was broadcast to select theaters in the United States.

Children's book

In 1958, Golden Books published an illustrated storybook, adapted by Barbara Shook Hazen and illustrated by Richard Scarry. The book is similar in story to the Max Fleischer cartoon short. Although it is one of the more memorable versions of the story in book form, it is apparently no longer in print. However, a revised Golden Books version of the storybook has since been issued.

Animated TV special

Main article: Rudolph the Red-Nosed Reindeer (TV special)

The reindeer made his television debut on NBC in 1964, when Rankin/Bass produced a stop-motion animated TV special. This version of the story adds several new characters, including the prospector Yukon Cornelius, a love interest for Rudolph named Clarice, and a Christmas elf named Hermey. (Hermey, like Rudolph, is a misfit: he suffers the disdain of the other elves because he would rather be a dentist than a toymaker). New subplots include Hermey and Rudolph running away to the "Island of Misfit Toys" where defective, anthropomorphic toys are left when they are deemed unfit for a child's care, and the capture of Rudolph's parents and Clarice by the Abominable Snowmonster.

In 1975, a sequel to the Rankin-Bass original special was produced, titled *Rudolph's Shiny New Year*, and then a third in 1979 titled *Rudolph and Frosty's Christmas in July*. The 2001 film *Rudolph the Red-Nosed Reindeer and the Island of Misfit Toys*, while it used the same characters, was produced by a different company, and it's unclear whether or not it should be considered as part of this particular canon (see the next section).

Animated feature-length film

Main article: Rudolph the Red-Nosed Reindeer: The Movie

An animated feature film remake of the story was produced in 1998, titled *Rudolph the Red-Nosed Reindeer: The Movie*. It received only a limited theatrical release before debuting on home video. Despite this it has garnered a base of dedicated fans as well as criticisms of many of the songs. Its inclusion of a villain character, Stormella, and a love interest, Zoey, for Rudolph as well as a small sidekick, Slyly, and a strong protector character, Leonard, are very derivative of the Rankin-Bass adaptation of the story as opposed to the original tale and song (the characters of Stormella, Zoey, Arrow, Slyly and Leonard closely parallel the Rankin-Bass characters of The Bumble, Clarice, Fireball, Hermey the Dentist, and Yukon Cornelius respectively). The movie amplifies the early back-story of Rudolph's harassment by his schoolmates (primarily an older fawn named Arrow) during his formative years.

GoodTimes Entertainment, the producers of this film, brought back most of the same production team for a CGI-animated sequel, *Rudolph the Red-Nosed Reindeer and the Island of Misfit Toys* in 2001. Unlike the film, the sequel licensed the original characters from the Rankin-Bass special.

Comic books

National Periodical Publications, also known as DC Comics, published a series of 13 annuals titled *Rudolph the Red-Nosed Reindeer* from 1950 to 1962. In 1972, DC published a 14th edition in an extra-large format. Subsequently, they published six more in that format: Limited Collectors' Edition C-24, C-33, C-42, C-50 and All-New Collectors' Edition C-53, C-60. Additionally, one digest format edition was published as The Best of DC #4 (Mar/Apr 1980).

Relatives in different adaptations

Main article: Santa Claus's reindeer#Additional reindeer

Two BBC animations carry on the legend by introducing Rudolph's son, Robbie the Reindeer. However, Rudolph is never directly mentioned by name (references are replaced by a character interrupting with the phrase "Don't say that name!" or something similar, presumably for copyright reasons.)

Rudolph is also given a brother, Rusty Reindeer, in the 2006 American special Holidaze: The Christmas That Almost Didn't Happen. Unlike in the "Robbie the Reindeer" cartoons, Rudolph's name is mentioned freely in the film.

Michael Fry and T. Lewis have recently given Rudolph another brother in a series of *Over the Hedge* comic strips; an overweight, emotionally-damaged reindeer named "Ralph, the Infra-Red nosed Reindeer", who has a red nose just like Rudolph's, but his is good for defrosting Santa's sleigh and warming up toast and waffles. He appeared before R.J., Verne, and Hammy, enviously complaining about his brother's publicity and his anonymity.

Rudolph has a cousin, Leroy, in Joe Diffie's 1995 song "Leroy the Redneck Reindeer".

In the animated specials produced by both Rankin-Bass and GoodTimes Entertainment, Rudolph has been given different sets of parents. In Rankin-Bass's holiday special, he is Donner's son and his mother is an unnamed tan doe with long eyelashes who is simply called "Mrs. Donner." In GoodTimes's retelling, Rudolph's father is Blitzen, possibly to avoid plagiarism, and his mother, played by Debbie Reynolds, is named Mitzi. In this film, Rudolph's three uncles are the three reindeer Dasher, Comet, and Cupid. Arrow, Rudolph's rival, is Cupid's son, making the two cousins. Robert L. May's original book does not name Rudolph's parents.

See also

- Santa Claus's reindeer

External links

- Official Licensor for Rudolph the Red-Nosed Reindeer [1]
- Official CBS website for Rudolph the Red-Nosed Reindeer [2]
- Rudolph The Red Nosed Reindeer (1948) [3]
- Rudolph The Red Nosed Reindeer (1948) Full Film (public domain footage) [4]
- **Lyrics To** Rudolph The Red Nosed Reindeer [5]

Père Noël

Père Noël is a legendary gift-giver during Christmas in France and French-speaking areas, identified with Father Christmas or Santa Claus in English speaking territories.

According to tradition, on Christmas Eve children leave their shoes by the fireplace filled with carrots and treats for Père Noël's donkey, Gui (French for "Mistletoe") before they go to bed. Père Noël takes the offerings and, if the child has been good, leaves presents in their place. Presents are traditionally small enough to fit in the shoes; candy, money or small toys.

Père Noël is sometimes confused with another character. In Eastern France (Alsace and Lorraine regions) there is a parallel tradition to celebrate *Saint Nicolas* on December 6. He is followed by *Le Père Fouettard*, who exists also in different parts of Germany (*Knecht Ruprecht* or *Belsnickel*), Austria (*Krampus*), Holland and Belgium (*Zwarte Piet*). *Le Père Fouettard* is a sinister figure dressed in black who accompanies *Saint Nicolas* and spanks children who have behaved badly.

In Brazil, due to the influence of French culture in the 19th century, the name of Papai Noel was adopted, opposing for example the name of Pai Natal in Portugal. However he is dressed in the North American style.

Joulupukki

Joulupukki is a Finnish Christmas figure. The name Joulupukki literally means Yule Goat. The Finnish word "pukki" comes from the Swedish "bock" (equivalent of the English "buck" or "billy-goat") and is an old Scandinavian tradition. Over time, the figure became more or less merged with Santa Claus.

There is a long Finnish tradition of persons dressing in goat costume to solicit or perform for leftover food after Christmas. Historically, such a person was an older man, and the tradition refers to him as a *nuuttipukki*. The term now also describes the practice, reportedly continuing in some parts of Finland.

Today Joulupukki looks and behaves mostly like his American version, but there are differences. Joulupukki's house and workshop are situated in the mountains of Korvatunturi, whereas the American counterpart resides at the North Pole. Another difference is that instead of sneaking in through the chimney during the late night hours, Joulupukki knocks on the front door during the Christmas Eve celebrations. When he comes in, his first words are traditionally "*Onkos täällä kilttejä lapsia?*" (Are there (any) well-behaved children here?)

He usually wears warm red clothes, uses a walking stick, and travels in a sleigh pulled by a number of reindeer. The popular song "Rudolph the Red-Nosed Reindeer" in its Finnish translation, *Petteri Punakuono*, has led to Rudolph's general acceptance in the mythology as Joulupukki's lead reindeer.

Joulupukki has a wife, Joulumuori ("*Old Lady Christmas*"), but tradition doesn't have much to say about her.

Home

Joulupukki lives in Korvatunturi in Lapland Finland.

Joulupukki's assistants are called *tonttu* or more precisely *joulutonttu* (from Swedish *tomte*); they are not elves, but essentially human, often dwarflike in character. They usually wear similar attire as Joulupukki, and males also have a white beard, but are often smaller in size and may be of any age or gender. While only a rather large, aged person can convincingly dress as Joulupukki, conveniently everyone can dress as a *joulutonttu*, with less special attire required.

Trivia

- The location of Joulupukki's workshop comes from a children's radio show called *Markus-sedän lastentunti* ("Children's hour with Uncle Markus") hosted by Markus Rautio and broadcast by the Finnish Broadcasting Company between years 1927-1956.
- Finland's Joulupukki received over 700,000 letters from children all over the world in 2006, according to a news report by the Finnish Broadcasting Company, YLE.
- The US-based Coca-Cola Santa Claus was designed by the son of Finnish emigrants, Haddon Sundblom.

The origins of Joulupukki

One interesting theory about the origins of Joulupukki and his flying reindeer, comes from the aboriginal Saami people of Lapland. In the forests there is a common poisonous mushroom, Amanita muscaria that is red with white dots. The shamans of Sami used to feed this mushroom to the reindeer, whereby the intestinal tract of the reindeer would filter out the poison, but leave the intoxicating substances. The urine of the reindeer would then be collected, and used as a hallucinogenic by the shamans. The shamans would often have out-of-the-body experiences and fly in the sky, returning through the chimney hole of their tent or cottage to their bodies. This shamanistic tradition would explain the flying reindeer, the use of chimneys, and even the red-white colouring of Joulupukki.[citation needed]

Joulupukki's dark side

Pagans used to have festivities to ward off evil spirits. In Finland these spirits of darkness wore goat skins and horns. In the beginning this creature didn't give presents but demanded them. The Yule Goat was an ugly creature and frightened children.

It is unclear how this personality was transformed into the benevolent Father Christmas. Nowadays the only remaining feature is the name. The process was probably a continuous amalgamation of many old folk customs and beliefs from varied sources. One can speak of a Christmas pageant tradition consisting of many personages with roles partly Christian, partly pagan: A white-bearded saint, the Devil, demons, house gnomes. Nowadays the Joulupukki of Finland resembles the American Santa Claus.

Popular radio programs from the year 1927 onwards probably had great influence in reformatting the concept with the Santa-like costume, reindeer and Korvatunturi as its dwelling place. Because there really are reindeer in Finland, and Finns live up North, the popular American cult took root in Finland very quickly.

See also

- Yule Goat
- Korvatunturi
- Finland at Christmas around the world
- Santa Claus Village

External links

- Santa Club [1]
- Santa Claus Foundation [2]
- Weihnachtsmann - Santa Claus - Joulupukki ... in Finnland [3]

Ded Moroz

In some Slavic cultures, the traditional character **Ded Moroz** (Russian: Дед Мороз) plays a role similar to that of Santa Claus. The literal translation of the name would be **Grandfather Frost**, although the name is often translated as **Father Frost**. Ded Moroz brings presents to children. However, unlike the secretive ways of Santa Claus, he often brings them in person, at the celebrations of the New Year, at New Year parties for kids by the New Year Tree.

Ded Moroz at his residence in Veliky Ustyug.

The "in-person" gifts usually occur at organized celebrations at kindergartens, schools, circus performances around New Year time where the gifts can be "standardized." Various agencies provide Ded Moroz visits to families and offices. In such cases specific gifts can be chosen for particular members at the parties. The clandestine operations of placing the gifts under the New Year tree still occur when a Ded Moroz visit is not arranged for some reason. [citation needed]

Ded Moroz is commonly accompanied by Snegurochka (Russian: Снегурочка), or 'Snow Maiden,' his granddaughter. She is a unique attribute of the image of Father Frost – none of his foreign colleagues has a similar companion.

Ded Moroz in the Kharkiv Metro.

The traditional appearance of Ded Moroz has a resemblance to that of Santa Claus, with his coat, boots and long white beard. Specifically, Ded Moroz wears a heel-long fur coat, a semi-round fur hat, and white valenki or high boots (sapogi), silver or red with silver ornament. Unlike Santa Claus, he walks with a long magical staff, does not say "Ho, ho, ho," and drives no reindeer but a troika or just walks.

The official residence of Ded Moroz in Russia is the town of Veliky Ustyug. The residence of the Belarusian Ded Moroz (Dzied Maroz in Belarusian) is in Belavezhskaya Pushcha.

Slovenian Dedek Mraz

History

Initially Father Frost used to be a wicked and cruel sorcerer who liked to freeze people. He took after the Old Slavic gods: 'Pozvizd' — the god of wind and good and bad weather, 'Zimnik' — god of winter, and the terrifying 'Korochun' — an underworld god ruling over frosts. The peculiar character of those pagan gods determined the initial disposition of Ded Moroz — at first he stole children and brought them away in his gigantic sack. To ransom the kids, their parents had to give him presents. However, with the lapse of time, everything turned upside down: under the influence of Orthodox traditions Father Frost reformed, became kind and started to give presents to kids. Then he adopted certain traits from the Dutch Sinterklaas (or Saint Nicholas), the prototype of the Santa Claus.

Snow sculpture of Ded Moroz in Samara.

His roots are in pagan beliefs, but since the 19th century his attributes and legend have been shaped by literary influences. He, together with Snegurochka, were "fleshed out" from a kind of a winter sprite into what he is now. The fairy tale play *Snegurochka* by the famous Russian playwright Aleksandr Ostrovsky was influential in this respect, followed by

Rimsky-Korsakov's *Snegurochka* with libretto based on the play.

By the end of the 19th century Ded Moroz had become the most popular of the various mythical figures who were in charge of New Year gift bringing: including Grandfather Nicholas, Santa Claus, Ded Treskun, Morozko and simply Moroz. Ded Moroz perfectly fits the Russian traditions, so there is a widespread erroneous opinion that he has been known to Russians for centuries.

In 1916, in Imperial Russia the Holy Synod called to boycott Christmas trees as a tradition, originating from Germany (Russia's enemy during World War I). In the Russian SFSR and the Soviet Union Christmas trees were banned until 1935 because they were considered to be a "bourgeois and religious prejudice". In 1928 Ded Moroz was declared "an ally of the priest and kulak".. Nevertheless, the image of Father Frost took its final shape in the USSR: he became the main symbol of the New Year's Holiday that replaced Christmas as the most favourite and fairy holiday in the pre-revolutionary Russia. The New Year's tree was revived in the USSR after the famous letter by Pavel Postyshev, published in *Pravda* on December 28, 1935, where he asked for New Year trees to be installed in schools, children's homes, Young Pioneer Palaces, children's clubs, children's theaters and cinema theaters. Postyshev believed that the origins of the holiday, which were pre-Christian in any case, were less important than the benefits it could bring to Soviet children. In 1937, Ded Moroz for the first time arrived at the Moscow Palace of Unions. In subsequent years, an invitation to the New Year Tree at the Palace of Unions became a matter of honor for Soviet children. The image of "Soviet" Father Frost was established by Soviet filmmakers in the 1930s. The color of the coat that Ded Moroz wore was changed several times. So as not to be confused with Santa Claus, it was often blue. Joseph Stalin ordered Palace of Unions' Ded Morozes to wear only blue coats. During the times of the Soviet Union's dominance over Eastern Europe, Ded Moroz was officially introduced in many national traditions, despite being alien to them. Following the fall of the Soviet Union, there have been efforts to revive local characters. Russia has other gift givers like baboushaka and kolyada.

Ded Moroz in modern Russia

Ded Moroz is quite popular in modern Russia. In 1998 town Veliky Ustyug was declared the motherland of Russian Ded Moroz.

Regional differences

There are equivalents of Ded Moroz and Snegurochka all over the former USSR, as well as the countries once in the so-called Soviet bloc and in the former Yugoslavia.

Belarus

In Belarus Dzied Maroz is not a traditional character and is never mentioned in national folklore. [*citation needed*]

The official residence of *Dzied Maroz* (Belarusian: Дзед Мароз, Dzied Maróz ("Ded Moroz" in Belarussian language) is located in Biełavieskaja Pušča.

Former Yugoslavia

In socialist Yugoslavia (Bosnia and Herzegovina, Croatia, the Republic of Macedonia, Montenegro, Serbia and Slovenia the person who brought gifts to children was called "Grandfather Frost" (Croatian: Djed Mraz, Bosnian: Dedo Mraz, Macedonian: Дедо Мраз (*Dedo Mraz*), Serbian: Деда Мраз (*Deda Mraz*), Slovenian: Dedek Mraz). He brought gifts for New Year as celebration of Christmas was discouraged by the Communist regime.

Croatia

After breakup of Yugoslavia, Djed Mraz was labeled communist and Djed Božićnjak (literally: Grandfather Christmas) was (un)successfully introduced. In mass media and advertising Djed Božićnjak tried to take place of Djed Mraz, except for the timing of gift bringing: Djed Božićnjak brings presents on Christmas. After 1999 names of Djed Mraz and Djed Božićnjak are names more or less equally used for the same person - including the public television. In some families Djed Mraz still brings gifts on New Year.

In Croatia, children also get presents on December 6. The present are brought by a traditional figure called *Sveti Nikola* (Saint Nicholas) who is also very close in resemblance to Djed Mraz or Djed Božićnjak, except for the fact that he is accompanied by Krampus who takes misbehaving children away.

In some religious families, little Jesus brings gifts on Christmas instead of Djed Božićnjak.

Slovenia

In Slovenia the name was translated from Russian as *Dedek Mraz* (literally, 'Grandpa Frost'). He is slim, wears a grey leather coat, which has fur inside and is decorated outside, and a round dormouse fur cap based on traditional imagery, especially as depicted by Maksim Gaspari. Initially he was said to live in Siberia, but with the Informbiro crisis and the schism between Yugoslavia and the Soviet Union his home was relocated to Mt. Triglav, Slovenia's highest peak. The notion of Father Frost was ideologically useful because it served to reorient the December/January holidays away from religion (Saint Nicholas Day and Christmas) and towards (secular) New Year. After the demise of the Communist regime at the beginning of the 1990s, two other "good old men" (as they are currently styled in Slovenian) reappeared in public: *Miklavž* (Saint Nicholas) brings presents on December 6, and *Božiček* (Santa Claus) on Christmas Eve. St. Nicholas has had a strong traditional presence in

Slovenian ethnic territory and remained celebrated in family circles throughout the Communist period. Until late 1940s some areas in Slovenia also celebrated Christkind called Jezušček (little Jesus) or Božiček (little God) who brought gifts on Christmas Eve. Božiček is also the name for Santa Claus. Since the 1990s, Father Frost has started appearing during all of December and may top the gifts off on New Year's Eve. There are also family preferences according to political or religious persuasion. In public the three figures avoid conflict, and are even featured together [1], as friends. Popular culture has also started blending attributes of the characters — for example, mention of (Santa's) reindeer is sometimes mingled into the Father Frost narrative at public appearances. Due to his non-religious character and strong institutionalization, Father Frost continues to retain a public presence.

Bulgaria

The traditional local name of Santa Claus in Bulgaria is **Дядо Коледа** (Dyado Koleda, "Grandfather Christmas"), with Dyado Mraz (Дядо Мраз, "Grandfather Frost") being a similar Russian-imported character lacking the Christian connotations and thus popular during Communist rule. However, he has been largely forgotten since 1989, when Dyado Koleda again returned as the more popular figure.

Poland

While there is no traditional analog of Ded Moroz in Polish folklore, there was an attempt to introduce him as *Dziadek Mróz* during the communist period. In the People's Republic of Poland the figure *Dziadek Mróz* was used in propaganda, since the traditional Święty Mikołaj (Saint Nicholas, the Polish Santa Claus) was determined to be "ideologically hostile", as part of the campaign against religion, which included elimination of Christmas in favor of New Year. Often officials insisted on using the figure in Polish schools and preschools during celebrations and events for Polish children, instead of Santa Claus in order to give impression of traditional cultural links with the Soviet Union. Despite those efforts, Dziadek Mróz never gained any popular support among the Polish people, and after the fall of communism he disappeared from Poland.

Romania

Moş Gerilă was, in Communist Romania, a replacement of Father Christmas (*Moş Crăciun*), being part of the Communist offensive against religion. His name is a Romanian language adaptation of the Russian Ded Moroz.

In 1948, after the Communists gained power in Romania, it was decided that Christmas should not be celebrated in Romania. 25 December and 26 December became working days and no official celebrations were to be held. As a replacement of *Moş Crăciun*, a new character was introduced, *Moş Gerilă* (literally "Old Man Frosty"), who brought gifts to children on 31 December.

Officially, the New Year's Day celebrations began on 30 December, which was named the Day of the Republic, since it was the day when King Mihai I of Romania abdicated in 1947.

After the Romanian Revolution of 1989, Moş Gerilă lost his influence, being replaced by Moş Crăciun.

Tatarstan

In Tatar he is known as Qış Babay/Кыш Бабай (Winter Grandfather) and is accompanied by Qar Qızı/Кар Кызы (Snow Girl).

Yamal

In Nenets (Nenets are aborigens of Yamal) he is known as Yamal Iri (Grandfather of Yamal).

See also

- Christmas in Eastern Europe
- Old Man Winter
- Jack Frost
- Father Christmas

External links

- Just Don't Call Me Santa! A History of Ded Maroz in English. [2]
- Father Frost, the Red Nose. [3]
- Father Frost of Yamal (peninsula and region of Russia) [4] (in Russian).

Befana

In Italian folklore, **Befana** is an old woman who delivers gifts to children throughout Italy on Epiphany Eve (the night of January 5) in a similar way to Saint Nicholas or Santa Claus. This Italian gift-giving spirit is also known as Saint Befana, La Vecchia (the Old Woman), and La Strega (the Witch).

The character may have originated in central Italy, then spread as a tradition to the rest of Italy.[citation needed]

A popular belief is that her name derives from the Feast of Epiphany or in Italian, "La Festa dell'Epifania". Epifania (Epiphany in English) is a Latin word with Greek origins. Epiphany means either the *Feast of the Epiphany* (January 6) or "manifestation (of the divinity)."

There is evidence to suggest that Befana is descended from the Sabine/Roman goddess named Strina. In the book *Vestiges of Ancient Manners and Customs, Discoverable in Modern Italy and Sicily* by Rev. John J. Blunt (John Murray, 1823), the author says:

Three *Befane* with their brooms.

"This Befana appears to be heir at law of a certain heathen goddess called Strenia, who presided over the new-year's gifts, 'Strenae,' from which, indeed, she derived her name. Her presents were of the same description as those of the Befana—figs, dates, and honey. Moreover her solemnities were vigorously opposed by the early Christians on account of their noisy, riotous, and licentious character".

Judika Illes wrote, "Befana may predate Christianity and may originally be a goddess of ancestral spirits, forests, and the passage of time. Some identify this wandering, nocturnal crone with Hekate."

In popular folklore Befana visits all the children of Italy on the eve of the Feast of the Epiphany to fill their socks with candy and presents if they are good or a lump of coal or dark candy if they are bad. Being a good housekeeper, many say she will sweep the floor before she leaves. The child's family typically leaves a small glass of wine and a plate with a few morsels of food, often regional or local, for the Befana.

She is usually portrayed as an old lady riding a broomstick through the air wearing a black shawl and is covered in soot because she enters the children's houses through the chimney. She is often smiling and carries a bag or hamper filled with candy, gifts, or both.[citation needed]

Legend

Christian legend had it that Befana was approached by the biblical magi, also known as the Three Wise Men (or the three kings) a few days before the birth of the Infant Jesus. They asked for directions to where the Son of God was, as they had seen his star in the sky, but she did not know. She provided them with shelter for a night, as she was considered the best housekeeper in the village, with the most pleasant home. The magi invited her to join them on the journey to find the baby Jesus, but she declined, stating she was too busy with her housework. Later, La Befana had a change of heart, and tried to search out the astrologers and Jesus. That night she was not able to find them, so to this day, La Befana is searching for the little baby. She leaves all the good children toys and candy ("caramelle") or fruit, while the bad children get coal ("carbone"), onions or garlic.

Another Christian legend takes a slightly darker tone as La Befana was an ordinary woman with a child whom she greatly loved. However, her child died, and her resulting grief maddened her. Upon hearing news of Jesus being born, she set out to see him, delusional that he was her son. She eventually met Jesus and presented him with gifts to make him happy. The infant Jesus was delighted, and he gave La Befana a gift in return; she would be the mother of every child in Italy.

Also, popular tradition tells that if one sees La Befana one will receive a thump from her broomstick, as she doesn't wish to be seen. This aspect of the tradition may be designed to keep children in their beds while parents are distributing candy (or coal) and sweeping the floor on Epiphany Eve.

Also, another commonly heard Christian legend of la Befana starts at the time of the birth of baby Jesus. Befana spends her days cleaning and sweeping. One day the magi, also known as the three wise men, came to her door in search of baby Jesus. Befana turned them away because she was too busy cleaning. Befana notices a bright light in the sky; she thinks this is the way to baby Jesus. She brought some baked goods and gifts for baby Jesus in her bag and took her broom to help the new mother clean and began her search for baby Jesus. She searched and searched for Baby Jesus, but never found him. Befana still searches today, after all these centuries. On the eve of the Epiphany, Befana comes to a house where there is a child and leaves a gift. Although she has been unsuccessful in her search, she still leaves gifts for good young children because the Christ Child can be found in all children

History

Many people believe that the name Befana is derived from the Italians' mispronunciation of the Greek word *epifania* or *epiphaneia* (Greek, επιφάνεια = appearance, surface, English: epiphany). Others point to the name being a derivative of Bastrina, the gifts associated with the goddess Strina. In the book *Domestic Life in Palestine*, by Mary E. Rogers (Poe & Hitchcock, 1865) the author notes:

"But an 'Essay on the Fine Arts,' by E. L. Tarbuck, led me to believe that this custom is a relic of pagan worship, and that the word "Bastrina" refers to the offerings which used to be made to the goddess Strenia. We could hardly expect that the pagans who embraced Christianity could altogether abandon their former creeds and customs. Macaulay says, "Christianity conquered paganism, but paganism infected Christianity; the rites of the Pantheon passed into her 'worship, and the subtilties of the Academy into her creed.' Many pagan customs were adopted by the new Church. T. Hope, in his 'Essay on Architecture,' says: 'The Saturnalia were continued in the Carnival, and the festival with offerings to the goddess Strenia was continued in that of the New Year...'" – page 408

An interesting theory connects the tradition of exchanging gifts to an ancient Roman festivity in honour of Ianus and Strenia (in Italian a Christmas gift is called *strenna*), celebrated at the beginning of the year, when Romans were used to giving each other presents.

The tradition of La Befana appears to incorporate other pre-Christian popular elements as well, adapted to Christian culture and related to the celebration of the New Year. Historian Carlo Ginzburg relates her to Nicevenn. The old lady character should then represent the *old year* just passed, ready to be burned in order to give place to the new one. In many European countries the tradition still exists of burning a puppet of an old lady at the beginning of the New Year, called Giubiana in Northern Italy, with clear Celtic origins. Italian anthropologists Claudia and Luigi Manciocco, in their book *Una Casa Senza Porte* (House without a Door) trace Befana's origins back to Neolithic beliefs and practices. The team of anthropologists also write about Befana as a figure that evolved into a goddess associated with fertility and agriculture.

The Befana today

The Befana is celebrated throughout all of Italy; she has become a national icon. Le Marche, Umbria and Lazio are three places that are associated with the Papal States, where the Epiphany held the most importance. Urbania is thought to be her official home. Every year there is a big festival held to celebrate the holiday. About 30,000-50,000 people attend the festivities. Hundreds of Befana's are present, swinging from the main tower. They juggle, dance and greet all the children. Traditionally, all Italian children may expect to find a lump of "coal" in their stockings (actually rock candy made black with caramel coloring), as every child has been at least occasionally bad during the year.

Two places in Italy are nowadays associated with the Befana tradition:

Befana of Campomarino di Maruggio (Italy)

- Piazza Navona in central Rome is the site of a popular market each year between Christmas and the Epiphany, where toys, sugar charcoal and other candies are on sale. The feast of the Befana in Rome was immortalized in four famous sonnets in the Roman dialect by the 19th century Roman poet Giuseppe Gioacchino Belli. In Ottorino Respighi's 1928 Feste Romane ("Roman Festivals"), the fourth movement, titled *La Befana*, is an orchestral portrayal of this Piazza Navona festival. Romans believe that at the midnight January 6 the Befana shows herself from a window of Piazza Navona, and they always go there to watch her (it's a joke everybody tells while going to the feast to buy candies, toys and sweets).

- The town of Urbania in the Province of Pesaro Urbino within the Marche region, where the national Befana festival is held each year, usually between January 2 and 6. A "house of the Befana" is scheduled to be built and the post office has a mailbox reserved for letters addressed to the Befana, mirroring what happens with Santa Claus in Rovaniemi.

In other parts of the world where a vibrant Italian community exists, traditions involving Befana may be observed and shared or celebrated with the wider community. In Toronto, Canada for example, a Befana Choir shows up on Winter Solstice each December to sing in the Kensington Market Festival of Lights parade. Women, men, and children dressed in La Befana costume and nose sing love songs to serenade the sun to beckon its return. The singing hags gather in the street to give candy to children, to cackle and screech to accordion music, and to sing in every key imaginable as delighted parade participants join in the cacophony. Sometimes, the Befanas dance with parade goers and dust down the willing as parade goers walk by.

Poems & Songs

There are poems about Befana, which are known in slightly different versions throughout Italy. Here is one of the versions:

> *La Befana vien di notte*
> *Con le scarpe tutte rotte*
> *Col vestito alla romana*
> *Viva, Viva La Befana!*

The English translation is:

> *The Befana comes by night*
> *With her shoes all tattered and torn*
> *She comes dressed in the Roman way*
> *Long life to the Befana!*

Another version told by people in the Province of Trento (northern Lake Garda):

> *Viene, viene la Befana*
> *Vien dai monti a notte fonda*
> *neve e gelo la circondan..*
> *neve e gelo e tramontana!*
> *Viene, viene la Befana*

The English translation is:

> *Here comes, here come the Befana*
> *she comes from the mountains in the deep of the night*
> *snow and frost (ice) surrounds her*
> *snow and frost and the West wind*
> *here comes, here comes the Befana!*

Tramontana: English - Tramontane: "a classical name for a northern wind." OR from "tra i monti" = "from the mountains" = cold wind, typically from the north.

Another song, this one by Italian pop singer and entertainer Gianni Morandi:

> *Trullalà Trullalà Trullalà.*
> *La Befana vien di notte*
> *con le scarpe tutte rotte,*
> *con la calza appesa al collo,*
> *col carbone, col ferro e l'ottone.*
> *Sulla scopa per volare.*
> *Lei viene dal mare.*
> *Lei viene dal mare.*
> *E la neve scenderà*

sui deserti del Maragià,
dall'Alaska al Canadà.
E partire lei dovrà
e cantando partirà
da ciociara si vestirà,
con il sacco arriverà,
la bufera vincerà.
E cantando trullalà,
la Befana arriverà.
Trulalla' Trullalà Trullalà.
Un bambino, grande come un topolino,
si è infilato nel camino,
per guardarla da vicino.
Quando arriva la Befana
senza denti
salta, balla, beve il vino.
Poi di nascosto s'allontana
con la notte appiccicata alla sottana.
E un vento caldo soffierà
sui deserti del Maragià,
dall'Alaska al Canadà.
Solo una stella brillerà
e seguirla lei dovrà,
per volare verso il nord
e la strada è lunga
ma la bufera vincerà.
E cantando Trullalà,
la Befana se ne va.
E cantando Trullalà
Truallalero Trullalà
Trullalà Trullalà Trullalà

External links

- Roots of Befana Legend [1]
- Befana, an academic view [2]

Christkind

Das Christkind (German "The Christ-child", pronounced German pronunciation: [ˈkʁɪstkɪnt]) is the traditional Christmas gift-bringer in regions of Austria, the Czech Republic, Croatia, Slovenia, Germany, Italy, Liechtenstein, Switzerland, Slovakia, Hungary, parts of Hispanic America, in certain areas of southern Brazil and in the Acadiana region of Louisiana. In Italy it is called *Gesù Bambino* (Italian for "Baby Jesus"), in Hungary its name is *Jézuska* (Hungarian for "Little Jesus"), in Slovakia *Ježiško* ("Little Jesus") and in the Czech Republic *Ježíšek* ("Little Jesus"). Promulgated by Martin Luther, explicitly to discourage the figure of St. Nicholas, at the Reformation in 16th-17th century Europe, many Protestants changed the gift bringer to the Christ Child or *Christkindl*, and the date of giving gifts changed from December 6 to Christmas Eve. The Christkind was adopted in Catholic areas during the 19th century, while it began to be gradually replaced by the Weihnachtsmann ("Father Christmas", a secularized version of Saint Nicholas) in Protestant regions.

Christkind.

The Christkind is a sprite-like child, usually depicted with blond hair and angelic wings. Martin Luther intended it to be a reference to the incarnation of Jesus as an infant. It is presumed by some to be so, but seems to be rooted in the Alsatian-born myth of a child bringing gifts *to* the baby Jesus.[citation needed] Children never see the Christkind, as parents will always tell them that the Christkind just disappeared before they came.

Since the 1990s, the Christkind is facing increasing competition from the Weihnachtsmann in the American version of Santa Claus, caused by the use of Santa Claus as an advertising figure. (Need citation. Santa Claus as advertising figure has been prominently used in the United States since the Macy's Department Store Thanksgiving-to-Christmas marketing campaigns of the 1870s.)

Christkindl or Christkindel are diminutive versions of Christkind. Christkind and Belsnickel are also found among communities of Volga German descent in Argentina.

Christkindl is also a small pilgrimage town in Austria, named after the miraculous wax statue of Christkind in the town church.

See also

- Kris Kringle, an Americanized pronunciation and spelling of Christkindl
- Christkindl Markt, a traditional holiday market in Austria and Germany
- Ježíšek, the same figure in the Czech tradition

External links

- Landler, Mark (12 December 2002). "Vienna Journal; For Austrians, Ho-Ho-Ho Is No Laughing Matter" [1]. *The New York Times*. Retrieved 10 December 2009.
- Cain, Phil (December 14, 2009). "Austria campaign to save Christkind from Santa Claus" [2]. *BBC News* (Graz). Retrieved December 14, 2009.

Zwarte Piet

In the folklore and legends of the Netherlands and Flanders, **Zwarte Piet** (pronunciation) (meaning **Black Pete**) is a companion of Saint Nicholas (Dutch: *Sinterklaas*) whose yearly feast in the Netherlands is usually celebrated on the evening of the 5th of December (*Sinterklaas-avond*, that is St. Nicolas Eve) and the 6th of December in Flanders, when they distribute sweets and presents to all good children.

The character of Zwarte Piet appears only in the weeks before Saint Nicholas's feast, first when the saint is welcomed with a parade as he arrives in the country (generally by boat, allegedly travelling from Spain), and is mainly targeted at children, who come to meet the saint as he visits stores, schools etc. He is sometimes associated with Knecht Ruprecht, but in the Low Countries the tradition has not merged with Christmas.

History

- 1845: Jan Schenkman writes *Saint Nicholas and his Servant*; Piet is described in this book as a servant and as black, and is depicted as a dark man wearing Asian-style clothes. Steamboat travel becomes part of the mythos from this point. In the 1850 version of Schenkman's book, they are depicted looking much as they do today. The servant gets his African origin but still has no standard name. In later editions Piet was shown in the page costume, the book stayed (with some changes) in print until 1950 and can be seen as the foundation of the current celebration, even though it did use a lot of older ideas and customs.
- 1891: in the book *Het Feest van Sinterklaas* the servant is named Pieter, until 1920 there were several books giving him other names, and in live appearances the name and looks still varied considerably.

- In the early 20th century the Civilized Standard Celebration for children, with Zwarte Piet as the standard personal servant of the saint, spread throughout the country. In the 1930s urban adults become more involved too and the arrival of Saint Nicholas and Zwarte Piet are staged, which more or less explains the shift from the 6th to the 5th of December, as the adults would celebrate on the eve of the saint's day.
- During the 20th century, the number of Sinterklaas' servants multiplied. This paradigm shift opened possibilities to create (for TV and such) lots of different characters being "Zwarte Piet" at the same time. For example, there's a "Hoofd Piet" (Head Piet) who carries the book of Sinterklaas, "Rijm Piet" (Rhyme Piet), et cetera.

The Dutch now celebrate Sinterklaas (5 December) with an exchange of gifts. These presents are given anonymously, but are often accompanied by poems (Sinterklaasgedicht), signed by "Zwarte Piet" or "Sint", which are read aloud during Sinterklaas evening for the enjoyment of the ones assembled. The poems often are teasing in nature.

Origin and evolution

According to myths dating to the beginning of the 19th century, Saint Nicholas (Sinterklaas) operated by himself or in the companionship of a devil. Having triumphed over evil, it was said that on Saint Nicholas Eve, the devil was shackled and made his slave. A devil as a helper of the Saint can also still be found in Austrian Saint Nicholas tradition in the character of Krampus.

Some sources indicate that in Germanic Europe, Zwarte Piet originally was such an enslaved devil forced to assist his captor, but the character emerged in the 19th century within the Netherlands as a companion of Saint Nicholas resembling a Moor. Saint Nicholas is said to come from Spain. The relation of Zwarte Piet with Haji Firuz is incredibly close, Haji Firuz is a traditional herald of Nowruz, the Persian New Year celebration, exactly black in the face and comes with Amoo Nowruz a white beared old man who brings gifts for the children counter part of Western Santa.

The introduction of this new Zwarte Piet was paired with a change in the attitude of the Sinterklaas character that was often shown as being quite rough against bad children himself and thought unbefitting of a Bishop by teachers and priests. Soon after the introduction of Zwarte Piet as Sinterklaas' helper, both characters adapted to a softer character.

Until the second half of the 20th century, Saint Nicholas' helper was not too bright, in line with the old colonial traditions. Once immigration started from the former colonised countries Zwarte Piet became a more respected assistant of Saint Nicholas.[citation needed]

According to the more modern Saint Nicholas legend, Zwarte Piet is a servant who accompanies Saint Nicholas on his holiday travels. In some versions, it is alleged that Saint Nicholas once liberated a young slave named Peter, who decided to serve Nicholas (as a free servant) rather than enjoy liberty alone. Zwarte Piet is today commonly depicted as a black man in the colorful pantaloons, feathered cap and ruffles of a Renaissance European page, a tradition based on a single illustration in a book published in 1850.

Zwarte Piet is often portrayed as a mischievous but rarely a mean-spirited character. Parents used to tell their children that if they have been good, Zwarte Piet will bring them gifts and sweets, but if they have been bad, Piet will scoop them up, stuff them in his huge dufflebag and spirit them away to Spain as punishment. Though this is increasingly uncommon nowadays, he can still carry some type of whip or scourge (called a "roe"), especially a birch, which could be used for birching or in modern words, to chastise children who have been too naughty to deserve presents. The character is believed to have been derived from pagan traditions of evil spirits. Also told for decades is a story that the Zwarte Pieten are black because of chimney soot and/or in mockery of the darker Spanish occupiers of the Low Countries in centuries past.

The traditions of the Saint Nicholas feast are in part at least of medieval origin, if not much older. St. Nicholas himself, as described in the Dutch tradition shows some similarities to Wuotan/Odin, which suggests that the duo have a pre-Christian origin. Possible precursors to *Zwarte Piet* can be found in Odin's ravens Hugin and Munin.

Current affairs

During recent years the role of Zwarte Piet has become part of a recurring debate in the Netherlands. Present-day observations in the Netherlands under controversy include holiday revellers blackening their faces, wearing afro wigs, gold jewellery and bright red lipstick, speaking in a Surinamese accent, and walking the streets throwing candy to passers-by.

Zwarte Piet

The lyrics of traditional Sinterklaas songs and some parents warn that while Sinterklaas and Zwarte Piet will leave well-behaved children presents, they will punish those who have been naughty. They will kidnap bad children and carry these children off in a sack to their homeland of Spain, where, according to legend, Sinterklaas and Zwarte Piet dwell out of season.

Foreign tourists, particularly Americans, often experience culture shock upon encountering the character (to dress in blackface is a gross taboo in America). Since the last decade of the 20th century there have been several attempts to introduce a new kind of Zwarte Piet to the Dutch population. These Zwarte Pieten have replaced the traditional black make-up with all sorts of colours. In 2006 the NPS (en: Dutch Programme Foundation) replaced the black Pieten by these rainbow-coloured Pieten, but in 2007 they reverted to the traditional all-black Pieten.

In 2008, on CBS's "The Early Show" and the NBC syndicated "The Martha Stewart Show", comedian Stephen Colbert cited the story of Black Peter and Sinterklaas as his preferred means of celebrating Christmas, proclaiming himself a "Christmas Originalist". The appearances coincided with the release of his Christmas special, "A Colbert Christmas: The Greatest Gift of All!".

External links

- David Sedaris, Six To Eight Black Men [1]
- Caroline Nelissen, Dutch debate Sinterklaas' Zwarte Piet [2]

Krampus

Krampus is a mythical creature. In various regions of the world – especially Austria and Hungary – it is believed that Krampus accompanies St. Nicholas during the Christmas season, warning and punishing bad children, in contrast to St. Nicholas, who gives gifts to good children. Due to German and Austrian influence, the myth of Krampus is also prevalent in Croatia, the Czech Republic, Slovakia, Slovenia and northern Italy.

The word *Krampus* originates from the Old High German word for claw (*Krampen*). In the Alpine regions, Krampus is represented by an incubus-like creature. Traditionally, young men dress up as the Krampus in the first two weeks of December, particularly on the evening of 5 December, and roam the streets frightening children and women with rusty chains and bells. In some rural areas the tradition also includes birching – corporal punishment with a birch rod – by Krampus, especially of young girls. Images of Krampus usually show him with a basket on his back used to carry away bad children and dump them into the pits of Hell.

Modern Krampus costumes consist of *Larve* (wooden masks), sheep's skin, and horns. Considerable effort goes into the manufacture of the hand-crafted masks, and many younger adults in rural communities compete in the Krampus events.

In Oberstdorf, in the alpine southwestern part of Bavaria, the tradition of *der Wilde Mann* ("the wild man") is kept alive. He is like Krampus in that he is dressed in fur and frightens children (and adults) with rusty chains and bells, but has no horns, and is not an assistant of Saint Nicholas.

In the aftermath of the Austrian Civil War the Krampus tradition was a target of Austrian Fascists allied with Nazi Germany.

In popular culture

- On 9 December 2009, Krampus was featured on *The Colbert Report*.
- Krampus appeared on *The Venture Bros.* Christmas special, "A Very Venture Christmas".
- The Krampus was featured in the web-comic, *The Non-Adventures of Wonderella*.
- Krampus is mentioned on the television show *Supernatural* in the episode "A Very Supernatural Christmas".

Gallery

Krampus and Saint Nicholas visit the home of naughty children

Krampus

Krampus

Krampus at Morzger Pass in Salzburg, Austria

See also

- Perchta
- Companions of Saint Nicholas
    - Belsnickel
    - Black Peter
    - Le Père Fouettard
- Pre-Christian Alpine traditions
- Saint Nicholas
- Namahage

External links

- Photos of Krampus Monsters [2]
  - Swiss legends [3]
  - Austrian legends [4]
- Krampus in Tirol [1]

Belsnickel

Belsnickel is the fur-clad Santa of the Palatinate (Pfalz) in southwestern Germany along the Rhine, the Saarland, and the Odenwald region of Baden-Württemberg.

In Pennsylvania Dutch communities, it is also a mythical being who visits children at Christmas time. If they have not been good, they will find coal and/or switches in their stockings. The Belsnickel was a scary creature not well loved except by parents wanting to keep their children in line.

Belsnickel is similar to Krampus in German-Austrian legend, except compared to Krampus, Belsnickel is rather benign. Belsnickel is a man wearing fur which covers his entire body, and he sometimes wears a mask with a long tongue. Krampus, on the other hand, is a demonic looking creature whose purpose is to scare children through his looks as well as his discipline techniques.

Among some families of German descent, Belsnickel delivers socks or shoes full of candy to children on the feast day of St. Nicholas, December 6. St. Nicholas is purported to have enabled the three daughters of a poor man to pay the dowries for their weddings. The poor man couldn't afford his daughters' dowries so Nicholas came to the man's house at night and sneaked three sacks of gold into the house thus saving the daughters from the indignity of a solitary life or prostitution.

Belsnickel and Christkind are also found among population of Volga German descent in Argentina.

Spelling variations

In North America, it is often spelled Belsnickel, Belschnickel, Belznickle or Belznickel. In South America, it is spelled as it is in German language: Pelznikel.

See also

- Companions of Saint Nicholas
- Krampus
- Black Peter
- Le Père Fouettard

External links

- Belsnickel article [1]

Le Père Fouettard

Le Père Fouettard (French for *The whipping Father*) is a character who accompanies St. Nicholas in his rounds during St. Nicholas' Day (6 December) dispensing lumps of coal and/or floggings to the naughty children while St. Nick gives gifts to the well behaved. He is known mainly in the Eastern regions of France, although similar characters exist all over Europe (see Companions of Saint Nicholas). This "Whipping Father" was said to bring a stick with him to spank all of the naughty kids who misbehaved.

Origin

The most popular story about the origin of Le Père Fouettard was first told in the year 1150. An Inn Keeper (or in other versions a butcher) captures three boys who appear to be wealthy and on their way to enroll in a religious boarding school. Along with his wife, he kills the children in order to rob them. One gruesome version tells that they drug the children, slit their throats, cut them into pieces, and stew them in a barrel. St. Nicholas discovers the crime and resurrects the children. After this, Le Père Fouettard repents and becomes St. Nick's partner. A slightly altered version of this story claims that St. Nicholas forced Le Père Fouettard to become his assistant as a punishment for his crimes.

Another story states that during the siege of Metz (a city in Eastern France) in 1552, an effigy of king Charles Quint was burned and dragged through the city. Meanwhile, an association of tanners created a grotesque character (also a tanner) armed with a whip and bound in chains that punished children. After Metz was liberated, the charred effigy of Charles Quint and the character created by the tanners somehow assimilated into what is now known as Le Père Fouettard. Events surrounding the city's liberation and the burning of the effigy coincided with the passage of St. Nicholas, hence Le Père Fouettard became his "bad cop" counterpart.

In the 1930s, Le Père Fouettard appeared in the United States under the translated name Father Flog or Spanky. Although almost identical to the original French personification, Father Flog had nothing to do with Christmas and also had a female accomplice named Mother Flog. The two doled out specific punishments for specific childhood crimes (e.g. cutting out the tongue for lying).

Similar Characters

Le Père Fouettard is similar if not identical to numerous characters that perform the same function. Knecht Ruprecht, a tradition of the Germanic People, is probably the best known of these characters. In the Alsace region, Le Père Fouettard is known as Hans Trapp. In Switzerland, Schmutzli is nearly identical. Hans Muff, Pelzebock, Drapp or Buzeberg are also used in various parts of Bavaria. In the Netherlands and Flanders they have Zwarte Piet, although he isn't as scary to kids.

Similar traditions in the Alpine regions have characters that are more bestial and range from a goat to an actual demon or devil. The most popular of these characters is Krampus, other similar/identical characters include Klaubauf, Bartel, Bellzebub, and Čert (Devil).

In some traditions, the bringer of gifts and the bringer of punishment are fused into one. Rumpelklas, Pelzebock, Pelznickel, Belzeniggl, and Belsnickel are examples of this tradition.

In Alsace, Le Père Fouettard is synonymous with the bogeyman.

Appearance

The most common depiction of Le Père Fouettard would be of a man with a sinister face dressed in dark robes with scraggly unkempt hair and a long beard. He is armed with either a whip, a large stick, or with bundles of switches. Some incarnations of the character have him wearing a wicker back pack in which children can be placed and carried away. Sometimes he merely carries a large bundle of sticks on his back (some speculate that the photograph on the cover of *Led Zeppelin IV* is Le Père Fouettard). Often, his face is darkened to varying degrees. Some say it is because of his being born of a burned effigy, others say that it is from the soot in the chimneys that he goes down with St. Nicholas. In other representations, Le Père Fouettard is identical to the Dutch character Zwarte Piet (Black Peter). Further renderings of the character show him as being nearly identical to Saint Nicholas or Santa Claus, but wearing a black suit instead of a red one.

Le Père Fouettard in Pop Culture

- Jacques Dutronc mentions Le Père Fouettard in his song "*La Fille du Père Noël*" ("Father Christmas's daughter").
- Another French pop star, Alain DeLorme mentioned him in the song "*Venez Venez St. Nicolas*"
- There is a restaurant named Le Père Fouettard at 9 Rue Pierre Lescot, in Paris which features "Classic Parisian Fare".
- Robert Schumann composed a piano piece in 1848 most commonly known as Knecht Ruprecht (a similar character, see Companions of Saint Nicholas), but in some cases the piece is called Le Père Fouettard.

See also

- Belsnickel
- Krampus
- Zwarte Piet

North Pole

Geographical coordinates: 90°N 0°W

The **North Pole**, also known as the **Geographic North Pole** or **Terrestrial North Pole**, is, subject to the caveats explained below, defined as the point in the northern hemisphere where the Earth's axis of rotation meets the Earth's surface. It should not be confused with the North Magnetic Pole.

The North Pole is the northernmost point on Earth, lying diametrically opposite the South Pole. It defines geodetic latitude 90° North, as well as the direction of True North. At the North Pole all directions point south; all lines of longitude converge there, so its longitude can be defined as any degree value.

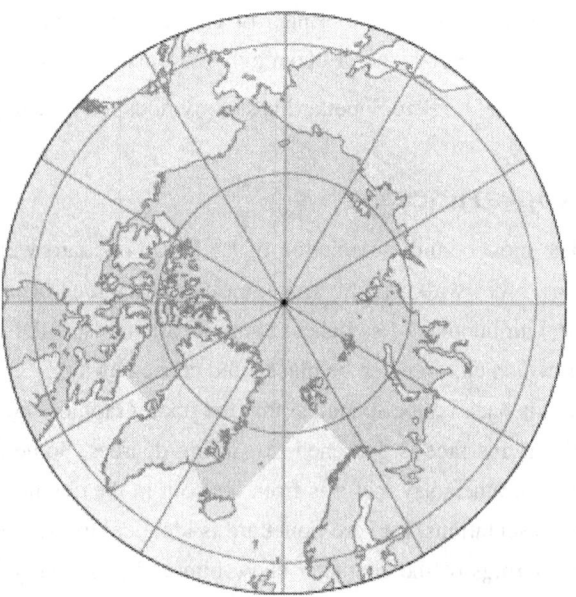

An Azimuthal projection showing the Arctic Ocean and the North Pole.

While the South Pole lies on a continental land mass, the North Pole is located in the middle of the Arctic Ocean amidst waters that are almost permanently covered with constantly shifting sea ice. This makes it impractical to construct a permanent station at the North Pole (unlike the South Pole). However, the Soviet Union, and later Russia, have constructed a number of manned drifting stations, some of which have passed over or very close to the Pole. In recent years, a number of studies have predicted that the North Pole may become seasonally ice-free due to Arctic shrinkage, with timescales varying from a few years to fifty years or more.

The sea depth at the North Pole has been measured at 4,261 metres (13,980 ft). The nearest land is usually said to be Kaffeklubben Island, off the northern coast of Greenland about 700 km (440 mi) away, though some perhaps non-permanent gravel banks lie slightly closer.

North Pole scenery

Precise definition

See also: Polar motion

The Earth's axis of rotation – and hence the position of the North Pole – was commonly believed to be fixed (relative to the surface of the Earth) until, in the 18th century, the mathematician Leonhard Euler predicted that the axis might "wobble" slightly. Around the beginning of the 20th century astronomers noticed a small apparent "variation of latitude," as determined for a fixed point on Earth from the observation of stars. Part of this variation could be attributed to a wandering of the Pole across the Earth's surface, by a range of a few meters. The wandering has several periodic components and an irregular component. The component with a period of about 435 days is identified with the 8 month wandering predicted by Euler and is now called the Chandler wobble after its discoverer. The exact point of intersection of the Earth's axis and the Earth's surface, at any given moment, is called the "instantaneous pole", but because of the "wobble" this cannot be used as a definition of a fixed North Pole (or South Pole) when metre-scale precision is required.

It is desirable to tie the system of Earth coordinates (latitude, longitude, and elevations or orography) to fixed landforms. Of course, given plate tectonics and Isostasy, there is no system in which all geographic features are fixed. Yet the International Earth Rotation and Reference Systems Service and the International Astronomical Union have defined a framework called the International Terrestrial Reference System.

Expeditions

See also: Arctic exploration, Farthest North and List of Arctic expeditions

Pre-1900

As early as the sixteenth century, many eminent people correctly believed that the North Pole was in a sea, which in the nineteenth century was called the Polynia or Open Polar Sea. It was therefore hoped that passage could be found through ice floes at favorable times of the year. Several expeditions set out to find the way, generally with whaling ships, already commonly used in the cold northern latitudes.

One of the earliest expeditions to set out with the explicit intention of reaching the North Pole was that of British naval officer William Edward Parry, who in 1827 reached latitude 82°45′ North. In 1871 the Polaris expedition, an American attempt on the Pole led by Charles Francis Hall, ended in disaster. An 1879–1881 expedition commanded by US naval officer George Washington DeLong also ended tragically when their ship, the USS *Jeanette*, was crushed by ice. Over half the crew, including DeLong, were lost.

In April 1895 the Norwegian explorers Fridtjof Nansen and Fredrik Hjalmar Johansen struck out for the Pole on skis after leaving Nansen's icebound ship *Fram*. The pair reached latitude 86°14′ North before they abandoned the attempt and went southwards, eventually reaching Franz Josef Land.

Nansen's ship *Fram* in the Arctic ice

In 1897 Swedish engineer Salomon August Andrée and two companions tried to reach the North Pole in the hydrogen balloon *Örnen* ("Eagle"), but were stranded 300 km north of Kvitøya, the northeasternmost part of the Svalbard Archipelago, and perished on this lonely island. In 1930 the remains of this expedition were found by the Norwegian Bratvaag Expedition.

The Italian explorer Luigi Amedeo, Duke of the Abruzzi and Captain Umberto Cagni of the Italian Royal Navy (Regia Marina) sailed the converted whaler *Stella Polare* from Norway in 1899. On March 11, 1900 Cagni led a party over the ice and reached latitude 86° 34' on April 25, setting a new record by beating Nansen's result of 1895 by 35 to 40 kilometres. Cagni barely managed to return back to the camp, remaining there until June 23. On August 16 the *Stella Polare* left Rudolf Island heading south and the expedition returned to Norway.

1900–1940

The American explorer Frederick Albert Cook claimed to have reached the North Pole on April 21, 1908 with two Inuit men, Ahwelah and Etukishook, but he was unable to produce convincing proof and his claim is not widely accepted.

The conquest of the North Pole was for many years credited to American Navy engineer Robert Peary, who claimed to have reached the Pole on April 6, 1909, accompanied by American Matthew Henson and four Inuit men named Ootah, Seeglo, Egingwah, and Ooqueah. However, Peary's claim remains controversial. The party that accompanied Peary on the final stage of the journey included no one who was trained in navigation and could independently confirm his own navigational work, which some claim to have been particularly sloppy as he approached the Pole.

Peary's sledge party "at the North Pole," 1909. From left: Ooqueah, Ootah, Henson, Egingwah, Seeglo.

The distances and speeds that Peary claimed to have achieved once the last support party turned back seem incredible to many people, almost three times that which he had accomplished up to that point. Peary's account of a journey to the Pole and back while traveling along the direct line – the only strategy that is consistent with the time constraints that he was facing – is contradicted by Henson's account of tortuous detours to avoid pressure ridges and open leads.

The British explorer Wally Herbert, initially a supporter of Peary, researched Peary's records in 1989 and concluded that they must have been falsified and that Peary had not reached the Pole. Support for Peary came again in 2005, however, when the British explorer Tom Avery and four companions recreated the outward portion of Peary's journey with replica wooden sleds and Canadian Eskimo Dog teams, reaching the North Pole in 36 days, 22 hours – nearly five hours faster than Peary. Avery writes on his web site that "The admiration and respect which I hold for Robert Peary, Matthew Henson and the four Inuit men who ventured North in 1909, has grown enormously since we set out from Cape Columbia. Having now seen for myself how he travelled across the pack ice, I am more convinced than ever that Peary did indeed discover the North Pole."

The first claimed flight over the Pole was made on May 9, 1926 by US naval officer Richard E. Byrd and pilot Floyd Bennett in a Fokker tri-motor aircraft. Although verified at the time by the US Navy and a committee of the National Geographic Society, this claim has since been disputed.

The first undisputed sighting of the Pole was on May 12, 1926 by Norwegian explorer Roald Amundsen and his American sponsor Lincoln Ellsworth from the airship *Norge*. *Norge*, though Norwegian owned, was designed and piloted by the Italian Umberto Nobile. The flight started from Svalbard and crossed the icecap to Alaska. Nobile, along with several scientists and crew from the *Norge*, overflew the Pole a second time on May 24, 1928 in the airship *Italia*. The *Italia* crashed on its return from the Pole, with the loss of half the crew.

1940–2000

In May 1945 an RAF Lancaster of the *Aries* expedition became the first Commonwealth aircraft to overfly the North Geographic and North Magnetic Poles. The plane was piloted by David Cecil McKinley of the Royal Air Force. It carried an 11-man crew, with Kenneth C. Maclure of the Royal Canadian Air Force in charge of all scientific observations. In 2006, Maclure was honoured with a spot in the Canadian Aviation Hall Of Fame.

Discounting Peary's disputed claim, the first men to set foot at the North Pole were, according to some sources, a Soviet Union party. These are variously described as including Pavel Gordiyenko (or Geordiyenko) and three or five others, or Aleksandr Kuznetsov and 23 others, who landed a plane (or planes) there on April 23, 1948. According to Antarctica.org, three Li-2 planes landed, carrying a total of seven men.

On May 3, 1952, U.S. Air Force Lieutenant Colonel Joseph O. Fletcher and Lieutenant William P. Benedict, along with scientist Albert P. Crary, landed a modified C-47 Skytrain at the North Pole. Some sources consider this (rather than the Soviet mission) to be the first ever landing at the Pole.

The United States Navy submarine *USS Nautilus* (SSN-571) crossed the North Pole on August 3, 1958, and on March 17, 1959, the *USS Skate* (SSN-578) surfaced at the Pole, becoming the first naval vessel to do so.

USS *Skate* at the North Pole, 1959

Setting aside Peary's claim, the first confirmed surface conquest of the North Pole was that of Ralph Plaisted, Walt Pederson, Gerry Pitzl and Jean Luc Bombardier, who traveled over the ice by snowmobile and arrived on April 19, 1968. The United States Air Force independently confirmed their position.

On April 6, 1969, Wally Herbert and companions Allan Gill, Roy Koerner and Kenneth Hedges of the British Trans-Arctic Expedition became the first men to reach the North Pole on foot (albeit with the aid of dog teams and air drops). They continued on to complete the first surface crossing of the Arctic

Ocean – and by its longest axis, Barrow, Alaska to Svalbard – a feat that has never been repeated. Because of suggestions of Plaisted's use of air transport, some sources classify Herbert's expedition as the first confirmed to reach the North Pole over the ice surface by any means.

On August 17, 1977, the Soviet nuclear powered icebreaker *Arktika* completed the first surface vessel journey to the North Pole.

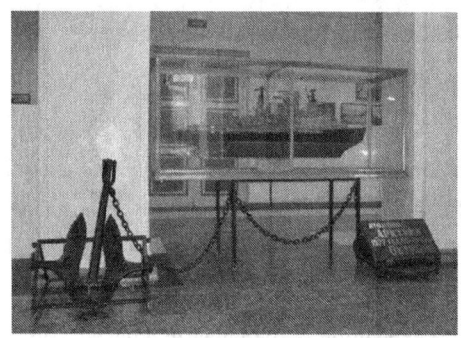

Memorial in honor of icebreaker *Arktika* conquest of the North Pole in 1977 in hall of museum of local lore of the Murmansk region

In 1982 Sir Ranulph Fiennes and Charles Burton became the first people to cross the Arctic Ocean in a single season. They departed from Cape Crozier, Ellesmere Island, on 17 February 1982 and arrived at the geographic North Pole on 10 April 1982. They travelled on foot and skidoo. From the Pole, they travelled towards Svalbard but, due to the unstable nature of the ice, ended their crossing at the ice edge after drifting south on an ice floe for 99 days. They were eventually able to walk to their expedition ship "MV Benjamin Bowring" and boarded it on 4 August 1982 at position 80:31N 00:59W. As a result of this journey, which formed a section of the three-year Transglobe Expedition 1979–1982, Fiennes and Burton became the first people to complete a circumnavigation of the world via both North and South Poles, by surface travel alone. This achievement remains unchallenged to this day.

On September 7, 1991, the German research vessel RV Polarstern and the Swedish ice breaker Oden reached the North Pole as the first conventional powered vessels. Both scientific parties and crew took oceanographic and geological samples and had a common tug of war and a football game on an ice floe. Polarstern again reached the pole exactly 10 years later together with the USCGC Healy.

21st century

In recent years, journeys to the North Pole by air (landing by helicopter or on a runway prepared on the ice) or by icebreaker have become relatively routine, and are even available to small groups of tourists through adventure holiday companies.

In 2005, the United States Navy submarine *USS Charlotte* (SSN-766) surfaced through 155 cm (61 inches) of ice at the North Pole and spent 18 hours there.

In July 2007, British endurance swimmer Lewis Gordon Pugh completed a 1 km swim at the North Pole. His feat, undertaken to highlight the effects of climate change, took place in clear water that had opened up between the ice floes. His later attempt to paddle a kayak to the North Pole in late 2008, following the erroneous prediction of clear water to the Pole, was stymied when his expedition found itself stuck in thick ice after only three days. The expedition was then abandoned.

A 2007 episode of the BBC motoring show *Top Gear*, in which the presenters were described as journeying to the "North Pole," was in fact an expedition to the 1996 position of the North *Magnetic* Pole.

2007 descent to North Pole seabed

Main article: Arktika 2007

On August 2, 2007, a Russian VASUWikipedia:Please clarify made the first ever manned descent to the ocean bottom at the North Pole, to a depth of 4.3 km, as part of a research programme in support of Russia's 2001 territorial claim to a large swathe of the Arctic Ocean. The descent took place in two MIR submersibles and was led by Soviet and Russian polar explorer Arthur Chilingarov. In a symbolic act, the Russian flag was placed on the seabed at the exact position of the Pole.

The expedition is the latest in a decades-long series of moves by Russia intended to show that it is the dominant influence in the Arctic. The warming Arctic climate and summer retreat of sea ice there has suddenly turned the attention of countries from China to the United States toward the top of the world, where resources and shipping routes may soon be exploitable.

Day and night

See also Midnight sun and Polar night

At the North Pole, the sun is permanently above the horizon during the summer months and permanently below the horizon during the winter months. Sunrise is just before the vernal equinox (around March 19); the sun then takes three months to reach its highest point of near 23½° elevation at the summer solstice (around June 21), after which time it begins to sink, reaching sunset just after the autumnal equinox (around September 24). When the sun is visible in the polar sky, it appears to move in a clockwise circle above the horizon. This circle gradually rises from near the horizon just after the vernal equinox to its maximum elevation (in degrees) above the horizon at summer solstice and then sinks back toward the horizon before sinking below it at the autumnal equinox.

A civil twilight period of about two weeks occurs before sunrise and after sunset, a nautical twilight period of about five weeks occurs before sunrise and after sunset and an astronomical twilight period of about seven weeks occurs before sunrise and after sunset.

These effects are caused by a combination of the Earth's axial tilt and its revolution around the sun. The direction of the Earth's axial tilt, as well as its angle relative to the plane of the Earth's orbit around the sun, remains very nearly constant over the course of a year (both change very slowly over long time periods). At northern midsummer the North Pole is facing towards the sun to its maximum extent. As the year progresses and the Earth moves around the sun, the North Pole gradually turns away from the sun until at midwinter it is facing away from the Sun to its maximum extent. A similar sequence is observed at the South Pole, with a six-month time difference.

Time

In most places on Earth, local time is determined by longitude, such that the time of day is more-or-less synchronised to the position of the sun in the sky (for example, at midday the sun is roughly at its highest). This line of reasoning fails at the North Pole, where the sun rises and sets only once per year, and all lines of longitude, and hence all time zones, converge. There is no permanent human presence at the North Pole, and no particular time zone has been assigned. Polar expeditions may use any time zone that is convenient, such as GMT, or the time zone of the country they departed from.

Climate

The North Pole is significantly warmer than the South Pole because it lies at sea level in the middle of an ocean (which acts as a reservoir of heat), rather than at altitude in a continental land mass.

Winter (January) temperatures at the North Pole can range from about −43 °C (−45 °F) to −26 °C (−15 °F), perhaps averaging around −34 °C (−30 °F). Summer temperatures (June, July and August) average around the freezing point (0 °C, 32 °F).

The sea ice at the North Pole is typically around two or three meters thick, though there is considerable variation and occasionally the movement of floes exposes clear water. Studies have shown that the average ice thickness has decreased in recent years. Many attribute this decrease to global warming, though this conclusion is disputed by some. Reports have also predicted that within a few decades the Arctic Ocean will be entirely free of ice in the summer months. This may have significant commercial implications; see "Territorial Claims," below.

Flora and fauna

Polar bears are believed rarely to travel beyond about 82° North owing to the scarcity of food, though tracks have been seen in the vicinity of the North Pole, and a 2006 expedition reported sighting a polar bear just one mile (1.6 km) from the Pole. The ringed seal has also been seen at the Pole, and Arctic foxes have been observed less than 60 km away at 89°40′ N.

Birds seen at or very near the Pole include the Snow Bunting, Northern Fulmar and Black-legged Kittiwake, though some bird sightings may be distorted by the tendency of birds to follow ships and expeditions.

Fish have been seen in the waters at the North Pole, but these are probably few in number. A member of the Russian team that descended to the North Pole seabed in August 2007 reported seeing no sea creatures living there. However, it was later reported that a sea anemone had been scooped up from the seabed mud by the Russian team and that video footage from the dive showed unidentified shrimps and amphipods.

Territorial claims to the North Pole and Arctic regions

Main article: Territorial claims in the Arctic

Under international law, no country currently owns the North Pole or the region of the Arctic Ocean surrounding it. The five surrounding Arctic countries, Russia, Canada, Norway, Denmark (via Greenland), and the United States, are limited to a 200-nautical-mile (370 km; 230 mi) Exclusive Economic Zone around their coasts, and the area beyond that is administered by the International Seabed Authority.

Upon ratification of the United Nations Convention on the Law of the Sea, a country has a ten year period to make claims to extend its 200 mile zone. Norway (ratified the convention in 1996), Russia (ratified in 1997), Canada (ratified in 2003) and Denmark (ratified in 2004) have all launched projects to base claims that certain Arctic sectors should belong to their territories.

Cultural associations

In some Western cultures, the geographic North Pole is the residence of Santa Claus. Canada Post has assigned postal code H0H 0H0 to the North Pole (referring to Santa's traditional exclamation of "Ho-ho-ho!").

This association reflects an age-old esoteric mythology of Hyperborea that posits the North Pole, the otherworldly world-axis, as the abode of God and superhuman beings (see Joscelyn Godwin, *Arktos: The Polar Myth*). The popular figure of the pole-dwelling Santa Claus thus functions as an esoteric archetype of spiritual purity and transcendence ([1]). As Henry Corbin has documented, the North Pole plays a key part in the cultural worldview of esoteric Sufism and Iranian mysticism. "The Orient sought by the mystic, the Orient that cannot be located on our maps, is in the direction of the north, beyond the north."

Owing to its remoteness, the Pole is sometimes identified with a mysterious mountain of ancient Islamic tradition called Mount Qaf (Jabal Qaf), the "farthest point of the earth". According to certain authors, the Jabal Qaf of Muslim cosmology is a version of Rupes Nigra, a mountain whose ascent, like Dante's climbing of the Mountain of Purgatory, represents the pilgrim's progress through spiritual states. In Iranian theosophy, the heavenly Pole, the focal point of the spiritual ascent, acts as a magnet to draw beings to its "palaces ablaze with immaterial matter."

Fantasy flights often refer to a flight to the North Pole for these same reasons.

See also

- South Pole
- Arctic exploration
- Polaris
- Inuit Circumpolar Council
- Arctic Council
- Arctic Circle
- Biome
- North Pole, Alaska
- Global warming
- Santa Claus

External links

- Arctic Council [2]
- The Northern Forum [3]
- North Pole travel guide from Wikitravel
- North Pole Web Cam [4]
- The short Arctic summer of 2004 [5]
- The puzzling Arctic summer of 2003 [6]
- Review of surface melting from 2002 to the present [7] *revealed by the North Pole Web Cam*
- FAQ on the Arctic and the North Pole [8]
- Polar Controversies Still Rage [9] article by Roderick Eime
- Magnetic Poles locations since 1600 [10] Download the KMZ file. For Google Earth Users.
- The Polar Race [11] a biennial race to the 1996 certified position of the Magnetic North Pole
- The Polar Challenge [12] an annual race to the Magnetic North Pole
- Daylight, Darkness and Changing of the Seasons at the North Pole [13]
- Video of scientists on sea ice at the North Pole as it begins to crack underfoot [14]
- Experts warn North Pole will be 'ice free' by 2040 [15]
- Goudarzi, Sara, "*Meltdown: Ice Cracks at North Pole.*" Sept 2006, LiveScience, <Web Link [16]>, Accessed 29 January 2007.
- "The North Pole Was Here: Puzzles and Perils at the Top of the World (first chapter)" [17]
- Video of the Nuclear Icebreaker Yamal visiting the North Pole in 2001 [18]
- Polar Discovery: North Pole Observatory Expedition [19]

krc:Шимал полюс pnb:بطق الت

Santa's workshop

The Legend of Santa's Workshop

Santa's Workshop or **Santa's Grotto**, is the workshop where Santa Claus makes the toys and presents given out at Christmas. In Santa Claus mythology, the workshop is a sprawling complex located at the North Pole. In addition to housing the factory where toys are either manufactured or distributed by the elves, the complex also houses the residence of Santa Claus, his wife, and all of the reindeer.

Department Store Santa's Grotto

In the 20th century it became common during December in large shops or department stores to have a "cavern" in which an actor dressed up as Santa Claus to give gifts to children. Grottos can be large-walk through fantasy cavern-like areas incorporating animatronic characters such as elfs and pantomime characters. This tradition started in Britain in 1879 and then extended in the 1890s to Australian and American department stores seeking to attract customers.

Santa in his workshop, (postcard, 1911)

The world's first Christmas grotto was in Lewis's Bon Marche Department Store in Liverpool. The grotto was opened in 1879, entitled "Christmas Fairyland". Many generations of people across Britain first visited Father Christmas here and it is a tradition which is carried on by Lewis's to this day. The grotto now covers over 10000 square feet (930 m^2) and is a staple of Liverpool's festive season. The grotto will be 130 years old in 2009.

In Adelaide, South Australia, the first "Magic Cave" was set up in 1896 at the John Martin's department store on Rundle Street. An annual store-sponsored parade, Adelaide Christmas Pageant, was initiated in 1933 during which Father Christmas was conducted to the Magic Cave to formally herald the holiday season. Since the closure of John Martin's, the David Jones stores, the world's oldest department store chain (est. 1838) still operating under the same name, have continued the tradition of the Magic Cave, in Adelaide as well as in other Australian capitals while the annual South Australia parade marked its 75th anniversary in 2007.

Nowadays department stores and shopping centres in the UK still host Santa's Grottos.

It is traditional that the children receive a toy from Father Christmas upon visiting his Grotto be it in a shopping mall or a little garden centre. Grottos are sometimes free and sometimes they charge parents to let their kids see Santa and receive a surprise gift.

Santa's Workshop reproductions

A themed attraction in Santa Claus, IN, named Santa's Candy Castle emulates the traditional depiction of Santa's Workshop.

Location of Santa's Workshop

In 1879, Thomas Nast, revealed to the world in a series of drawings that Santa's Workshop is at the North Pole. However, it is less clear which North Pole Thomas Nast was referring to. The two commonly referred to North Pole's for Santa's workshop are the Geographic North Pole and the Magnetic North Pole. However, one can deduce from film and pictures the aurora borealis centres on Santa's Workshop, indicating the workshop is at the Magnetic North Pole in Northern Canada. Once a year a train, the Polar Express travels to the Santa's Workshop. It is doubtful train tracks could be rebuilt on polar ice each winter. In 1994, United States Air Force pilots reported they have seen no signs of a workshop at the Geographic North Pole in the physical realm.. In the same year, Canada Post issued Santa's Workshop its own postal code H0 H0 H0.. In 2004 nuclear submarines surfaced at the North Pole, proving once and for all Santa Workshop is not at the Geographic North Pole.

See also

- Santa's Workshop (amusement park)

Korvatunturi

Geographical coordinates: 68°04′25″N 29°18′55″E

Korvatunturi	
Range	
Country	Finland
Province	Lapland
Municipality	Savukoski
Elevation	486 m (1594 ft)
Prominence	210 m (689 ft)
Coordinates	68°04′25″N 29°18′55″E
For public	Yes; Requires border zone permission and border guard escort
Location within Finland	

Korvatunturi is a fell in Urho Kekkonen National Park, Lapland, on the border of Finland (in the municipality of Savukoski) and Russia. Its height is 486 metres (roughly 1594 feet) from sea level. It has three peaks. The border is drawn through the middle peak. The name translates to "Ear Fell".

Korvatunturi is the place where *Father Christmas* (or *Joulupukki* in Finnish) lives. This legend comes from a children's radio show called *Markus-sedän lastentunti* ("Children's hour with Uncle Markus") hosted by Markus Rautio and broadcast by the Finnish Broadcasting Company between years 1927 and 1956. Uncle Markus told children that from this "Ear Fell" Father Christmas can hear what all the children are saying so he can find out if the children behave and obey their parents (and therefore may receive gifts next Christmas). This legend is an important plot point in the 2010 film *Rare Exports: A Christmas Tale*.

360 degree panorama from Korvatunturi

See also

- Christmas in Finland
- Santa Claus Village

External links

- Korvatunturi [1]
- Site with photograph [2]

Knecht Ruprecht

In the folklore of Germany, **Knecht Ruprecht**, which translates as *Farmhand Rupert* or *Servant Rupert*, is a companion of Saint Nicholas. Tradition holds that he appeared in homes on Christmas Eve, and was a man with a long beard, wearing fur or covered in pea-straw. Knecht Ruprecht sometimes carrying a long staff and a bag of ashes, and wore little bells on his clothes.

Sometimes he rides on a white horse, and sometimes he is accompanied by fairies or men in blackface dressed as old women.

According to tradition, Knecht Ruprecht asks children whether they can pray. If they can, they receive apples, nuts, and gingerbread. If they cannot, he beats the children with his bag of ashes. In other (presumably more modern) versions of the story, Knecht Ruprecht gives naughty children useless, ugly gifts such as lumps of coal, sticks, and stones, while well-behaving children receive sweets from Saint Nicholas.

In the Mittelmark he was known as *De hêle Christ* ("The Holy Christ"). He was also known as *Hans Ruprecht*, *Rumpknecht*, and in Mecklenburg, was called *Rû Clås* (Rough Nicholas). In the Altmark and in East Friesland, he was known as *Bûr* and *Bullerclås*.

Ruprecht was a common name for the Devil in Germany, and Grimm states that "Robin fellow is the same home-sprite whom we in Germany call Knecht Ruprecht and exhibit to children at Christmas..." Knecht Ruprecht first appears in written sources in the 17th century, as a figure in a Nuremberg Christmas procession.

According to Alexander Tille, Knecht Ruprecht originally represented an archetypal manservant, "and has exactly as much individuality of social rank and as little personal individuality as the *Junker Hanns* and the *Bauer Michel*, the characters representative of country nobility and peasantry respectively." Tille also states that Knecht Ruprecht originally had no connection with Christmastime.

Knecht Ruprecht is commonly cited as a servant and helper of St. Nicholas, and is sometimes associated with Saint Rupert.

According to some stories, Ruprecht began as a farmhand; in others, he is a wild foundling whom St. Nicholas raises from childhood. Ruprecht sometimes walks with a limp, because of a childhood injury. Often, his black clothes and dirty face are attributed to the soot he collects as he goes down chimneys.

Christmas Traditions

Twelve Days of Christmas

12 Days of Christmas	
The Adoration of the Magi. Fresco in Lower Church, Basilica of San Francesco d'Assisi	
Observed by	Christians
Type	Christian
Date	1st day **26-Dec** to 12th day **6-Jan**
Observances	varies by culture, country
Related to	Christmas Day, Twelfth Night, Epiphany

The **Twelve Days of Christmas** are the festive days beginning Christmas Day (25 December). This period is also known as Christmastide. The Twelfth Day of Christmas is 5 January, with the celebrations of Christmas traditionally ending on Twelfth Night and is followed by the Feast of the Epiphany on 6 January. In some traditions the first day of Epiphany and the twelfth day of Christmas overlap.

Over the centuries, differing churches and sects of Christianity have changed the actual traditions, time frame and their interpretations. St. Stephen's Day (or Boxing Day), for example, is 26 December in the Western Church and 27 December in the Eastern Church. Boxing Day, the first weekday after Christmas, is observed as a legal holiday in parts of the Commonwealth of Nations and was traditionally marked by the giving of Christmas boxes to service workers (such as postal workers and trades people) in the United Kingdom; 28 December is Childermas or the Feast of the Innocents. Currently, the twelve days and nights are celebrated in widely varying ways around the world. For example, some give gifts only on Christmas Night, some only on Twelfth Night and some each of the twelve nights.

Eastern Christianity

In Eastern Christianity (the Eastern Orthodox, Oriental Orthodox and Eastern Catholic churches) the Great Feast of Theophany (Epiphany) on 6 January is considered a higher-ranked feast than the Nativity (Christmas), and commemorates the Baptism of Jesus rather than the arrival of the Wise Men. The twelve days beginning on 25 December are observed as a fast-free period of celebration. The Armenian Apostolic Church and the Armenian Catholic Church, however, observe the Nativity of Christ on 6 January, and thus do not have a twelve day period between Christmas and 5 January.

Orthodox Churches

Icon of the Nativity of Christ.

In the Eastern Orthodox Church (and those Eastern Catholic churches which follow the Byzantine Rite) The Great Feast of the Nativity of our Lord begins on the Eve of 25 December (for those Orthodox churches which follow the Julian Calendar, 25 December falls on 7 January of the modern Gregorian Calendar).

The Twelve Days of Christmas are a festive period linking together two Great Feasts of the Lord: Nativity and Theophany. During this period one celebration leads into another. The Nativity of Christ is a three day celebration: the formal title of the first day is "The Nativity According to the Flesh of our Lord, God and Saviour Jesus Christ", and celebrates not only the Nativity of Jesus, but also the Adoration of the Shepherds of Bethlehem and the arrival of the Maji; the second day is referred to as the "Synaxis of the Theotokos", and commemorates the role of the Virgin Mary in the Incarnation; the third day is known as the "Third Day of the Nativity", and is also the feast day of the Protodeacon and Protomartyr Saint Stephen.

29 December is the Orthodox Feast of the Holy Innocents.

The Afterfeast of the Nativity (similar to the Western octave) continues until 31 December (that day is known as the Apodosis or "leave-taking" of the Nativity).

The Saturday following the Nativity is commemorated by special readings from the Epistle (Tim 1 6:11-16) and Gospel (Matt 12:15-21) during the Divine Liturgy. The Sunday after Nativity has its own liturgical commemoration in honour of "The Righteous Ones: Joseph the Betrothed, David the King and James the Brother of the Lord".

1 January, at the center of the festal period, is another feast of the Lord (though not ranked as a Great Feast): the Feast of the Circumcision of the Lord. On this same day is the feast day of Saint Basil the Great, and so the service celebrated on that day is the Divine Liturgy of Saint Basil.

2 January begins the Forefeast of the Theophany.

The Eve of the Theophany (5 January) is a day of strict fasting, on which the devout will not eat anything until the first star is seen at night. This day is known as Paramony ("preparation"), and follows the same general outline as Christmas Eve. That morning is the celebration of the Royal Hours and then the Divine Liturgy of Saint Basil combined with Vespers, at the conclusion of which is celebrated the Great Blessing of Waters, in commemoration of the Baptism of Jesus in the Jordan River. There are certain parallels between the hymns chanted on Paramony and those of Good Friday, to show that, according to Orthodox theology, the steps that Jesus took into the Jordan River were the first steps on the way to the Cross. That night the All-Night Vigil is served for the Feast of the Theophany.

Russian icon of the Theophany.

Western Christianity

Middle Ages

In England in the Middle Ages, this period was one of continuous feasting and merrymaking, which climaxed on Twelfth Night, the traditional end of the Christmas season. In Tudor England, Twelfth Night itself was forever solidified in popular culture when William Shakespeare used it as the setting for one of his most famous stage plays, titled *Twelfth Night*. Often a Lord of Misrule was chosen to lead the Christmas revels.

Some of these traditions were adapted from the older pagan customs, including the Roman Saturnalia and the Germanic Yuletide. Some also have an echo in modern day pantomime where traditionally authority is mocked and the principal male lead is played by a woman, while the leading older female character, or 'Dame', is played by a man.

Colonial America

The early North American colonists brought their version of the Twelve Days over from England, and adapted them to their new country, adding their own variations over the years. For example, the modern day Christmas wreath may have originated with these colonials. A homemade wreath would be fashioned from local greenery and if fruits were available, they were added. Making the wreaths was one of the traditions of Christmas Eve; they would be hung on each home's front door beginning on Christmas Night (1st night of Christmas) through Twelfth Night or Epiphany morning. As was already the tradition in their native England, all decorations would be taken down by Epiphany morning and the remainder of the edibles would be consumed. A special cake, the king cake, was also baked then for Epiphany.

Modern Western secular customs

United Kingdom and Commonwealth

Many in the United Kingdom and other Commonwealth nations still celebrate some aspects of the Twelve Days of Christmas. Boxing Day (26 December) is a national holiday in many Commonwealth nations, being the first full day of Christmas. Victorian era stories by Charles Dickens (and others), particularly *A Christmas Carol*, hold key elements of the celebrations such as the consumption of plum pudding, roasted goose and wassail. While these foods are consumed more at the beginning of the Twelve Days in the UK, some dine and dance in the traditional way throughout, all the way to Twelfth Night.

Nowadays, the Twelfth Day is the last day for decorations to be taken down, and it is held to be bad luck to take decorations down after this date. This is in contrast to the custom in Elizabethan England, when decorations were left up until Candlemas; this is still done in some other Western European countries such as Germany.

United States

With the onset of more Americanized and secular traditions throughout the past two centuries (such as the American "Santa Claus"), the rise in popularity of Christmas Eve itself as if it were also an actual holiday, and of New Year's Eve parties, the traditions of the Twelve Days of Christmas have been largely forgotten in the U.S. This is also heightened by the commercial practice to have *after*-Christmas sales begin on 26 December and run usually until New Year's Eve. Indeed, contemporary marketing and media tend to espouse the (erroneous) belief that the Twelve Days *end* on Christmas and thus begin 14 December.

However, a small percentage of Christians of many sects have held on to their own favorite ways to celebrate and those who choose to also have their own church to guide them in a spiritual way of marking this reverent holiday. Americans who celebrate in various ways include Christians of all backgrounds: Catholics, Orthodox Christians, Lutherans, Episcopalians, Moravians and those of the Amish and Mennonite communities.

Today, some celebrants give gifts each of the Twelve Days, feast and otherwise celebrate the entire time through to Epiphany morning. Lighting a candle for each day has become a modern tradition in the U.S. and of course, singing the appropriate verses of the famous song each day is also an important and fun part of the American celebrations.

Some still celebrate Twelfth Night as the biggest night for parties and gift-giving and some also light a Yule Log on the first night (Christmas) and let it burn some each of the twelve nights. Some Americans also have their own traditional foods to serve each night.

Twelfth Night costumers in New Orleans.

As in olden days, Twelfth Night to Epiphany morning is then the traditional time to take down the Christmas tree and decorations.

References

- "Christmas" [1]. *Catholic Encyclopedia*. Retrieved 22 December 2005. Primarily subhead *Popular Merrymaking* under *Liturgy and Custom*.
- Bowler, Gerald (2000). *The World Encyclopedia of Christmas*. Toronto: M&S. ISBN 9780771015311. OCLC 44154451 [2].
- Caulkins, Mary (2002). *Christmas Trivia: 200 Fun & Fascinating Facts About Christmas*. New York: Gramercy. ISBN 9780517220702. OCLC 49627774 [3].
- Collins, Ace; Clint Hansen (2003). *Stories Behind the Great Traditions of Christmas*. Grand Rapids, Michigan: Zondervan. ISBN 9780310248804. OCLC 52311813 [4].
- Evans, Martin Marix (2002). *The Twelve Days of Christmas*. White Plains, New York: Peter Pauper Press. ISBN 9780880887762. OCLC 57044650 [5].
- Wells, Robin Headlam (2005). *Shakespeare's Humanism*. Cambridge: Cambridge University Press. ISBN 9780521824385. OCLC 62132881 [6].
- Hoh, John L., Jr. (2001). *The Twelve Days of Christmas: A Carol Catechism*. Vancouver: Suite 101 eBooks.

Christmas tree

The **Christmas tree** is a decorated evergreen coniferous tree, real or artificial, and a tradition associated with the celebration of Christmas, or originally Yule. The Christmas tree is often brought into a home, but can also be used in the open, and can be decorated with Christmas lights (originally candles), ornaments, garlands and tinsel during the days around Christmas. An angel or star is often placed at the top of the tree, representing the host of angels or the Star of Bethlehem from the Nativity. The tradition of decorating an evergreen tree at Christmas started in Germany in the 16th century.

An artificial Christmas tree inside a home.

Origin

According to Christian lore, the Christmas tree is associated with St Boniface and the German town of Geismar. Sometime in St Boniface's lifetime (c. 672-754) he cut down the tree of Thor in order to disprove the legitimacy of the Norse gods to the local German tribe. St. Boniface saw a fir tree growing in the roots of the old oak. Taking this as a sign of the Christian faith, he said "...let Christ be at the center of your households..." using the fir tree as a symbol of Christianity.

The tradition of the Christmas tree as it is today known is fairly young. It was established by Martin Luther as a Protestant counterpart to the Catholic Nativity scene. Luther established the Christmas tree as a symbol of the Tree of Life in the Garden of Eden.

The custom of erecting a Christmas Tree can be historically traced to 16th century Northern Germany and Livonia (a colony of the Livonian Brothers of the Sword in present-day Estonia and northern Latvia). According to the first documented uses of a Christmas tree in Estonia, in 1441, 1442, and 1514 the Brotherhood of the Blackheads erected a tree for the holidays in their brotherhood

A Christmas tree in Chile.

house in Reval (now Tallinn). At the last night of the celebrations leading up to the holidays, the tree was taken to the Town Hall Square where the members of the brotherhood danced around it. In 1584, the pastor and chronicler Balthasar Russow wrote of an established tradition of setting up a decorated spruce at the market square where the young men "went with a flock of maidens and women, first sang and danced there and then set the tree aflame". In that period, the guilds started erecting Christmas trees in front of their guildhalls: Ingeborg Weber-Kellermann (Marburg professor of European ethnology) found a Bremen guild chronicle of 1570 which reports how a small tree was decorated with "apples, nuts, dates, pretzels and paper flowers" and erected in the guild-house, for the benefit of the guild members' children, who collected the dainties on Christmas Day.

18th and 19th century

By the early 18th century, the custom had become common in towns of the upper Rhineland, but it had not yet spread to rural areas. Wax candles are attested from the late 18th century. The Christmas tree remained confined to the upper Rhineland for a relatively long time. It was regarded as a Protestant custom by the Roman Catholic majority along the lower Rhine and was spread there only by Prussian officials who were moved there in the wake of the Congress of Vienna in 1815. Just like Christmas (Germanic Yuletide), the Christmas tree was more or less accepted by the Roman Catholic Church because it could not prevent its use.

The tradition was introduced to Canada in the winter of 1781 by Brunswick soldiers stationed in the Province of Quebec to garrison the colony against American attack. General Friedrich Adolf Riedesel and his wife, the Baroness von Riedesel, held a Christmas party at Sorel, delighting their guests with a fir tree decorated with candles and fruits.

In the early 19th century, the custom became popular among the nobility and spread to royal courts as far as Russia. Princess Henrietta of Nassau-Weilburg introduced the Christmas tree to Vienna in 1816, and the custom spread across Austria in the following years. In France, the first Christmas tree was introduced in 1840 by the duchesse d'Orléans.

In Britain, the Christmas tree was introduced in the time of the personal union with Hanover, by George III's Queen Charlotte of Mecklenburg-Strelitz in early 1800s, but the custom hadn't yet spread much beyond the royal family. Queen Victoria as a child was familiar with the custom. In her journal for Christmas Eve 1832, the delighted 13-year-old princess wrote, "After dinner...we then went into the drawing-room near the dining-room...There were two large round tables on which were placed two trees hung with lights and sugar ornaments. All the presents being placed round the trees..". After her marriage to her German cousin Prince Albert, by 1841 the custom became even more widespread throughout Britain. In 1847, Prince Albert wrote: "I must now seek in the children an echo of what Ernest [his brother] and I were in the old time, of what we felt and thought; and their delight in the Christmas-trees is not less than ours used to be".

A woodcut of the British Royal family with their Christmas tree at Windsor Castle, initially published in the *Illustrated London News* December 1848, was copied in the United States at Christmas 1850, in *Godey's Lady's Book* (illustration, left). *Godey's* copied it exactly, except for the removal of the Queen's crown and Prince Albert's mustache, to remake the engraving into an American scene. The republished *Godey's* image became the first widely circulated picture of a decorated evergreen Christmas tree in America. Art historian Karal Ann Marling called Prince Albert and Queen Victoria, shorn of their royal trappings, "the first influential American Christmas tree". Folk-culture historian Alfred Lewis Shoemaker states, "In all of America there was no more important medium in spreading the Christmas tree in the decade 1850-60 than *Godey's Lady's Book*". The image was reprinted in 1860, and by the 1870s, putting up a Christmas tree had become common in America.

Several cities in the United States with German connections lay claim to that country's first Christmas tree: Windsor Locks, Connecticut, claims that a Hessian soldier put up a Christmas tree in 1777 while imprisoned at the Noden-Reed House, while the "First Christmas Tree in America" is also claimed by Easton, Pennsylvania, where German settlers purportedly erected a Christmas tree in 1816. In his diary, Matthew Zahm of Lancaster, Pennsylvania, recorded the use of a Christmas tree in 1821, leading Lancaster to also lay claim to the first Christmas tree in America. Other accounts credit Charles Follen, a German immigrant to Boston, for being the first to introduce to America the custom of decorating a Christmas tree. August Imgard, a German immigrant living in Wooster, Ohio, is the first to popularise the practice of decorating a tree with candy canes. In 1847, Imgard cut a blue spruce tree from a woods outside town, had the Wooster village tinsmith construct a star, and placed the tree in his house, decorating it with paper ornaments and candy canes. The National Confectioners' Association officially recognises Imgard as the first ever to put candy canes on a Christmas tree; the canes were all-white, with no red stripes. Imgard is buried in the Wooster Cemetery, and every year, a large pine tree above his grave is lit with Christmas lights. German immigrant Charles Minnegerode accepted a position as a professor of humanities at the College of William and Mary in Williamsburg in 1842, where he taught Latin and Greek. Entering into the social life of the Virginia Tidewater, Minnigerode introduced the German custom of decorating an evergreen tree at Christmas at the home of law professor St. George Tucker, thereby becoming another of many influences that prompted Americans to adopt the practice at about that time.

20th century

Many cities, towns, and department stores put up public Christmas trees outdoors, such as the Rich's Great Tree in Atlanta, the Rockefeller Center Christmas Tree in New York City and the large Christmas tree at Victoria Square in Adelaide. During most of the 1970s and 1980s, the largest decorated Christmas tree in the world was put up every year on the property of *The National Enquirer* in Lantana, Florida. This tradition grew into one of the most spectacular and celebrated events in the history of southern Florida, but was discontinued on the death of the paper's founder in the late 1980s.

Rockefeller Center tree

In some cities, a Festival of Trees is organised around the decoration and display of multiple trees as charity events. In some cases the trees represent special commemorative gifts, such as in Trafalgar Square in London, where the City of Oslo, Norway presents a tree to the people of London as a token of appreciation for the British support of Norwegian resistance during the Second World War; in Boston, where the tree is a gift from the province of Nova Scotia, in thanks for rapid deployment of supplies and rescuers to the 1917 ammunition ship explosion that levelled the city of Halifax; and in Newcastle upon Tyne, where the 15 m-tall main civic Christmas tree is an annual gift from the city of Bergen, Norway, in thanks for the part played by soldiers from Newcastle in liberating Bergen from Nazi occupation. Norway also annually gifts a Christmas tree to Washington D.C. as a symbol of friendship between Norway and the US and as an expression of gratitude from Norway for the help received from the US during World War II.

The United States' National Christmas Tree is lit each year on the South Lawn of the White House. Today, the lighting of the National Christmas Tree is part of what has become a major holiday event at the White House. President Jimmy Carter lit only the crowning star atop the Tree in 1979 in honour of the Americans being held hostage in Iran. The same was true in 1980, except the tree was fully lit for 417 seconds, one second for each day the hostages had been in captivity.

The term *Charlie Brown Christmas tree* is used in the United States and Canada to describe any poor-looking or malformed little tree. Some tree buyers intentionally adopt such trees, feeling sympathetic to their plights. The term comes from the appearance of Charlie Brown's Christmas tree in the TV special *A Charlie Brown Christmas*.

In New Zealand, Pōhutukawa trees are described as "native Christmas trees", as they bloom at Christmas time, and look like Christmas trees with their red flowers and green foliage.

In Russia, the Christmas tree was banned shortly after the October Revolution but then reinstated as a *New-year fir-tree* (Новогодняя ёлка) in 1935. It became a fully secular icon of the New year holiday, e.g. the crowning star was regarded not as a symbol of Bethlehem Star, but as the Red Star. Decorations, such as figurines of airplanes, bicycles, space rockets, cosmonauts, and characters of Russian fairy tales, were produced. This tradition persists after the fall of the USSR, with the New Year holiday outweighting the Christmas (7 January) for a wide majority of Russians[citation needed].

Dates

Both setting up and taking down a Christmas tree are associated with specific dates. Traditionally, Christmas trees were not brought in and decorated until Christmas Eve (24 December) or, in the traditions celebrating Christmas Eve rather than first of day of Christmas, the 23 December, and then removed the day after twelfth night (6 January); to have a tree up before or after these dates was even considered bad luck.

Christmas trees lit by candles, Denmark.

Modern commercialization of Christmas has resulted in trees being put up much earlier; in shops often as early as late October — in the UK, Selfridges's Christmas department is up by early September, complete with Christmas trees, and in New York City, street Christmas tree vendors set up their stands shortly after Thanksgiving. Some households in the U.S. do not put up the tree until the second week of December, and leave it up until the 6th of January (Epiphany). In Germany, traditionally the tree is put up on the 24th of December and taken down on the 7th of January, though many start one or two weeks earlier, and in Roman Catholic homes the tree may be kept until late January. In Australia, the Christmas tree is usually put up on the 1st of December, which occurs about a week before the school summer holidays; except for South Australia, where most people put up their tree after the Adelaide Credit Union Christmas Pageants in early December.The christmas tree traditionally is covered with pine cones in Egypt.[citation needed] Some traditions suggest that Christmas trees may be kept up until no later than the 2nd of February, the feast of the Presentation of Jesus in the Temple (Candlemas), when the Christmas season effectively closes. Superstitions say it's a bad sign if Christmas greenery is not removed by Candle mas Eve.]

Types of trees used

Natural trees

See also: Christmas tree cultivation

The most commonly used species are fir (*Abies*), which have the benefit of not shedding their needles when they dry out, as well as retaining good foliage colour and scent; but species in other genera are also used.

In northern Europe most commonly used are:

- Silver Fir *Abies alba* (the original species)
- Nordmann Fir *Abies nordmanniana* (as in the photo)
- Noble Fir *Abies procera*
- Norway Spruce *Picea abies* (generally the cheapest)
- Serbian Spruce *Picea omorika*
- Scots Pine *Pinus sylvestris*
- Stone Pine *Pinus pinea* (as small table-top trees)
- Swiss Pine *Pinus cembra*

In North America, Central America and South America most commonly used are:

- Douglas-fir *Pseudotsuga menziesii*
- Balsam Fir *Abies balsamea*
- Fraser Fir *Abies fraseri*
- Grand Fir *Abies grandis*
- Guatemalan Fir *Abies guatemalensis*
- Noble Fir *Abies procera*
- Red Fir *Abies magnifica*
- White Fir *Abies concolor*
- Pinyon Pine *Pinus edulis*
- Jeffrey Pine *Pinus jeffreyi*
- Scots Pine *Pinus sylvestris*
- Stone Pine *Pinus pinea* (as small table-top trees)
- Norfolk Island Pine *Araucaria heterophylla*

Several other species are used to a lesser extent. Less-traditional conifers are sometimes used, such as Giant Sequoia, Leyland Cypress, Monterey Cypress and Eastern Juniper. Various types of spruce tree are also used for Christmas trees (including the Blue Spruce and, less commonly, the White Spruce); but spruces (unlike firs) begin to lose their needles rapidly upon being cut, and spruce needles are often sharp, making decorating uncomfortable. Virginia Pine is still available on some tree farms in the southeastern United States, however its winter colour is faded. The long-needled Eastern White Pine is also used there, though it is an unpopular Christmas tree in most parts of the country, owing also to its faded winter coloration and limp branches, making decorating difficult with all but the lightest ornaments. Norfolk Island Pine is sometimes used, particularly in Oceania, and in Australia some species of the genera *Casuarina* and *Allocasuarina* are also occasionally used as Christmas trees but by far the most common tree is the Monterey Pine. *Adenanthos sericeus* or Albany Woolly Bush is commonly sold in southern Australia as a potted living Christmas tree. Hemlock species are generally considered unsuitable as Christmas trees due to their poor needle retention and inability to support the weight of lights and ornaments.

Some trees, frequently referred to as Living Christmas trees, are sold live with roots and soil, often from a nursery, to be stored at nurseries in planters or planted later outdoors and enjoyed (and often decorated) for years or decades. Others are produced in a container and sometimes as topiary for a porch or patio. However, when done improperly, the combination of root loss caused by digging, and the indoor environment of high temperature and low humidity is very detrimental to the tree's health; additionally, the warmth of an indoor climate will bring the tree out of its natural winter dormancy, leaving it little protection when put back outside into a cold outdoor climate. Thus, the survival rate of these trees is low. However, replanting when done properly provides higher survival rates.

European tradition prefers the open aspect of naturally-grown, unsheared trees, while in North America (outside western areas where trees are often wild-harvested on public lands) there is a preference for close-sheared trees with denser foliage, but less space to hang decorations.

In the past, Christmas trees were often harvested from wild forests, but now almost all are commercially grown on tree farms. Almost all Christmas trees in the United States are grown on Christmas tree farms where they are cut after about ten years of growth and new trees planted. According to the United States Department of Agriculture (USDA) agriculture census for 2002 (the census is done every five years) there were 21,904 farms were producing conifers for the cut Christmas tree market in America, 180897 hectares (447006 acres) were planted in Christmas trees, and 13,849 farms harvested cut trees. The top 5 percent of the farms (40 hectares / 100 acres or more) sold 61 percent of the trees. The top 26 percent of the farms (8 hectares / 20 acres or more) sold 84 percent of the trees. Farms less than 0.8 hectare (two acres) comprised 21 percent of the farms, and sold an average of 115 trees per farm.

The life cycle of a Christmas tree from the seed to a 2-metre (7 ft) tree takes, depending on species and treatment in cultivation, between 8 and 12 years. First, the seed is extracted from cones harvested from older trees. These seeds are then usually grown in nurseries and then sold to Christmas tree farms at an age of 3–4 years. The remaining development of the tree greatly depends on the climate, soil quality, as well as the cultivation and tendance by the Christmas tree farmer.

Artificial trees

Main article: Artificial Christmas trees

The first artificial Christmas trees were developed in Germany during the 19th century, though earlier examples exist. These "trees" were made using goose feathers that were dyed green. The German feather trees were one response by Germans to continued deforestation in Germany. Feather Christmas trees ranged widely in size, from a small 2-inch (51 mm) tree to a large 98-inch (2500 mm) tree sold in department stores during the 1920s. Often, the tree branches were tipped with artificial red berries which acted as candle holders.

A tree with fibre optic lights

Over the years, other styles of artificial Christmas trees have evolved and become popular. In 1930, the U.S.-based Addis Brush Company created the first artificial Christmas tree made from brush bristles. Another type of tree, the aluminum Christmas tree, is made from aluminum. The trees were manufactured in the United States, first in Chicago in 1958, and later in Manitowoc, Wisconsin, where the majority of the trees were produced.

Most modern artificial Christmas trees are made from 100% recycled plastics of used packaging materials, such as polyvinyl chloride (PVC) or other plastics. Approximately 10% of artificial Christmas trees are using virgin suspension PVC resin and despite being plastic most artificial trees are not recyclable or biodegradable.

Other gimmicks have developed as well. Fiber optic Christmas trees come in two major varieties, one resembles a traditional Christmas tree. One Dallas-based company offers "holographic mylar" trees in many hues. Tree-shaped objects made from such materials as cardboard, glass, ceramic or other materials can be found in use as tabletop decorations. Upside-down artificial Christmas trees became popular for a short time and were originally introduced as a marketing gimmick; they allowed consumers to get closer to ornaments for sale in retail stores as well as opened up floor space for more products.

Artificial trees became increasingly popular during the late 20th century. Users of artificial Christmas trees assert that they are more convenient, and, because they are reusable, much cheaper than their natural alternative. Between 2001 and 2007 artificial Christmas tree sales jumped from 7.3 million to 17.4 million.

Evolution of Artificial Christmas Trees to adapt to changing modern styles and trends.

Environmental issues

Artificial

The debate about the environmental impact of artificial trees is ongoing. Generally, natural tree growers contend that artificial trees are more environmentally harmful than their natural counterpart. On the other side of the debate, trade groups such as the American Christmas Tree Association, continue to refute that artificial trees are more harmful to the environment and maintain that the PVC used in Christmas trees has excellent recyclable properties. In the past, lead was often used as a stabilizer in PVC, but is now banned by Chinese laws. Most trees are made of recycled PVC rigid sheets using Tin stabilizer in the recent years. Its use of Lead stabilizer in the old Chinese imported trees has been an issue of concern among politicians and scientists over recent years. A 2004 study found that while in general artificial trees pose little health risk from lead contamination, there do exist

An artificial Christmas tree.

"worst-case scenarios" where major health risks to young children exist. Another report, this time a 2008 U.S. Environmental Protection Agency report, found that as the PVC in artificial Christmas trees aged it began to degrade. The report determined that of the 50 million artificial trees in the United States approximately 20 million were 9 or more years old, the point where dangerous lead contamination levels are reached. A professional study on the Life Cycle Assessment (LCA) of both real and fake Christmas trees revealed that one must use its artificial Christmas tree at least during 20 years to leave an environmental footprint as small as the natural Christmas tree.

A small amount of real-tree material is used in some artificial trees. For instance, the bark of a real tree can be used to surface an artificial trunk.

Natural

Natural Christmas trees on the other hand are entirely biodegradable and are often reused by tree farms or local governments as woodchips or mulch.

Real or Cut trees are used only for a short time, but can be recycled and used as mulch or used to prevent erosion. Real trees are carbon-neutral, they emit no more carbon dioxide by being cut down and disposed of than they absorb while growing. An independent Life Cycle Assessment (LCA) study, conducted by a firm of experts in sustainable development, states that a natural tree will generate 3.1 kg of greenhouse gases whereas the artificial tree will produce 8.1 kg per year. Some people use Living

Christmas or potted trees, so they plant it later to help ease the CO_2 levels, making it the greenest choice.[citation needed] Living Christmas trees can be reused for several seasons, providing a longer life cycle for each tree. Living Christmas trees can be purchased or rented in by local market growers. Rentals are picked up after the holidays, while purchased trees can be planted by the owner after use or donated to local tree adoption/urban reforestation services.

Live trees are typically grown as a crop and replanted in rotation after cutting, often providing suitable habitat for wildlife.[citation needed] In some cases management of Christmas tree crops can result in poor habitat since it sometimes involves heavy input of pesticides.[citation needed]

Concerns have been risen about people cutting down old and rare confers , such as the Keteleeria evelyniana, for Christmas trees.

Decoration and ornaments

Tree trimming decorations

A bauble decorating a Christmas tree

Tinsel and several types of garland or ribbon are commonly used to decorate a Christmas tree. Delicate mould-blown and painted coloured glass Christmas ornaments were a speciality of the glass factories in the Thuringian Forest especially in Lauscha in the late 19th century, and have since become a large industry, complete with famous-name designers. Lighting with candles or electric lights (fairy lights) is commonly done and a tree topper, traditionally either an angel or a star, completes the ensemble.

Silvered saran based tinsel was introduced later, which many have found to be unsatisfactory, since it did not drape well, leading to the demise of tinsel in tree decorating in the United States (it remains popular in many European countries). Baubles are another extremely common decoration, and usually consist of a fairly small hollow glass or plastic sphere coated with a thin metallic layer to make them reflective, and then with a further coating of a thin pigmented polymer in order to provide colouration.

Individuals' decorations vary widely, typically being an eclectic mix of family traditions and personal tastes; even a small unattractive ornament, if passed down from a parent or grandparent, may come to carry considerable emotional value and be given a place of pride on the tree. Conversely, trees decorated by professional designers for department stores and other institutions will usually have a "theme"; a set of predominant colours, multiple instances of each type of ornament, and larger decorations that may be more complicated to set up correctly. Some churches decorate with Chrismon trees, which use handmade ornaments depicting various Chrismon symbols.

Many people also decorate outdoor trees with food that birds and other wildlife will enjoy, such as garlands made from unsalted popcorn or cranberries, orange halves, and seed-covered suet cakes.

Tree mats and skirts

Since candles were used to light trees until electric bulbs came about, a mat (UK) or skirt (US) was often placed on the floor below the tree to protect it by catching the dripping candle wax, and also to collect any needles that fall. Even when dripless candles, electric lights and artificial trees have been used, a skirt is still usually used as a decorative feature: among other things, it hides the Christmas tree stand, which may be unsightly but which is an important safety feature of home trees. What began as ordinary cloth has now often become much more ornate, some having embroidery or being put together like a quilt.

A nativity scene, model train, or Christmas village may be placed on the mat or skirt. As Christmas presents arrive, they are generally placed underneath the tree on the tree skirt (depending on tradition, all Christmas gifts, or those too large to be hung on the tree, as in "presents on the tree" of the song "I'll Be Home for Christmas").

Generally, the difference between a mat and skirt is simply that a mat is placed *under* the Christmas tree stand, while a skirt is placed *over* it, having a hole in the middle for the trunk, with a slot cut to the outside edge so that it can be placed around the tree (beneath the branches) easily. A plain mat of fabric or plastic may also be placed under the stand and skirt to protect the floor from scratches or water.

Christmas tree stand

A Christmas tree stand is an object designed to support a cut, natural Christmas tree or an artificial Christmas tree. Christmas tree stands appeared as early as 1876 and have had various designs over the years. Those stands designed for natural trees have a water reservoir to hydrate the live tree. Artificial Christmas trees usually have a plastic or metal stand, with 3 legs shaping like a Y.

Flocking

In the 1940s and 1950s flocking was very popular on the West Coast of the United States. There were home flocking kits that could be used with vacuum cleaners. In the 1980s some trees were sprayed with fluffy white flocking to simulate snow. Typically it would be sprayed all over the tree from the sides, which produced a look different from real snow, which settles in clumps atop branches. Flocking can be done with a professional sprayer at a tree lot (or the manufacturer if it is artificial), or at home from a spray can, and either can be rather messy. This tradition seems to be most popular on the West Coast and Southern parts of the United States.

Because flock contains flame retardants, a flocked tree can be placed in a public building in accordance with local fire codes.

Controversy

The Christmas tree has seen an amount of controversy, mainly involving separation of church and state, the secular and non-secular usage of the tree as well as groups who oppose usage of the tree on the grounds of interpretation of scripture and pagan origins or pagan character of the custom.

In 2005, the Seattle-Tacoma International Airport removed all of its Christmas trees in the middle of the night rather than allow a rabbi to put up a menorah near the largest tree display. Officials feared that one display would open the door for other religious displays, and, in 2006, they opted to display a grove of birches in polyethylene terephthalate snow rather than religious symbols or Christmas trees.

In 2005, the city of Boston renamed the spruce tree used to decorate the Boston Common a "Holiday Tree" rather than a "Christmas Tree". The name change drew a poor response from the public and was changed back to "Christmas Tree" after being threatened with several lawsuits by Rev. Jerry Falwell and the Alliance Defense Fund. In the same year, Speaker of the House, Dennis Hastert, R-Ill., asked that the tree that decorates the Capitol grounds to be renamed back to "Christmas tree". It had been renamed "Holiday tree" in the 1990s.

Christianity

Jeremiah 10:1-5 in the Bible says the following (King James Version):

> [1] Hear ye the word which the Lord speaketh unto you, O house of Israel:
> [2] Thus saith the Lord, Learn not the way of the heathen, and be not dismayed at the signs of heaven; for the heathen are dismayed at them.
> [3] For the customs of the people are vain: for one cutteth a tree out of the forest, the work of the hands of the workman, with the axe.
> [4] They deck it with silver and with gold; they fasten it with nails and with hammers, that it move not.
> [5] They are upright as the palm tree, but speak not: they must needs be borne, because they cannot go. Be not afraid of them; for they cannot do evil, neither also is it in them to do good.

Christmas tree in front of Notre Dame in Paris, France.

This is interpreted by some fundamentalist Christians as referring to a Christmas tree, and that therefore the Bible would explicitly forbid the practice. However, the more common interpretation is that the passage refers to idol worship, and it is the practice of making an object out of wood, silver, and gold, and then worshiping that idol. Others feel that since "Christmas Trees" are not biblically ordained, they should not be used. Such individuals and Christian denominations are unlikely to celebrate Christmas at all, for the same reason, such as the United Church of God.

Isaiah 55: 13, refers to the evergreen tree as a joyful sign to the Lord in celebration of life everlasting, that shall not be cut off.

[Isaiah 55:13 is saying that the Messiah will live forever just like an evergreen tree never dies, it doesn't lose it leaves when Autumn comes.]

Some churches however use Christmas trees as decoration at Christmas time. Others use the same stripped Christmas tree as a Christian cross at Easter. See the poem The Dream of the Rood. Both Ezekiel 47:12 and the Book of Revelation 22:2 use trees as a symbol of new fruitful life, compared to the Tree of life denied Adam in Genesis 3:22-23. Paul makes the link between Adam and Christ clear in Romans chapter 5:

> Adam is *a type of the one who was to come. (v. 14)*

In the same way the Christmas tree can be seen as mirroring the tree of life, a symbol or type of the Crucifix which brings redemption.

In some Catholic countries, the tree is seen as a recent Protestant or American influence detracting from the Mediterranean traditions of the Christmas crib. However in many Catholic homes, both types of decoration coexist.

Judaism

Jewish parentsWikipedia:Avoid weasel words in Christian societies may find that their children feel omitted of traditions during the Christmas season.[*citation needed*] This has led to the increasing importance of the Hanukkah celebrations, traditionally less important than other holidays such as Yom Kippur or Passover, because of its rabbinic origins. Children now receive gifts and toys instead of the *gelt* of Ashkenazi tradition. Some mixed-religion families or those wanting to blend better with their Christian environment will dub their trees "Hanukkah bushes". Typically, these trees will incorporate a Jewish motif, with blue colour schemes and ornaments featuring menorahs, dreidels and other typical symbols of Hanukkah.

Syncretising traditions in Northern Spain, the Bilbao airport displays the foreign tree and the Basque Olentzero.

Industry

See also: Christmas tree production

Each year, 33 to 36 million Christmas trees are produced in America, and 50 to 60 million are produced in Europe. In 1998, there were about 15,000 growers in America (a third of them "choose and cut" farms). In that same year, it was estimated that Americans spent $1.5 billion on Christmas trees.

See also

- Chrismon tree
- Festive ecology
- Festivus Pole
- Hanukkah bush
- Holiday tree
- New Year tree
- Star of Bethlehem
- Tree (mythology)
- Weihnachten
- Yule log

Notes

Nordmanntannen24 Weihnachtsbaum Kulturen [1]

References

- Hewitt, James. *The Christmas Tree*, (Google Books [2]), Lulu.com, 2007, (ISBN 1430308206).

External links

- Christmas trees [3] at the Open Directory Project
- British Royal Family Christmas trees [4]
- *Christmas Tree Survives War, A-Bomb* [5] By Eric Talmadge; 21 December 2007
- Riga, Latvia purported home of the original Christmas Tree [6]
- Christmas Lights around the World [7]
- History of the Christmas Tree [8]

Wassailing

Wassailing as a practice falls into two distinct categories. The House-Visiting wassail, very much similar to caroling, is the practice of people going door-to-door singing Christmas carols. In modern times, it is most commonly known through reference in various English traditional Christmas carols (e.g., "Here we come a-wassailing / among the leaves so green"). The Orchard-Visiting wassail refers to the practice of singing to trees in apple orchards in cider-producing regions of England to promote a good harvest for the coming year.

Origins of wassailing

Some scholars prefer a pre-Christian explanation of the old traditional ceremony of wassailing. How far the tradition dates back is unknown but it has undeniable connections with Anglo-Saxon pagan ritual. Of recent times the word Wassail (from the Anglo-Saxon toast *wæs þu hæl*, "be thou hale" — i.e., "be in good health") has come to be synonymous with Christmas. The word wassail is old English (OE) and so may predate the Norman conquest in 1066. According to the Oxford English Dictionary "waes hael" is the Middle English spelling parallel to OE "wes hal". The American Heritage Dictionary, fourth edition, gives Old Norse "ves heill" as the source of Middle English "waeshaeil".

Christmas was not celebrated anywhere before the third century, and only gradually moved northwards through Europe. Charlemagne was crowned on Christmas day 800. It was probably the Normans who brought the celebration to England. Traditionally, the wassail is celebrated on Twelfth Night January 6. However most people insist on wassailing on 'Old Twelvey Night' (January 17) as that would have been the correct date before the introduction of the Gregorian Calendar in 1752.

The practice has its roots in the middle ages as a reciprocal exchange between the feudal lords and their peasants as a form of recipient initiated charitable giving, to be distinguished from begging. This point is made in the song "Here We Come A-Wassailing", when the wassailers inform the lord of the house that

> "we are not daily beggars that beg from door to door but we are friendly neighbours whom you have seen before."

The lord of the manor would give food and drink to the peasants in exchange for their blessing and goodwill, i.e...

> "Love and joy come to you,
>
> And to you your wassail too;
>
> And God bless you and send you
>
> a Happy New Year"

... which would be given in the form of the song being sung. Wassailing is the background practice against which an English carol such as "We Wish You a Merry Christmas" dating back to sixteenth century England, can be made sense of. The carol lies in the English tradition where wealthy people of the community gave Christmas treats to the carolers on Christmas Eve such as 'figgy puddings'.

Although wassailing is often described in innocuous and sometimes nostalgic terms, the practice has not always been considered so innocent. In fact in early New England wassailing was associated with rowdy bands of young men who would enter the homes of wealthy neighbors and demand free food and drink in a trick-or-treat fashion. If the householder refused, he was usually cursed, and occasionally his house was vandalized.

The example of the exchange is seen in their demand for "figgy pudding" and "good cheer", i.e., the wassail beverage, without which the wassailers in the song will not leave, "we won't go until we've got some."

The Orchard-Visiting Wassail

In the cider-producing West of England (primarily the counties of Devon, Somerset, Dorset, Gloucestershire and Herefordshire) wassailing also refers to drinking (and singing) the health of trees in the hopes that they might better thrive.

An old rhyme goes: "Wassaile the trees, that they may beare / You many a Plum and many a Peare: / For more or lesse fruits they will bring, / As you do give them Wassailing."

The purpose of wassailing is to awake the cider apple trees and to scare away evil spirits to ensure a good harvest of fruit in the Autumn.{"England In Particular", Common Ground 2007} The ceremonies of each wassail vary from village to village but they generally all have the same *core* elements. A wassail King and Queen lead the song and/or a processional tune to be played/sung from one orchard to the next, the wassail Queen will then be lifted up into the boughs of the tree where she will place toast soaked in Wassail from the Clayen Cup as a gift to the tree spirits (and to show the fruits created the previous year). Then an incantation is usually recited such as

Here's to thee, old apple tree, That blooms well, bears well. Hats full, caps full, Three bushel bags full, An' all under one tree. Hurrah! Hurrah!

Then the assembled crowd will sing and shout and bang drums and pots & pans and generally make a terrible racket until the gunsmen give a great final volley through the branches to make sure the work is done and then off to the next orchard. Perhaps unbeknown to the general public, this ancient English tradition is still very much thriving today. The West Country is the most famous and largest cider producing region of the country and some of the most important wassails are held annually in Carhampton (Somerset) and Whimple (Devon), both on 17 January (old Twelfth Night). In Canada the Orchard Group of the Heron Rocks Friendship Society, Hornby Island, also holds a wassailing event in late January, where a Queen and King present toasts to the old apple trees.

Private readings about people in Somerset in the 1800s revealed that inhabitants of Somerset practised the old Wassailing Ceremony, singing the following lyrics after drinking the cider until they were "merry and gay:"

"Apple tree, apple tree, we all come to wassail thee, Bear this year and next year to bloom and to blow, Hat fulls, cap fulls, three cornered sack fills, Hip, Hip, Hip, hurrah, Holler biys, holler hurrah."

Wassail bowls

Wassail bowls, generally in the shape of goblets, have been preserved. The Worshipful Company of Grocers made a very elaborate one in the seventeenth century, decorated with silver. It is so large that it must have passed around as a "loving cup" so that many members of the guild could drink from it.

In the British Christmas carol "Wassail, Wassail, All Over the Town", the singers tell that their "bowl is made of the white maple tree, with a wassailing bowl we'll drink to thee". White maple is a completely tasteless wood, commonly used even today to make some kitchen utensils, and likely was what many simple peasant wassail bowls were made from.

There are surviving examples of "puzzle wassail bowls", with many spouts. As you attempt to drink from one of the spouts, you are drenched from another spout. The drink was either punch, mulled wine or spicy ale.

See also
- Apple Wassail
- Wish Tree
- Yule Goat

References
- Oxford English Dictionary [1]
- Merriam-Webster Online Dictionary "wassail." [2]
- Birmingham Museums & Art Gallery [3] Wassail Bowl
- "Reminiscences of Life in the parish of Street, Somersetshire dated 1909 at pages 25-26 written by an "old inhabitant" William Pursey of Street 1836-1919. This is the art of wassail.

External links

- Pictures of Wassail Bowls [4]
- Wassailing [5]
- Wassailing: Caroling for Beer [6]

Yule log

A **Yule log** is a large wooden log which is burned in the hearth as a part of traditional Yule or Christmas celebrations in several European cultures. It can be a part of the Winter Solstice festival or the Twelve Days of Christmas, Christmas Eve, Christmas Day, or Twelfth Night.

The expression "Yule log" has also come to refer to log-shaped Christmas cakes, also known as "chocolate logs" or *"Bûche de Noël"*. The Yule log is related to other Christmas and Yuletide traditions such as the Ashen faggot.

An illustration of people collecting a yule log from *Chambers Book of Days* (1832) p. 736

Etymology

The term "Yule log" is not the only term used to refer to the custom. In the north-east of England it was commonly called a "**Yule Clog**", and in the country's Midlands and West Country, the term "**Yule Block**" was also used. In the county of Lincolnshire, the term "**Gule Block**" was found, and in Cornwall, the term "Stock of the Mock" was as well. In other parts of the British Isles, different terms were used, for instance in Wales, the log was often referred to as *Y Bloccyn Gwylian*, meaning "the Festival Block", whilst in Scotland, *Yeel Carline* (meaning "the Christmas Old Wife") was used, and in Ireland, the term, *Bloc na Nollaig*, which meant "the Christmas Block", was used. The Yule log was originally an entire tree, that was carefully chosen and brought into the house with great ceremony with the purpose being to provide maximum warmth and endurance. In some European traditions, the largest end of the log would be placed into the fire hearth while the rest of the tree stuck out into the room. While references are anecdotal, it seems to be a tradition that morphed into early European Christian tradition of the Twelve Days of Christmas. Within 20th century Europe and North America was predominantly a reference to the burning of the largest log possible at or around Christmas.

In Germany, the log is referred to as **Christklotz**, **Christbrand** or **Weihnachtsscheit** ("Christ-log" or "Christmas-log"). Kindled on Christmas Eve, the log in German tradition functioned as a lightning charm.[citation needed]

Historical origins

The Yule log has frequently been associated with having its origins in the historical Germanic paganism which was practiced across northern Europe prior to Christianisation. One of the first people to do so was the British Henry Bourne, who, writing in the 1720s, described the practice occurring in the Tyne valley. Bourne theorised that the practice derives from customs in 6th to 7th century Anglo-Saxon paganism.

Robert Chambers, in his 1832 work, *Book of Days* notes that "two popular observances belonging to Christmas are more especially derived from the worship of our pagan ancestors—the hanging up of the mistletoe and the burning of the Yule log." James George Frazer in his work on anthropology, *The Golden Bough* (p. 736) holds that "the ancient fire-festival of the winter solstice appears to survive" in the Yule log custom. Frazer records traditions from England, France, among the South Slavs, in Central Germany (Meiningen) and western Switzerland (the Bernese Jura).

However, some historians have disagreed with this claim, for instance the Swedish folklorist Carl Wilhelm von Sydow attacked Frazer's theories, claiming that the Yule log had never had any religious significance, and was instead simply a festive decoration with practical uses.

Modern folklore

Great Britain

Because there are no accounts of the custom in Great Britain prior to the 17th century, some historians and folklorists have theorised that it was not an ancient British custom but was in fact imported into Britain from continental Europe in the early modern period, possibly from Flanders in Belgium, where the tradition thrived in this period.

The first mention of the Yule log in Britain is a written account by the clergyman Robert Herrick, from the 1620s or 1630s. Herrick called the tradition a "Christmas log" and said that it was brought into the farmhouse by a group of males, who were then rewarded with free beer from the farmer's wife. Herrick claimed that the fire used to burn the log was always started with a remnant from the log that had been burned in the previous year's festivities. He also said that the log's role was primarily one of bringing prosperity and protection from evil - by keeping the remnant of the log all the year long the protection was said to remain across the year.

The Yule log was not only seen as a magical protective amulet in traditional British rural culture. There are many reports of rivalries occurring between members of a community as to who had the largest log.

The traditions of the Yule log died out in Britain in the latter 19th and early 20th century because of, according to historian Ronald Hutton, "the reduction in farm labour and the disappearance of the old-fashioned open hearths".

In English folklore, Father Christmas was often depicted carrying a Yule Log.

French-speaking Europe

Main article: Bûche de Noël

In France and Wallonia, and thence also in Quebec and in Lebanon, the *Bûche de Noël* ("christmas log") is a traditional dessert, in origin a facsimile of the actual yule log. The tradition of the yule log was discontinued as large fireplaces became an increasingly rarer feature of the average living room. The dessert is usually in the form of a large rectangular yellow cake spread with frosting and rolled up into a cylinder - one end is then lopped off and stood on end to indicate the rings of the "log." It is not known when the dessert, or its name, originated. It is known to have existed by 1945, and apparently[citation needed], a tradition of jelly rolls served at Christmas is attested for Poitou-Charentes since the 19th century.

Durian-flavoured log

Southern Europe

In the most traditional of the Catalan homes, the old custom of "fer cagar el tió" is still followed for Christmas. A log is wrapped with a blanket several days in advance of Christmas and is "fed" grass. On Christmas Eve the log is repeatedly hit in order to make the log go "cagar." The blanket is then removed to reveal the gifts that have been "expelled" by the log.

In Tuscany, there is a *Festa del Ceppo* ("festival of the log").

Balkans

In Croatia, Christmas Eve is called *Badnjak* (Christmas Eve Day: *Badnji dan*, Christmas Eve night: *Badnja večer*), after the traditional log that is cut on Christmas Eve and lit in the hearth of the home in the evening. In villages, the father of the family cuts down a piece of wood from a tree at dawn, reciting the Lord's Prayer and making the sign of the cross, invoking God to bless the family. In the cities, logs are usually bought instead of cut down. The log is brought to the home, but left inside until the evening, where it is brought in and placed in the hearth or fireplace. Holy water is then poured on the log, usually accompanied by the Apostle's Creed. It is then lit and the father praises Jesus and welcomes Christmas Eve.

The badnjak is a central feature in the traditional Serbian Christmas celebration. It is the log that a family solemnly brings into the house and places on the fire in the evening of Christmas Eve. The tree used for the badnjak, preferably a young and strait oak, is ceremoniously felled in the early morning of Christmas Eve. The burning of the log is accompanied by prayers to God so that the coming year may bring much happiness, love, luck, riches, and food. It would burn on through Christmas Day, whether rekindled or kept burning from the Eve. The first person to visit the family on that day should strike the burning badnjak with a poker or a branch to make sparks fly from it, at the same time uttering a wish that the happiness, prosperity, health, and joy of the family be as abundant as the sparks. The ideal environment to fully carry out these customs is the traditional multi-generation country household. Since most Serbs today live in towns and cities, the badnjak is symbolically represented by several leaved oak twigs that can be bought at marketplaces or received in churches. The origin of the badnjak is explained by events surrounding the Nativity of Jesus Christ. Scholars, however, regard these customs as practices inherited from the old Slavic religion.

In Bulgaria, it is an important part of Christmas Eve preparations. Traditionally a young man of the family was sent dressed in his best clothes to cut down an oak, elm, or pear tree. That tree is used as the *Budnik* (bg:Бъдник). A pray for forgiveness was necessary before it could be chopped down and carried on one's right shoulder as it is not allowed to touch the ground. An indication of the importance of the ritual is that Christmas Eve translates to *Budnik* or *Budnik Eve* (bg:Бъдни вечер) in Bulgaria. In some regions, upon the man's return he asks "Do you glorify the Young God?" three times and receive a positive answer "We glorify Him, welcome". After that a hole is bored in one end of the badnik and filled with Chrism made of wine, cooking oil, and incense. The hole is plugged, and that end of the log is wrapped with a white linen cloth before the badnik is festively burned on the hearth. The log is considered to poses special healing powers and the ritual includes songs and uttering of wishes as the log is lit much like the Serbian ritual described above. The log has to burn all night and it is believed that its warmth and light symbolise the coming of Christ as well as providing a warm welcome to Virgin Mary and the family's ancestors who are believed to be guests at the table according to traditions in some regions. Sometimes the fire is put off using wine in the morning. Remains of the log are cherished and sometimes used to make personal crosses, also to make a plough and ashes are simply spread over a field or vineyard to induce better yields.

See also
- Yule goat
- *Yule Log* - the televised burning of the log.
- Christmas ham
- Wassail
- Tió de Nadal - a Christmas log tradition in Catalonia.
- Badnjak - a Christmas log tradition of Serbs.

References
- Margaret Baker, *Discovering Christmas Customs and Folklore* (1992), pp. 16 ff.
- Walsh, William Shepard. *Curiosities of Popular Customs And of Rites, Ceremonies, Observances, and Miscellaneous Antiquities* (1897), p. 1014

External links
- Several variations of Yule Logs [1] created by Pastry Chef Eric Hubert
- "The Yule Log" [2], a page with information about the Yule log

Christmas stocking

A **Christmas stocking** is an empty sock or sock-shaped bag that children hang on Christmas Eve so that Santa Claus (or Father Christmas) can fill it with small toys, candy, fruit, coins or other small gifts when he arrives. These small items are often referred to as **stocking stuffers** or **stocking fillers**. In some Christmas stories, the contents of the Christmas stocking are the only toys the child receives at Christmas from Santa Claus. Other presents are wrapped up in wrapping paper and placed under the Christmas tree. Tradition in Western culture dictates that a child who behaves badly during the year will receive only a piece of coal. However, coal is rarely left in a stocking, as it is considered cruel.

US soldiers hang stockings on a gun rack, Christmas 1941.

History

While there are no written records of the origin of the Christmas stocking, there are popular legends that attempt to tell the history of this Christmas tradition. One such legend has several variations, but the following is a good example: Very long ago, there lived a poor man and his three very beautiful daughters. He had no money to get his daughters married, and he was worried what would happen to them after his death.

Saint Nicholas was passing through when he heard the villagers talking about the girls. St. Nicholas wanted to help, but knew that the old man wouldn't accept charity. He decided to help in secret. He waited until it was night and crept through the chimney.

He had three bags of gold coins with him, one for each girl. As he was looking for a place to keep those three bags, he noticed stockings of the three girls that were hung over the mantelpiece for drying. He put one bag in each stocking and off he went. When the girls and their father woke up the next morning, they found the bags of gold coins and were of course, overjoyed. The girls were able to get married and live happily ever after.

This led to the custom of children hanging stockings or putting out shoes, eagerly awaiting gifts from Saint Nicholas. Sometimes the story is told with gold balls instead of bags of gold. That is why three gold balls, sometimes represented as oranges, are one of the symbols for St. Nicholas. And so St. Nicholas is a gift-giver.

A tradition that began in many European countries, originally, children simply used one of their everyday socks, but eventually special Christmas stockings were created for this purpose. The Christmas stocking custom is derived from the Germanic figure Odin. According to Phyllis Siefker, children would place their boots, filled with carrots, straw, or sugar, near the chimney for Odin's flying horse, Sleipnir, to eat. Odin would reward those children for their kindness by replacing Sleipnir's food with gifts or candy. This practice, she claims, survived in Germany, Belgium and the Netherlands after the adoption of Christianity and became associated with Saint Nicholas as a result of the process of Christianization. Today, stores carry a large variety of styles and sizes of Christmas stockings, and Christmas stockings are also a popular homemade craft.

Many families create their own Christmas stockings with each family member's name applied to the stocking so that Santa will know which stocking belongs to which family member.

A 'Square Stocking' is a box sent by the charity Uk4u Thanks! to UK servicemen who are overseas or injured at Christmas.

A lump of anthracite coal in a Xmas stocking originally meant the family had arrived financially. That if everyone put their coal together, they could make a nice, symbolic fire. The wrong kind of coal could create quite a mess. It could even dirty the stocking. Young children did not understand; they merely complained.

The World's Largest Christmas Stocking

The World's Biggest Christmas Stocking was created by supporters of The Children's Society in December 2007. Guinness World Records awarded the stocking the title of the Largest Christmas Stocking on 14 December 2007 at ExCel in London. The previous holder of the title had broken the record in Canada just weeks before this attempt with a stocking measuring 19.25m by 8.23m.

It was made out of over 6,000 squares of red knitting and measured 32.56m long and 14.97m wide (heel to toe). It weighed the equivalent of three reindeer and was filled with 1000 presents, which were then given to children in The Children's Society's projects.

The stocking was created as part of The Children's Society's knitting fundraising appeal, 'The Big Stitch' . £33,000 was raised through sponsorship.

See also

- Christmas shopping
- Christmas decorations

References

- New York Times - The Christmas Stocking [1]
- Holidays.net - The Legend of the Christmas Stocking [2]
- AllThingsChristmas - Christmas stockings [3]
- CreativeHomeMaking.com - The History of the Christmas Stocking [4]
- Bronners.com - Christmas Stockings [5]

External links

- The History of the Christmas Stocking [6]
- How to Fill a Christmas Stocking [7]

Christmas ornament

Christmas ornaments are decorations (usually made of glass, metal, wood or ceramics) that are used to festoon a Christmas tree. Ornaments take many different forms, from a simple round ball to highly artistic designs. Ornaments are almost always reused year after year, rather than purchased annually, and family collections often contain a combination of commercially produced ornaments and decorations created by family members. Such collections are often passed on and augmented from generation to generation.

Common thin blown glass ornament empty inside, a typical frosted glass bauble

Santa Claus is a commonly used figure. Candy canes, fruit, animals, snowmen, angels and snowflake imagery are also popular choices.

Lucretia P. Hale's story "The Peterkins' Christmas-Tree" offers a short catalog of the sorts of ornaments used in the 1870s:

> "There was every kind of gilt hanging-thing, from gilt pea-pods to butterflies on springs. There were shining flags and lanterns, and bird-cages, and nests with birds sitting on them, baskets of fruit, gilt apples, and bunches of grapes."

The modern-day Christmas ornament was originally invented in the small German town of Lauscha in the mid 19th century.

Bauble

A **bauble** is a spherical decoration that it commonly used to adorn Christmas trees. The bauble is one of the most popular Christmas ornament designs, and they have been in production since 1847. Baubles can have various designs on them, from "baby's first Christmas," to a favorite sports team. The Polish name for these things is *bombka* (which translates as "a little bomb").

A handcrafted Christmas ornament.

Invention

The first decorated trees were adorned with apples, strings of popcorn, white candy canes and pastries in the shapes of stars, hearts and flowers. Glass baubles were first made in Lauscha, Germany, by Hans Greiner who produced garlands of glass beads similar to the popcorn strands and tin figures that could be hung on trees. The popularity of these decorations grew into the production of glass figures made by highly skilled artisans with clay molds.

The artisans heated a glass tube over a flame, then inserted the tube into a clay mold, blowing the heated glass to expand into the shape of the mold. The original ornaments were only in the shape of fruits and nuts.

After the glass cooled, a silver nitrate solution was swirled into it, a silvering technique developed in the 1850s by Justus von Liebig. After the nitrate solution dried, the ornament was hand-painted and topped with a cap and hook.

Export

Other glassblowers in Lauscha recognised the growing popularity of Christmas baubles and began producing them in a wide range of designs. Soon, the whole of Germany began buying Christmas glassware from Lauscha. On Christmas Eve 1832, a young Queen Victoria wrote about her delight at having a tree, hung with lights, ornaments, and presents placed round it. In the 1840s, after a picture of Victoria's Christmas tree was shown in a London newspaper decorated with glass ornaments and baubles from her husband Prince Albert's native Germany, Lauscha began exporting its products throughout Europe.

In the 1880s, American F. W. Woolworth discovered Lauscha's baubles during a visit to Germany. He made a fortune by importing the German glass ornaments to the U.S.A.

Mass production

The first American-made glass ornaments were created by William DeMuth in New York in 1870. In 1880, Woolworth's began selling Lauscha glass ornaments. Other stores began selling Christmas ornaments by the late 1800s and by 1910, Woolworth's had gone national with over 1000 stores bringing Christmas ornaments across America. New suppliers popped up everywhere including Dresden die-cut fiberboard ornaments which were popular among families with small children.

Glass ornaments

By the 1900s, Woolworth's had imported 200,000 ornaments and topped $25 million in sales from Christmas decorations alone. As of 2009, the Christmas decoration industry ranks second to gifts in seasonal sales.. Gloria Duchin, Inc., just one of the industry's Christmas ornament manufacturers and designers today, has over 100 million ornaments in circulation and produces millions of new ornaments each year.

Post World War II

After World War II, the East German government turned most of Lauscha's glassworks into state-owned entities, and production of baubles in Lauscha ceased. After the Berlin Wall came down, most of the firms were reestablished as private companies. As of 2009, there are still about 20 small glass-blowing firms active in Lauscha that produce baubles. One of the producers is Krebs Glas Lauscha, part of the Krebs family which is now one of the largest producers of glass ornaments worldwide.

The modern bauble

Although glass baubles are still produced, baubles are now frequently made from plastic and available worldwide in a huge variety of shapes, colors and designs.

Tree-topper

Post-War NOMA plastic, electrified angel tree topper, circa middle twentieth century

It is common to place a large star or angel at the top of the Christmas tree. Hans Christian Andersen's story of The Fir-Tree describes the decoration of a Danish Christmas tree:

> On one branch there hung little nets cut out of colored paper, and each net was filled with sugarplums; and among the other boughs gilded apples and walnuts were suspended, looking as though they had grown there, and little blue and white tapers were placed among the leaves. Dolls that looked for all the world like men—the Tree had never beheld such before—were seen among the foliage, and at the very top a large star of gold tinsel was fixed.

In American English, this is called a "**tree-topper**". Glass spire-like ornaments are popular. Plastic tree toppers are often electrified and, once connected with the tree's strings of colored lights, glow from within. Following WWII, various Christmas icons, such as Santa Claus, were introduced as electrified tree toppers. The angel and star however remained the preferred topper.

Chrismons

Chrismons are a specific type of ornament. The word "Chrismon" is a portmonteau derived from "CHRISt's MONogram." All Chrismons are hand-made. Their colors are predominantly white with gold and pearl beads. White, the liturgical color for Christmas, symbolizes the Christian belief in Jesus' purity and perfection. Gold refers to his majesty and glory. Pearls represent the work of God. Chrismons are placed on an evergreen tree, itself symbolic of eternal life.

A Chrismon cannot be bought or sold; they can only be made and give in love and in celebration of Christ's birth.

Chrismons were first made at the Ascension Lutheran Church in Danville, Virginia in 1957. The idea has spread to Christians all over the world.

See also

- Bauble
- Christmas tree
- Snow baby
- Pleated Christmas hearts

Nutcracker

A **nutcracker** is a mechanical device for cracking nuts. Usually they work on the principle of moments as described in Archimedes' analysis of the lever. The earliest use of the term *nutcracker* in English dates to 1481.

Functional

A nutcracker with a functional design

Manufacturers produce modern nutcrackers — designed to crack nuts — usually somewhat resembling pliers, but with the pivot point at the end beyond the nut, rather than in the middle. These are also used for cracking the shells of crab and lobster to make the meat inside available for eating.

Parrots use their beaks as natural nutcrackers, in much the same way smaller birds crack seeds. In this case, the pivot point stands opposite the nut, at the jaw.

Decorative

Nutcrackers in the form of wooden carvings of a soldier, knight, king, or other profession have existed since at least the 15th century. These nutcrackers portray a person with a large mouth which the operator opens by lifting a lever in the back of the figurine. Originally one could insert a nut in the big-toothed mouth, press down and thereby crack the nut. Modern nutcrackers in this style serve mostly for decoration, mainly at Christmas time. The ballet *The Nutcracker* derives its name from this festive holiday decoration.

The carving of nutcrackers—as well as of religious figures and of cribs—developed as a cottage industry in forested rural areas of Germany. The most famous nutcracker carvings come from Sonneberg in Thuringia (also a center of dollmaking) and from the Ore Mountains. Wood-carving usually provided the only income for the people living there. Today the travel industry supplements their income by bringing visitors to the remote areas.

Steinbach Nutcrackers have become popular in the United States as well, and the recreated "Bavarian village" of Leavenworth, Washington, even features a nutcracker museum. Many other materials also serve to make decorated nutcrackers, such as porcelain, silver, and brass; the museum displays samples.

Carvings by famous names like Junghanel, Klaus Mertens, Karl, Olaf Kolbe, Petersen, Christian Ulbricht and especially the Steinbach nutcrackers have become collectors' items.

The United States Postal Service (USPS) in October 2008 issued four stamps with Nutcrackers for the first time. These featured custom-made Nutcrackers made by Richmond, Virginia, artist Glenn Crider.

Decorative brass populuxe nutcracker by the industrial designer Maurice Ascalon

External links

- Smithsonian Museum Nutcrackers [1]
- Leavenworth Nutcracker Museum [2]
- History of Christian Ulbricht Nutcrackers [3]
- Nutcracker videos [4] on the Internet Bird Collection

Christmas lights

The use of decorative, festive lighting during the Christmas holiday season is a long standing tradition in many Christian cultures, and has been adopted as a secular practice in a number of other non-Christian, or predominantly non-Christian, cultures (notably in Japan).

While the use of celebratory lighting during winter solstice festivals pre-dates Christianity, it is the European (and later North American) partly secularised traditions associated with Christmas which are now commonly recognised and enjoyed as Christmas (or festive, holiday-season) lights.

A string electric of Christmas lights, unlit, decorating the edge of a roof on a house in Keswick, Ontario, Canada; Christmas 2008

History

Early Christians were persecuted for having worship gatherings ("mass"). A candle in the window signified where worship would be occurring for Christians in a community.

The illuminated Christmas tree became a Christmas tradition in Germany during the Early Modern period. The illuminated Christmas tree became established in the United Kingdom during Queen Victoria's reign, and through emigration spread to North America and Australia. In her journal for Christmas Eve 1832, the delighted 13-year-old princess wrote, "After dinner..we then went into the drawing-room near the dining-room. There were two large round tables on which were placed two trees hung with lights and sugar ornaments. All the presents being placed round the trees". Until the development of inexpensive electrical power in the mid nineteenth century, miniature candles were commonly (and in some cultures still are) used.

In the United Kingdom electrically powered christmas lights are generally known as fairy lights. The British physicist William Thomson was aked by the London Savoy Theatre to equip the principal fairies with miniature lighting for the opening night of the Gilbert and Sullivan operetta Iolanthe on 25th November 1882. The battery powered lights were supplied by the Swan United Electric Lamp Company founded by Sir Joseph Swan. This term for a string of electrically powered christmas lights has been in common usage in the UK ever since.

Trafalgar Square Christmas Tree with lights in London, United Kingdom.

The first known electrically illuminated Christmas tree was the creation of Edward H. Johnson, an associate of inventor Thomas Edison. While he was vice president of the Edison Electric Light Company, a predecessor of today's Con Edison electric utility, he had Christmas tree light bulbs especially made for him. He proudly displayed his Christmas tree, which was hand-wired with 80 red, white and blue electric incandescent light bulbs the size of walnuts, on December 22, 1882 at his home on Fifth Avenue in New York City. Local newspapers ignored the story, seeing it as a publicity stunt. However, it was published by a Detroit newspaper reporter, and Johnson has become widely regarded as the Father of Electric Christmas Tree Lights. By 1900, businesses started stringing up Christmas lights behind their windows. Christmas lights were too expensive for the average person; as such, electric Christmas lights did not become the majority replacement for candles until 1930.

In 1895, U.S. President Grover Cleveland proudly sponsored the first electrically lit Christmas tree in the White House. It was a huge specimen, featuring more than a hundred multicolored lights. The first commercially produced Christmas tree lamps were manufactured in strings of multiples of eight sockets by the General Electric Co. of Harrison, New Jersey. Each socket took a miniature two-candela carbon-filament lamp.

The Christmas tree at Rockefeller Center in New York City

From that point on, electrically illuminated Christmas trees, but only indoors, grew with mounting enthusiasm in the United States and elsewhere. San Diego in 1904 and Appleton, WI in 1909, and New York City in 1912 were the first recorded instances of the use of Christmas lights outside. McAdenville North Carolina claims to have been the first in 1956. The Library of Congress credits the town for inventing "the tradition of decorating evergreen trees with Christmas lights dates back to 1956 when the McAdenville Men's Club conceived of the idea of decorating a few trees around the McAdenville Community Center." However, the The Tree at Rockefeller Center has had "lights" since 1931, but did not have real electric lights until 1956. Furthermore, Philadelphia's Christmas Light Show and Disney's Christmas Tree also began in 1956. Though General Electric sponsored community lighting competitions during the 1920s, it would take until the mid 1950s for the use of such lights to be adopted by average households.

Over a period of time, strings of Christmas lights found their way into use in places other than Christmas trees. Soon, strings of lights adorned mantles and doorways inside homes, and ran along the rafters, roof lines, and porch railings of homes and businesses. In recent times, many city skyscrapers are decorated with long mostly-vertical strings of a common theme, and are activated simultaneously in Grand Illumination ceremonies.

In the mid 2000s, the video of the home of Carson Williams was widely distributed on the internet as a viral video. It garnered national attention in 2005 from The Today Show on NBC, Inside Edition and the CBS Evening News and was featured in a Miller television commercial. Williams turned his hobby into a commercial venture, and was commissioned to scale up his vision to a scale of 250,000 lights at a Denver shopping center, as well as displays in parks and zoos.

Technology

Main article: Christmas lighting technology

The technology used in Christmas lighting displays is highly diverse, ranging from simple light strands, *Christmas lights* (aka *Fairy lights* in the UK), through to full blown animated tableaux, involving complex illuminated animatronics and statues.

Christmas lights (also called **twinkle lights, holiday lights,** and **mini lights** in the US and **fairy lights** in the UK), that are strands of electric lights used to decorate homes, public/commercial buildings and Christmas trees during the Christmas season are amongst the most recognized form of Christmas lighting. Christmas lights come in a dazzling array of configurations and colors. The small "midget" bulbs commonly known as fairy lights are also called **Italian lights** in some parts of the U.S., such as Chicago.

The types of lamps used in Christmas lighting also vary considerably, reflecting the diversity of modern lighting technology in general. Common lamp types are incandescent light bulbs and now light-emitting diodes (LEDs), which are being increasingly encouraged as being more energy efficient. Less common are neon lamp sets. Fluorescent lamp sets were produced for a limited time by Sylvania in the mid-1940s.

Outdoor displays

The Marshall, Texas courthouse outlined in Christmas lights

Public venues

Displays of Christmas lights in public venues and on public buildings are a popular part of the annual celebration of Christmas, and may be set up by businesses or by local governments. The displays utilise Christmas lights in many ways, including decking towering Christmas trees in public squares, street trees and park trees, adorning lampposts and other such structures, decorating significant buildings such as town halls and department stores, and lighting up popular tourist attractions such as the Eiffel Tower and the Sydney Opera House.

Annual displays in Oxford Street, London, England are adored by the public and local businesses alike, have been erected for decades.

Neighborhoods

In the U.S. from the 1960s, beginning in tract housing, it became increasingly the custom to completely outline the house (but particularly the eaves) with weatherproof Christmas lights. The Holiday Trail of Lights is a joint effort by cities in east Texas and northwest Louisiana that had its origins in the Festival of Lights and Christmas Festival in Natchitoches, started in 1927, making it one of the oldest light festivals in the United States.

Colorful Christmas light arrangement in a residential neighborhood in Champaign, Illinois.

It is often a pastime to drive or walk around neighborhoods in the evening to see the lights displayed on and around other homes traditionally called a Tacky Light Tour [1]. While some homes have no lights, others may have incredibly ornate displays which require weeks to construct. A rare few have even made it to the *Extreme Christmas* TV specials shown on HGTV, at least one requiring a generator and another requiring separate electrical service to supply the amount of electrical power required.

In Australia and New Zealand, chains of Christmas lights were quickly adopted as an effective way to provide ambient lighting to verandas, where cold beer is often served in the long hot summer evenings. For many years the use of Christmas lights on Australian homes was mainly limited to this simple form. From about 1990 increasingly elaborate Christmas lights have been displayed and driving around between 8 and 10 p.m. to look at the lights has become a popular family entertainment. While in some areas there is fierce competition, with town councils offering awards for the best decorated house, in other areas it is seen as a co-operative effort, with residents priding themselves on their street or their neighbourhood.

Other holidays

In the United States, lights have been produced for many other holidays. These may be simple sets in typical holiday colors, or the type with plastic ornaments which the light socket fits into. Light sculptures are also produced in typical holiday icons.

Halloween is the most popular, with miniature light strings having black-insulated wires and semi-opaque orange bulbs. Later sets had some transparent purple bulbs (a representation of black, similar to blacklight), a few even have transparent green, or a translucent or semi-opaque lime green (possibly representing slime as in *Ghostbusters*, or creatures like goblins or space aliens). Two types of icicle lights are sold at Halloween: all-orange, and a combination of purple and green known as "slime lights."

Easter lights are often produced in pastels. These typically have white wire and connectors.

Red, white, and blue lights are produced for Independence Day, as well as U.S. flag and other patriotic-themed ornaments. Net lights have been produced with the lights in a U.S. flag pattern. In 2006 some stores carried stakes with LEDs that light fiber-optics, looking similar to fireworks.

These above light strings are occasionally used on Christmas Trees anyway, usually to add extra variety to the colors of the lights on the tree.

Closeup of a mini light

Various types of patio lighting with no holiday theme are also made for summertime. These are often clear white lights, but most are ornament sets, such as lanterns made of metal or bamboo, or plastic ornaments in the shape of barbecue condiments, flamingos and palm trees, or even various beers. Some are made of decorative wire or mesh, in abstract shapes such as dragonflies, often with glass "gems" or marbles. Light sculptures are also made in everything from wire-mesh frogs to artificial palm trees outlined in rope lights.

In India, fairy lights are often used to decorate in celebration of Eid ul-Fitr, which occurs at the end of Ramadan. For example see the holiday decorations in the movie, Saawariya.

Light sculptures

Christmas light sculptures are light sculptures used as Christmas decorations and for other holidays. Originally, these were large wireframe metalwork pieces made for public displays, such as for a municipal government to place on utility poles, and shopping centers to place on lampposts. Since the 1990s, these are also made in small plastic home versions that can be hung in a window, or on a door or wall. Attached to them are strings of Christmas lights, typically the large C7 screw-in bulbs for outdoor types, and miniature lights for indoor ones.

Light sculptures can be either flat (most common) or three-dimensional. Most flat ones are bare frames, but garland can also be attached to outdoor ones, and indoor ones often have a multicolored plastic backing sheet, often holographic. 3D ones include deer or reindeer (even moose) in various positions, and with or without antlers, often with a motor to move the head up and down or side to side as if grazing. These and other 3D displays may be bare-frame, or be covered with garland, looped and woven transparent plastic cord or acrylic, or natural or goldtone-painted vines. Snowflakes are a popular design for municipal displays, so as not to be misconstrued as a government endorsement of religion, or so they can be left up all winter.

Some places make huge displays of these during December, such as Callaway Gardens, Life University, and Lake Lanier Islands in the U.S. state of Georgia. In east Tennessee, the cities of Chattanooga, Sevierville, Pigeon Forge, and Gatlinburg have light sculptures up all winter. Gatlinburg also has custom ones for Valentine's Day and St. Patrick's Day, while Pigeon Forge puts flowers on its tall lampposts for spring, and for winter has a steamboat and the famous picture of U.S. Marines *Raising the Flag on Iwo Jima*, in addition to the city's historic Old Mill.

Some sculptures have microcontrollers that sequence circuits of lights, so that the object appears to be in motion. This is used for things such as snowflakes falling, Santa Claus waving, a peace dove flapping its wings, or train wheels rolling.

Examples

Toronto, Ontario, Canada

LED light sculptures over ice skating rink in Nathan Phillips Square

Auckland, New Zealand

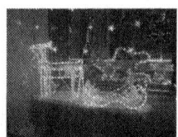

Rope light sculpture

Lisbon in 2005

LED light sculpture in Gänserndorf, Austria

Place de la République in Limoges, France

Guimarães, Portugal

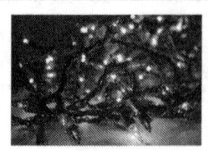

External links

- Quantum Wells in the Seasonal Department, The Technology of LED Christmas Lights [2]
- Christmas Lights Company, Lighting up Christmas with Indoor, Outdoor and LED Christmas Lights [3]

Yule Goat

The **Yule Goat** is one of the oldest Scandinavian and Northern European Yule and Christmas symbols and traditions. Originally denoting the goat that was slaughtered during the Germanic pagan festival of Yule, "Yule Goat" now typically refers to a goat-figure made of straw. It is also associated with the custom of wassailing, sometimes referred to as "going Yule Goat" in Scandinavia.

The Swedish Gävle Goat in 2006.

History

Its origins might go as far back as to pre-Christian days, where goats were connected to the Norse god Thor, who rode the sky in a chariot drawn by two goats, Tanngrisnir and Tanngnjóstr, and carried his hammer Mjöllnir. The "Prose Edda", written by Snorri Sturluson in the 13th century, relates that when Thor kills and cooks the goats, their flesh provides sustenance for the god and his guests, and after Thor resurrects them with his hammer they are brought back to life the next day.

A folk tale depiction of Father Christmas riding on a goat. Perhaps an evolved version of the Swedish Tomte.

The function of the Yule Goat has differed throughout the ages. In Finland, the Yule Goat was originally said to be an ugly creature that frightened children, and demanded gifts at Christmas. In Scandinavia, people thought of the Yule Goat as an invisible creature that would appear some time before Christmas to make sure that the Yule preparations were done right. During the 19th century its role shifted towards becoming the giver of Christmas gifts, in Finland as well as the rest of Scandinavia, with one of the men in the family dressing up as the Yule Goat. The goat was replaced by *jultomte* or *julenisse* (Father Christmas/Santa Claus) at the end of the century, , although he is still called the Yule Goat (*Joulupukki*) in Finland, and the tradition of the man-sized goat disappeared.

Ornamental Yule Goats made of straw, used for Yule decoration in Scandinavia.

A Swedish custom that has continued up to this century is the "Yule Sacrifice" (*Juleoffer*) involving a person dressed as a goat which, after undergoing a mock-sacrifice, is resurrected. Sir James George Frazer described its performance as follows:

> "The actor, hidden by a coverlet made of skins and wearing a pair of formidable horns, is led into the room by two men, who make believe to slaughter him, while they sing verses referring to the mantles of various colours, red, blue, white, and yellow, which they laid on him, one after the other. At the conclusion of the song, the Yule Goat, after feigning death, jumps up and skips about to the amusement of the spectators."

The Yule Goat is nowadays best known as a Christmas ornament often made out of straw or roughly-hewn wood. In older Scandinavian society a popular prank was to place the Yule Goat in a neighbour's house without them noticing; the family successfully pranked had to get rid of it in the same way. The modern version of the Yule Goat figure is a decorative goat made out of straw and bound with red ribbons, a popular Christmas ornament often found under the Yule tree or Christmas tree. Large versions of this ornament are frequently erected in towns and cities around Christmas time — these goats tend to be illegally set on fire before Christmas. The Gävle goat was the first of these goats, and remains the most famous.

See also

- Christmas ham
- Christmas tree
- Julebukking
- Joulupukki
- Santa Claus
- Yule log

References

- Frazer, James G. (1994). *The Golden Bough: A Study in Magic and Religion*. Oxford: Oxford University Press.
- Reade, Arthur (1914). *Finland and the Finns*. London: Methuen.

A Yule Goat from Uppland, Sweden

- Rossel, Sven H.; Elbrönd-Bek, Bo (1996). *Christmas in Scandinavia*. Lincoln: University of Nebraska Press.

External links

- The Gävle Goat webcam [1]
- A website with pictures of decorative straw goats [2]
- The Gävle Goat has been fire proofed for Christmas 2006 [3]
- Traditional Christmas games [4]
- Information about the Norwegian Yule Goat tradition [5]
- Webcamplaza.net Christmas Cams [6]

Julbocken by John Bauer

Article Sources and Contributors

Christmas Eve *Source*: http://en.wikipedia.org/?oldid=390126514 *Contributors*: StAnselm

Christmas *Source*: http://en.wikipedia.org/?oldid=388600011 *Contributors*: Hmains

Father Christmas *Source*: http://en.wikipedia.org/?oldid=388872648 *Contributors*: Vrenator

Santa Claus *Source*: http://en.wikipedia.org/?oldid=390629626 *Contributors*: Tbhotch

Pre-Christian Alpine traditions *Source*: http://en.wikipedia.org/?oldid=368899218 *Contributors*: Pigman

Sinterklaas *Source*: http://en.wikipedia.org/?oldid=389621211 *Contributors*: 1 anonymous edits

Saint Nicholas *Source*: http://en.wikipedia.org/?oldid=390590863 *Contributors*: 1 anonymous edits

Mrs. Claus *Source*: http://en.wikipedia.org/?oldid=383074748 *Contributors*: Kubigula

Christmas elf *Source*: http://en.wikipedia.org/?oldid=389919656 *Contributors*: Dbachmann

Santa Claus's reindeer *Source*: http://en.wikipedia.org/?oldid=390418301 *Contributors*: 1 anonymous edits

Rudolph the Red-Nosed Reindeer *Source*: http://en.wikipedia.org/?oldid=389272637 *Contributors*: Giovannii84

Père Noël *Source*: http://en.wikipedia.org/?oldid=336014581 *Contributors*: GL

Joulupukki *Source*: http://en.wikipedia.org/?oldid=389798560 *Contributors*: 1 anonymous edits

Ded Moroz *Source*: http://en.wikipedia.org/?oldid=378865083 *Contributors*: 1 anonymous edits

Befana *Source*: http://en.wikipedia.org/?oldid=385836289 *Contributors*: 1 anonymous edits

Christkind *Source*: http://en.wikipedia.org/?oldid=377232232 *Contributors*: 1 anonymous edits

Zwarte Piet *Source*: http://en.wikipedia.org/?oldid=388427582 *Contributors*: Hrafieik

Krampus *Source*: http://en.wikipedia.org/?oldid=381677374 *Contributors*:

Belsnickel *Source*: http://en.wikipedia.org/?oldid=354625776 *Contributors*: Rvolz

Le Père Fouettard *Source*: http://en.wikipedia.org/?oldid=367023990 *Contributors*: Andreas Philopater

North Pole *Source*: http://en.wikipedia.org/?oldid=390668000 *Contributors*: 1 anonymous edits

Santa's workshop *Source*: http://en.wikipedia.org/?oldid=384848160 *Contributors*: 1 anonymous edits

Korvatunturi *Source*: http://en.wikipedia.org/?oldid=388039472 *Contributors*: Nihonjoe

Knecht Ruprecht *Source*: http://en.wikipedia.org/?oldid=388452616 *Contributors*:

Twelve Days of Christmas *Source*: http://en.wikipedia.org/?oldid=383076215 *Contributors*: Walter Görlitz

Christmas tree *Source*: http://en.wikipedia.org/?oldid=390134424 *Contributors*: Ohnoitsjamie

Wassailing *Source*: http://en.wikipedia.org/?oldid=375473528 *Contributors*: Mike in Aus

Yule log *Source*: http://en.wikipedia.org/?oldid=376601053 *Contributors*: Pinethicket

Christmas stocking *Source*: http://en.wikipedia.org/?oldid=379980084 *Contributors*: 1 anonymous edits

Christmas ornament *Source*: http://en.wikipedia.org/?oldid=339429130 *Contributors*: PurpleChez

Nutcracker *Source*: http://en.wikipedia.org/?oldid=390336245 *Contributors*: 1 anonymous edits

Christmas lights *Source*: http://en.wikipedia.org/?oldid=387776753 *Contributors*: Fotaun

Yule Goat *Source*: http://en.wikipedia.org/?oldid=355522625 *Contributors*: Sigurd Dragon Slayer

Image Sources, Licenses and Contributors

File:Nativity Icon.jpg *Source*: http://bibliocm.bibliolabs.com/mwAnon/index.php?title=File:Nativity_Icon.jpg *License*: unknown *Contributors*: -

Image:Wigilia potrawy 554.jpg *Source*: http://bibliocm.bibliolabs.com/mwAnon/index.php?title=File:Wigilia_potrawy_554.jpg *License*: unknown *Contributors*: -

Image:Oplatki.w.koszyczku.jpg *Source*: http://bibliocm.bibliolabs.com/mwAnon/index.php?title=File:Oplatki.w.koszyczku.jpg *License*: unknown *Contributors*: -

Image:Hundreds of candles and a Christian Cross at a cemetery on Christmas eve.jpg *Source*: http://bibliocm.bibliolabs.com/mwAnon/index.php?title=File:Hundreds_of_candles_and_a_Christian_Cross_at_a_cemetery_on_Christmas_eve.jpg *License*: unknown *Contributors*: -

Image:Khaki-chums-xmas-truce-1914-1999.redvers.jpg *Source*: http://bibliocm.bibliolabs.com/mwAnon/index.php?title=File:Khaki-chums-xmas-truce-1914-1999.redvers.jpg *License*: unknown *Contributors*: -

Image:commons-logo.svg *Source*: http://bibliocm.bibliolabs.com/mwAnon/index.php?title=File:Commons-logo.svg *License*: logo *Contributors*: User:3247, User:Grunt

File:Nativity_tree.jpg *Source*: http://bibliocm.bibliolabs.com/mwAnon/index.php?title=File:Nativity_tree.jpg *License*: unknown *Contributors*: -

Image:Adorazione del Bambino - Beato Angelico.jpg *Source*: http://bibliocm.bibliolabs.com/mwAnon/index.php?title=File:Adorazione_del_Bambino_-_Beato_Angelico.jpg *License*: unknown *Contributors*: -

Image:Ilex-aquifolium (Europaeische Stechpalme-1.jpg *Source*: http://bibliocm.bibliolabs.com/mwAnon/index.php?title=File:Ilex-aquifolium_(Europaeische_Stechpalme-1.jpg *License*: unknown *Contributors*: -

File:Steaua, Bucharest, 1842 crop.jpg *Source*: http://bibliocm.bibliolabs.com/mwAnon/index.php?title=File:Steaua,_Bucharest,_1842_crop.jpg *License*: unknown *Contributors*: -

File:Greeting Card Christmas Victorian 1870.jpg *Source*: http://bibliocm.bibliolabs.com/mwAnon/index.php?title=File:Greeting_Card_Christmas_Victorian_1870.jpg *License*: unknown *Contributors*: -

Image:Sinterklaas 2007.jpg *Source*: http://bibliocm.bibliolabs.com/mwAnon/index.php?title=File:Sinterklaas_2007.jpg *License*: unknown *Contributors*: -

Image:ChristAsSol.jpg *Source*: http://bibliocm.bibliolabs.com/mwAnon/index.php?title=File:ChristAsSol.jpg *License*: unknown *Contributors*: User:Leinad-Z

Image:FatherChristmastrial.jpg *Source*: http://bibliocm.bibliolabs.com/mwAnon/index.php?title=File:FatherChristmastrial.jpg *License*: unknown *Contributors*: -

Image:Scrooges third visitor-John Leech,1843.jpg *Source*: http://bibliocm.bibliolabs.com/mwAnon/index.php?title=File:Scrooges_third_visitor-John_Leech,1843.jpg *License*: unknown *Contributors*: -

Image:MerryOldSanta.jpg *Source*: http://bibliocm.bibliolabs.com/mwAnon/index.php?title=File:MerryOldSanta.jpg *License*: unknown *Contributors*: -

Image:Boyana Angel.jpg *Source*: http://bibliocm.bibliolabs.com/mwAnon/index.php?title=File:Boyana_Angel.jpg *License*: unknown *Contributors*: -

Image:Santaandgoat.gif *Source*: http://bibliocm.bibliolabs.com/mwAnon/index.php?title=File:Santaandgoat.gif *License*: Public Domain *Contributors*: M2545, Man vyi, Olivier2, Square87, 1 anonymous edits

Image:Santa Claus 1863 Harpers.png *Source*: http://bibliocm.bibliolabs.com/mwAnon/index.php?title=File:Santa_Claus_1863_Harpers.png *License*: unknown *Contributors*: -

Image:1918eatonssantaclausparade.jpg *Source*: http://bibliocm.bibliolabs.com/mwAnon/index.php?title=File:1918eatonssantaclausparade.jpg *License*: unknown *Contributors*: -

Image:Wea01250.jpg *Source*: http://bibliocm.bibliolabs.com/mwAnon/index.php?title=File:Wea01250.jpg *License*: unknown *Contributors*: -

file:Why NORAD Tracks Santa.jpg *Source*: http://bibliocm.bibliolabs.com/mwAnon/index.php?title=File:Why_NORAD_Tracks_Santa.jpg *License*: unknown *Contributors*: -

File:Uummannaq-santa-claus-turf-hut.jpg *Source*: http://bibliocm.bibliolabs.com/mwAnon/index.php?title=File:Uummannaq-santa-claus-turf-hut.jpg *License*: unknown *Contributors*: -

File:Ded Moroz.jpg *Source*: http://bibliocm.bibliolabs.com/mwAnon/index.php?title=File:Ded_Moroz.jpg *License*: unknown *Contributors*: -

File:Krampus at Perchtenlauf Klagenfurt.jpg *Source*: http://bibliocm.bibliolabs.com/mwAnon/index.php?title=File:Krampus_at_Perchtenlauf_Klagenfurt.jpg *License*: Creative Commons Attribution 2.0 *Contributors*: Anita Martinz

File:Krampus Salzburg 5.jpg *Source*: http://bibliocm.bibliolabs.com/mwAnon/index.php?title=File:Krampus_Salzburg_5.jpg *License*: unknown *Contributors*: -

File:Krampus Morzger Pass Salzburg 2008 04.jpg *Source*: http://bibliocm.bibliolabs.com/mwAnon/index.php?title=File:Krampus_Morzger_Pass_Salzburg_2008_04.jpg *License*: Creative Commons Attribution-Sharealike 3.0 *Contributors*: User:MatthiasKabel

Image:Perchten4.jpg *Source*: http://bibliocm.bibliolabs.com/mwAnon/index.php?title=File:Perchten4.jpg *License*: GNU Free Documentation License *Contributors*: Adziura, Crux, Holt, XcepticZP

Image:Badalisc Andrista 1 (Foto Luca Giarelli).jpg *Source*: http://bibliocm.bibliolabs.com/mwAnon/index.php?title=File:Badalisc_Andrista_1_(Foto_Luca_Giarelli).jpg *License*: Creative Commons Attribution-Sharealike 3.0 *Contributors*: Luca Giarelli

Image:Perchtenlauf2009.jpg *Source*: http://bibliocm.bibliolabs.com/mwAnon/index.php?title=File:Perchtenlauf2009.jpg *License*: GNU Free Documentation License *Contributors*: Giessauf A, JuTa, 1 anonymous edits

Image:Sinter-claes-saint-nicolas-dam800.jpg *Source*: http://bibliocm.bibliolabs.com/mwAnon/index.php?title=File:Sinter-claes-saint-nicolas-dam800.jpg *License*: unknown *Contributors*: -

File:Pieterbaas.png *Source*: http://bibliocm.bibliolabs.com/mwAnon/index.php?title=File:Pieterbaas.png *License*: Free Art License *Contributors*: User:12Danny12

Image:Sint-intocht-boot.jpg *Source*: http://bibliocm.bibliolabs.com/mwAnon/index.php?title=File:Sint-intocht-boot.jpg *License*: unknown *Contributors*: -

Image:Chocoladeletter A.jpg *Source*: http://bibliocm.bibliolabs.com/mwAnon/index.php?title=File:Chocoladeletter_A.jpg *License*: unknown *Contributors*: -

File:Nikola from 1294.jpg *Source*: http://bibliocm.bibliolabs.com/mwAnon/index.php?title=File:Nikola_from_1294.jpg *License*: unknown *Contributors*: -

File:Grab Nikolaus.jpg *Source*: http://bibliocm.bibliolabs.com/mwAnon/index.php?title=File:Grab_Nikolaus.jpg *License*: unknown *Contributors*: -

File:MHS przeniesienie relikwi Mikolaja XVII w p.jpg *Source*: http://bibliocm.bibliolabs.com/mwAnon/index.php?title=File:MHS_przeniesienie_relikwi_Mikolaja_XVII_w_p.jpg *License*: unknown *Contributors*: -

Image Sources, Licenses and Contributors

File:Gentile da Fabriano 063.jpg *Source*: http://bibliocm.bibliolabs.com/mwAnon/index.php?title=File:Gentile_da_Fabriano_063.jpg *License*: unknown *Contributors*: -

File:Nikolaus von Myra.jpg *Source*: http://bibliocm.bibliolabs.com/mwAnon/index.php?title=File:Nikolaus_von_Myra.jpg *License*: unknown *Contributors*: -

File:Saint Nicholas.jpg *Source*: http://bibliocm.bibliolabs.com/mwAnon/index.php?title=File:Saint_Nicholas.jpg *License*: unknown *Contributors*: -

File:Ilja Jefimowitsch Repin 005.jpg *Source*: http://bibliocm.bibliolabs.com/mwAnon/index.php?title=File:Ilja_Jefimowitsch_Repin_005.jpg *License*: unknown *Contributors*: -

File:Ferapontov.jpg *Source*: http://bibliocm.bibliolabs.com/mwAnon/index.php?title=File:Ferapontov.jpg *License*: unknown *Contributors*: -

File:Christmas Stamp of Ukraine 2006 2.jpg *Source*: http://bibliocm.bibliolabs.com/mwAnon/index.php?title=File:Christmas_Stamp_of_Ukraine_2006_2.jpg *License*: unknown *Contributors*: -

File:Sinter-claes-saint-nicolas-dam800.jpg *Source*: http://bibliocm.bibliolabs.com/mwAnon/index.php?title=File:Sinter-claes-saint-nicolas-dam800.jpg *License*: unknown *Contributors*: -

File:Sinterklaas 2007.jpg *Source*: http://bibliocm.bibliolabs.com/mwAnon/index.php?title=File:Sinterklaas_2007.jpg *License*: unknown *Contributors*: -

File:Nikolaus & Weihnachtsmann.jpg *Source*: http://bibliocm.bibliolabs.com/mwAnon/index.php?title=File:Nikolaus_&_Weihnachtsmann.jpg *License*: unknown *Contributors*: -

File:Nikolas myra.jpg *Source*: http://bibliocm.bibliolabs.com/mwAnon/index.php?title=File:Nikolas_myra.jpg *License*: unknown *Contributors*: -

File:Demre Noel Baba op Plein.JPG *Source*: http://bibliocm.bibliolabs.com/mwAnon/index.php?title=File:Demre_Noel_Baba_op_Plein.JPG *License*: unknown *Contributors*: -

Image:Mr&MrsSantaClaus.jpg *Source*: http://bibliocm.bibliolabs.com/mwAnon/index.php?title=File:Mr&MrsSantaClaus.jpg *License*: Public Domain *Contributors*: Author/artist unknown

Image:Lill's Travels.png *Source*: http://bibliocm.bibliolabs.com/mwAnon/index.php?title=File:Lill's_Travels.png *License*: unknown *Contributors*: -

Image:Goody Santa Claus.jpg *Source*: http://bibliocm.bibliolabs.com/mwAnon/index.php?title=File:Goody_Santa_Claus.jpg *License*: Public Domain *Contributors*: Artist unknown

File:Elf ornament.jpg *Source*: http://bibliocm.bibliolabs.com/mwAnon/index.php?title=File:Elf_ornament.jpg *License*: unknown *Contributors*: -

image:Two Zwarte Piet.jpg *Source*: http://bibliocm.bibliolabs.com/mwAnon/index.php?title=File:Two_Zwarte_Piet.jpg *License*: unknown *Contributors*: -

Image:Santa Claus Parade Toronto 2009 (2).jpg *Source*: http://bibliocm.bibliolabs.com/mwAnon/index.php?title=File:Santa_Claus_Parade_Toronto_2009_(2).jpg *License*: unknown *Contributors*: -

Image:Ded Moroz .jpg *Source*: http://bibliocm.bibliolabs.com/mwAnon/index.php?title=File:Ded_Moroz_.jpg *License*: unknown *Contributors*: -

Image:Dedek Mraz.JPG *Source*: http://bibliocm.bibliolabs.com/mwAnon/index.php?title=File:Dedek_Mraz.JPG *License*: GNU Free Documentation License *Contributors*: User:Andrejj

Image:SnowDedMoroz.jpg *Source*: http://bibliocm.bibliolabs.com/mwAnon/index.php?title=File:SnowDedMoroz.jpg *License*: Creative Commons Attribution 2.0 *Contributors*: Rogue Soul from Wales

Image:Befane.jpg *Source*: http://bibliocm.bibliolabs.com/mwAnon/index.php?title=File:Befane.jpg *License*: Creative Commons Attribution-Sharealike 2.5 *Contributors*: Mindmatrix, Square87, Twice25

Image:Befana - Campomarino di Maruggio.JPG *Source*: http://bibliocm.bibliolabs.com/mwAnon/index.php?title=File:Befana_-_Campomarino_di_Maruggio.JPG *License*: Creative Commons Attribution-Sharealike 2.5 *Contributors*: Piero Caramia

Image:Christkind.jpg *Source*: http://bibliocm.bibliolabs.com/mwAnon/index.php?title=File:Christkind.jpg *License*: GNU Free Documentation License *Contributors*: AndreasPraefcke, Square87, Test-tools

File:Nikolaus krampus.jpg *Source*: http://bibliocm.bibliolabs.com/mwAnon/index.php?title=File:Nikolaus_krampus.jpg *License*: Public Domain *Contributors*: unknown, not stated in the source

File:Krampus Morzger Pass Salzburg 2008 10.jpg *Source*: http://bibliocm.bibliolabs.com/mwAnon/index.php?title=File:Krampus_Morzger_Pass_Salzburg_2008_10.jpg *License*: Creative Commons Attribution-Sharealike 3.0 *Contributors*: User:MatthiasKabel

Image:Arctic Ocean.png *Source*: http://bibliocm.bibliolabs.com/mwAnon/index.php?title=File:Arctic_Ocean.png *License*: unknown *Contributors*: -

Image:Noaa3-2006-0602-1206.jpg *Source*: http://bibliocm.bibliolabs.com/mwAnon/index.php?title=File:Noaa3-2006-0602-1206.jpg *License*: unknown *Contributors*: -

File:Nansen-fram.jpg *Source*: http://bibliocm.bibliolabs.com/mwAnon/index.php?title=File:Nansen-fram.jpg *License*: unknown *Contributors*: -

File:Peary Sledge Party and Flags at the Pole .jpg *Source*: http://bibliocm.bibliolabs.com/mwAnon/index.php?title=File:Peary_Sledge_Party_and_Flags_at_the_Pole_.jpg *License*: unknown *Contributors*: -

File:USS Skate (SSN-578) surfaced in Arctic - 1959.jpg *Source*: http://bibliocm.bibliolabs.com/mwAnon/index.php?title=File:USS_Skate_(SSN-578)_surfaced_in_Arctic_-_1959.jpg *License*: unknown *Contributors*: -

File:Arctic 77.jpg *Source*: http://bibliocm.bibliolabs.com/mwAnon/index.php?title=File:Arctic_77.jpg *License*: unknown *Contributors*: -

File:Workshop 02.jpg *Source*: http://bibliocm.bibliolabs.com/mwAnon/index.php?title=File:Workshop_02.jpg *License*: unknown *Contributors*: -

Image:Finland locator map.svg *Source*: http://bibliocm.bibliolabs.com/mwAnon/index.php?title=File:Finland_locator_map.svg *License*: Public Domain *Contributors*: w:User:MysidMysid

Image:Locator Red.svg *Source*: http://bibliocm.bibliolabs.com/mwAnon/index.php?title=File:Locator_Red.svg *License*: unknown *Contributors*: -

File:Korvatunturi.jpg *Source*: http://bibliocm.bibliolabs.com/mwAnon/index.php?title=File:Korvatunturi.jpg *License*: Creative Commons Attribution-Sharealike 3.0 *Contributors*: eusa

File:Magnify-clip.png *Source*: http://bibliocm.bibliolabs.com/mwAnon/index.php?title=File:Magnify-clip.png *License*: GNU Free Documentation License *Contributors*: User:Erasoft24

File:Nativity.jpg *Source*: http://bibliocm.bibliolabs.com/mwAnon/index.php?title=File:Nativity.jpg *License*: Public Domain *Contributors*: User:Ranosonar

File:Bogojavlenie.jpg *Source*: http://bibliocm.bibliolabs.com/mwAnon/index.php?title=File:Bogojavlenie.jpg *License*: unknown *Contributors*: Mladifilozof, Shakko, 1 anonymous edits

File:TwelfthNightCostumers.jpg *Source*: http://bibliocm.bibliolabs.com/mwAnon/index.php?title=File:TwelfthNightCostumers.jpg *License*: GNU Free Documentation License *Contributors*: User:Infrogmation

Image Sources, Licenses and Contributors

File:12242008 ChristmasEve00028.JPG *Source*: http://bibliocm.bibliolabs.com/mwAnon/index.php?title=File:12242008_ChristmasEve00028.JPG *License*: unknown *Contributors*: -

File:ArbolNavidad.jpg *Source*: http://bibliocm.bibliolabs.com/mwAnon/index.php?title=File:ArbolNavidad.jpg *License*: unknown *Contributors*: -

Image:Rockefeller Center Tree.jpg *Source*: http://bibliocm.bibliolabs.com/mwAnon/index.php?title=File:Rockefeller_Center_Tree.jpg *License*: unknown *Contributors*: -

Image:CandleChristmas.JPG *Source*: http://bibliocm.bibliolabs.com/mwAnon/index.php?title=File:CandleChristmas.JPG *License*: unknown *Contributors*: -

Image:Fiber-optic Christmas tree.jpg *Source*: http://bibliocm.bibliolabs.com/mwAnon/index.php?title=File:Fiber-optic_Christmas_tree.jpg *License*: unknown *Contributors*: -

Image:Pencilpinepurple.jpg *Source*: http://bibliocm.bibliolabs.com/mwAnon/index.php?title=File:Pencilpinepurple.jpg *License*: unknown *Contributors*: -

Image:Balsam-Hill-artificial-Christmas-tree.jpg *Source*: http://bibliocm.bibliolabs.com/mwAnon/index.php?title=File:Balsam-Hill-artificial-Christmas-tree.jpg *License*: unknown *Contributors*: -

Image:Christmas tree bauble.jpg *Source*: http://bibliocm.bibliolabs.com/mwAnon/index.php?title=File:Christmas_tree_bauble.jpg *License*: unknown *Contributors*: -

File:Notre-dame-paris-xmas1.jpg *Source*: http://bibliocm.bibliolabs.com/mwAnon/index.php?title=File:Notre-dame-paris-xmas1.jpg *License*: unknown *Contributors*: -

Image:Noelentzero.jpg *Source*: http://bibliocm.bibliolabs.com/mwAnon/index.php?title=File:Noelentzero.jpg *License*: unknown *Contributors*: -

Image:Chambers Yule Log.png *Source*: http://bibliocm.bibliolabs.com/mwAnon/index.php?title=File:Chambers_Yule_Log.png *License*: Public Domain *Contributors*: Robert Chambers

Image:durianlog.JPG *Source*: http://bibliocm.bibliolabs.com/mwAnon/index.php?title=File:Durianlog.JPG *License*: Creative Commons Attribution-Sharealike 2.5 *Contributors*: BorgQueen, Chensiyuan, Man vyi

Image:Dec, 1941 US Army troops hang stockings on gun rack.jpg *Source*: http://bibliocm.bibliolabs.com/mwAnon/index.php?title=File:Dec,_1941_US_Army_troops_hang_stockings_on_gun_rack.jpg *License*: Public Domain *Contributors*: BrokenSphere, Cornellrockey04, Infrogmation, M2545

File:Czerwona bombka choinkowa ze stanu Tennessee USA zblizenie.jpg *Source*: http://bibliocm.bibliolabs.com/mwAnon/index.php?title=File:Czerwona_bombka_choinkowa_ze_stanu_Tennessee_USA_zblizenie.jpg *License*: unknown *Contributors*: -

Image:Ornament3.jpg *Source*: http://bibliocm.bibliolabs.com/mwAnon/index.php?title=File:Ornament3.jpg *License*: Creative Commons Attribution-Sharealike 3.0 *Contributors*: User:Durova

File:Christbaumschmuck.JPG *Source*: http://bibliocm.bibliolabs.com/mwAnon/index.php?title=File:Christbaumschmuck.JPG *License*: unknown *Contributors*: -

File:Topper Angel.jpg *Source*: http://bibliocm.bibliolabs.com/mwAnon/index.php?title=File:Topper_Angel.jpg *License*: Public Domain *Contributors*: RLogos

File:Notenkraker.JPG *Source*: http://bibliocm.bibliolabs.com/mwAnon/index.php?title=File:Notenkraker.JPG *License*: unknown *Contributors*: -

File:Maurice Ascalon, Pal-Bell Nutcracker.jpg *Source*: http://bibliocm.bibliolabs.com/mwAnon/index.php?title=File:Maurice_Ascalon,_Pal-Bell_Nutcracker.jpg *License*: unknown *Contributors*: -

Image:Christmaslightsnowyicyroof.jpg *Source*: http://bibliocm.bibliolabs.com/mwAnon/index.php?title=File:Christmaslightsnowyicyroof.jpg *License*: Creative Commons Attribution-Sharealike 3.0 *Contributors*: User:Carissa Starscream

File:Trafalgar Square Christmas Carols - Dec 2006.jpg *Source*: http://bibliocm.bibliolabs.com/mwAnon/index.php?title=File:Trafalgar_Square_Christmas_Carols_-_Dec_2006.jpg *License*: unknown *Contributors*: -

Image:Rockefeller Center christmas tree.jpg *Source*: http://bibliocm.bibliolabs.com/mwAnon/index.php?title=File:Rockefeller_Center_christmas_tree.jpg *License*: GNU Free Documentation License *Contributors*: IP 84.5, Infrogmation, Urban, 1 anonymous edits

File:MarshallCourthouse.JPG *Source*: http://bibliocm.bibliolabs.com/mwAnon/index.php?title=File:MarshallCourthouse.JPG *License*: GNU Free Documentation License *Contributors*: User:Kar98

Image:Christmas lights.jpg *Source*: http://bibliocm.bibliolabs.com/mwAnon/index.php?title=File:Christmas_lights.jpg *License*: unknown *Contributors*: -

File:Christmas light closeup.JPG *Source*: http://bibliocm.bibliolabs.com/mwAnon/index.php?title=File:Christmas_light_closeup.JPG *License*: unknown *Contributors*: -

File:Merry_Christmas_from_Toronto.jpg *Source*: http://bibliocm.bibliolabs.com/mwAnon/index.php?title=File:Merry_Christmas_from_Toronto.jpg *License*: Creative Commons Attribution-Sharealike 2.0 *Contributors*: Benson Kua

File:Arch Decorations.jpg *Source*: http://bibliocm.bibliolabs.com/mwAnon/index.php?title=File:Arch_Decorations.jpg *License*: Creative Commons Attribution-Sharealike 2.0 *Contributors*: Joseolgon, Mindmatrix, Túrelio

File:Auckland_Christmas_Lights1.jpg *Source*: http://bibliocm.bibliolabs.com/mwAnon/index.php?title=File:Auckland_Christmas_Lights1.jpg *License*: Creative Commons Attribution-Sharealike 2.5 *Contributors*: User:Antilived

File:Christmas_decorations_by_Albedo_001.JPG *Source*: http://bibliocm.bibliolabs.com/mwAnon/index.php?title=File:Christmas_decorations_by_Albedo_001.JPG *License*: unknown *Contributors*: -

File:Christmas_Lisbon_2005_a.JPG *Source*: http://bibliocm.bibliolabs.com/mwAnon/index.php?title=File:Christmas_Lisbon_2005_a.JPG *License*: Creative Commons Attribution-Sharealike 2.5 *Contributors*: EuTuga, Infrogmation, Jcornelius, Joseolgon, Lusitana, Olivier2, OsvaldoGago, Ranveig

File:Gaenserndorf_weihnachten_2008_1.jpg *Source*: http://bibliocm.bibliolabs.com/mwAnon/index.php?title=File:Gaenserndorf_weihnachten_2008_1.jpg *License*: Creative Commons Attribution 3.0 *Contributors*: User:Doronenko

File:Leuchtstern.jpg *Source*: http://bibliocm.bibliolabs.com/mwAnon/index.php?title=File:Leuchtstern.jpg *License*: Creative Commons Attribution 3.0 *Contributors*: User:Telrúnya

File:Place_de_la_République,_Limoges.PNG *Source*: http://bibliocm.bibliolabs.com/mwAnon/index.php?title=File:Place_de_la_République,_Limoges.PNG *License*: Creative Commons Attribution 3.0 *Contributors*: User:Babsy

File:Gualterianas.JPG *Source*: http://bibliocm.bibliolabs.com/mwAnon/index.php?title=File:Gualterianas.JPG *License*: Public Domain *Contributors*: Marcus Derencius

File:Gualterianas 2007 no Toural 01.jpg *Source*: http://bibliocm.bibliolabs.com/mwAnon/index.php?title=File:Gualterianas_2007_no_Toural_01.jpg *License*: Creative Commons Attribution 2.0 *Contributors*: Feliciano Guimarães

File:Christmas_lights_trees_and_snowman.jpg *Source*: http://bibliocm.bibliolabs.com/mwAnon/index.php?title=File:Christmas_lights_trees_and_snowman.jpg *License*: Creative Commons Attribution 2.0 *Contributors*: Mike Spasoff from Granada Hills, USA

File:Gabonak.jpg *Source*: http://bibliocm.bibliolabs.com/mwAnon/index.php?title=File:Gabonak.jpg *License*: Public Domain *Contributors*: User:Lumentzaspi

Image Sources, Licenses and Contributors

File:Christmas lights strung on snow-covered fence.JPG *Source*: http://bibliocm.bibliolabs.com/mwAnon/index.php?title=File:Christmas_lights_strung_on_snow-covered_fence.JPG *License*: Public Domain *Contributors*: User:Juliancolton

Image:Gavle christmas goat 2006.jpg *Source*: http://bibliocm.bibliolabs.com/mwAnon/index.php?title=File:Gavle_christmas_goat_2006.jpg *License*: Creative Commons Attribution-Sharealike 2.5 *Contributors*: Original uploader was Stefan at en.wikipedia

Image:Julbock gransmycke.jpg *Source*: http://bibliocm.bibliolabs.com/mwAnon/index.php?title=File:Julbock_gransmycke.jpg *License*: GNU Free Documentation License *Contributors*: User:Nordelch

Image:Julbock_(Uppland).png *Source*: http://bibliocm.bibliolabs.com/mwAnon/index.php?title=File:Julbock_(Uppland).png *License*: Public Domain *Contributors*: Amphis, Lokal Profil, Ludmiła Pilecka, Nicke L

Image:Julbocken 1912.jpg *Source*: http://bibliocm.bibliolabs.com/mwAnon/index.php?title=File:Julbocken_1912.jpg *License*: unknown *Contributors*: Ludmiła Pilecka, M2545, Nasko, Thuresson, 1 anonymous edits

The cover image herein is used under a Creative Commons License and may be reused or reproduced under that same license.

http://images.cdn.fotopedia.com/flickr-72682860-hd.jpg

CPSIA information can be obtained
at www.ICGtesting.com
Printed in the USA
LVHW061203241122
733812LV00006B/358